BRA

Behaviour problems
in young children

Behaviour problems
in young children
Assessment and management

Jo Douglas

Tavistock/Routledge
London and New York

First published in 1989
by Routledge
11 New Fetter Lane, London EC4P 4EE
29 West 35th Street, New York, NY 10001

© 1989 Jo Douglas

Typeset by Photoprint, Torquay, Devon
Printed and bound in Great Britain by
Mackays of Chatham PLC, Chatham, Kent

British Library Cataloguing in Publication Data

Douglas, Jo
  Behaviour problems in young children.
  1. Children, to 5 years. Behaviour
  modification
  I. Title
  649'.64   ~~649.64~~
                                155.453

Library of Congress Cataloging in Publication Data

Douglas, Jo., 1950–
  Behaviour problems in young children : assessment
    and management / Jo Douglas.
  p.   cm.
  Bibliography: p.
  Includes index.
  1. Behavior disorders in children. I. Title. II. Title:
  Behavior problems in young children.
  RJ506.B44D68   1989
  618.92'89—dc19   89-3550
                                                 CIP

ISBN 0-415-02247-9
ISBN 0-415-02248-7 (pbk)

Contents

Preface

Many primary health care professionals have commented that there is a lack of a book that comprehensively covers the areas of pre-school children's emotional and behavioural problems. This book aims to fill that gap. Its purpose is not only to provide an introduction to the recent research about the problems of young children and their families but also to provide a practical guide to assessing and managing these problems. The book can be used as a resource to further reading but is essentially practical in nature. Outlines are provided for assessments and interviews as well as details on a range of types of treatment methods. Case examples are provided in order to provide flavour and humanity to the text.

It will be a valuable resource not only for clinicians who advise parents on how to manage their children in their daily practice, but also for trainees of all health professionals who will be working with young families. The book can be read in conjunction with a new in-service training pack *Emotional and Behavioural Problems in Young Children: A Multidisciplinary Approach to Identification and Management*, Jo Douglas (ed.) (1988), Windsor, NFER/ Nelson, which is an active learning pack to stimulate discussion and treatment plans in the work-place.

Acknowledgements

I would like to express my gratitude to the staff of the Department of Psychological Medicine, Hospital for Sick Children, Great Ormond Street, London, who are all exciting and stimulating colleagues with whom to work, and particularly to the staff of the Day Centre and the Pre-school Programme, who have shared ideas and skills about helping families with pre-school children. I would also like to thank the families who have attended the Day Centre, many of whom are described in this book.

My special thanks go to Naomi Richman for her hard work reading the manuscript and making constructive comments.

This book could never have been written without my invaluable word-processor and tremendous support and consideration from my husband and children during the long evenings spent working on the computer. Alexandra and Amanda slept while Robin prepared the supper.

Chapter one

Introduction: causes of behaviour problems

All parents face uncertainty, make mistakes, and ask for advice about coping with their children at some point during their child's early years. These queries may be about how to manage a crying baby, at what age toilet training should start and how to do it, how much food should be offered at each meal, or how to cope with temper tantrums. But occasionally parents find that their child is so out of control that they become anguished, angry, distressed, and distraught. Such families have reached a point at which intervention from outside the family is required to help establish a happier and more fulfilling relationship between them.

This book aims to introduce the primary health care professional – the health visitor, the general practitioner, and the community physician – to the behaviour and emotional problems commonly seen in young children. Detailed plans for helping parents with management of these problems are outlined. Recent research findings are presented to provide a theoretical background to the advice being offered.

Prevalence

Richman and her colleagues (1982) carried out a research study into the behaviour problems of pre-school children that looked at 705 families living in central London. They found the following rates of behaviour disturbance in 3-year-olds:

15 per cent had mild problems
6.2 per cent had moderate problems
1.1 per cent had severe problems.

Other studies in both Britain and the USA have found similar prevalence rates (Jenkins *et al.* 1980; Earls 1980; 1982). These figures seem to be remarkably high when one considers that this means that a quarter of all pre-school children can be considered to show behaviour problems at some point in their early years. The stress that this causes in some families is very serious, particularly as many isolated young mothers are trying to cope alone for most of the day.

Another study found that only 2 per cent of mothers take their child to the GP for help about these behaviour problems but when they do they still tend to identify medical reasons for these visits (Bax and Hart 1976). So it appears that most of the problems either continue without help until the severity is so great that a referral is made to a child guidance centre, or that the problems resolve themselves as the child grows, or that health visitors manage a large number of the parental concerns without recourse to the GP.

Continuity

The behaviour problems that many children show in the early years will eventually resolve and disappear, but there is a group in which the difficulties persist. It is not possible to predict clearly which children these will be, but by grouping factors associated with the behaviour problems it is possible to guess which children will continue to show problems.

Richman *et al.* (1982) found that 63 per cent of 3-year-olds with problems were still considered to have problems one and five years later. They also found that the sex of the child was a very powerful indicator of whether problems would persist: 73 per cent of boys but only 47 per cent of girls still had problems at age 8. They also found some continuity in the type of problem. Children who were restless at 3 years were often diagnosed as having a conduct disorder at 8 years, while those who were fearful at 3 years were seen as showing emotional problems at 8 years. The severity of the behaviour problem was also predictive. Three-quarters of children who showed moderate or severe disorders at 3 years continued to show these at 8 years, while only a half of children with mild disorders continued to have problems. The most important feature of the child's behaviour that was related to continued difficulties was having poor relationships with other children. Richman concluded that the most accurate predictor of outcome was the severity of the early behaviour problems.

Young boys who have poor relations with other children and who show severe difficulties in their early years are more likely to carry on being difficult. This tells us nothing about the cause of the problems or what is likely to help but the fact that children don't just grow out of the problems is important when considering the need for help and intervention in some families with difficult young children.

Causes of behaviour problems

No direct causal links exist between predisposing factors and eventual behaviour problems in young children; all we can say is that certain factors are associated with behaviour problems. Butler and Golding (1986) found that the number of cigarettes the mother smokes is associated with frequency of temper tantrums in her child. This cannot be considered to be causal but there may be a mechanism that links these events that has as yet not been detected: perhaps tense mothers smoke more and tense mothers may find parenting a more difficult task. Even the fact that a certain management approach helps a problem gives us no clear indication of the cause of the difficulty.

The factors associated with behaviour problems can be grouped into two main categories:

1 Child factors where aspects related to the individual child affect his or her behaviour.

2 Environmental factors where family, housing, and the social situation affect the child.

This is not a nature–nurture split, as most people would now agree that there is a complex interaction between these various factors.

Child factors

Temperament Temperamental traits are considered to be important differences in personality development. Definitions that have been suggested include the following characteristics:

1 temperament has a constitutional basis
2 it appears in infancy and shows some continuity
3 it is an objectively definable characteristic of an individual
4 it is affected by the environment (Bates 1980).

One of the concerns about attributing problems to a child's temperament is that it is often felt to be an unalterable and immutable state that induces despair in adults. This is not a helpful frame of mind when attempting to engender enthusiasm for change and coping with a problem. The use of temperamental explanations does not provide any understanding of the mechanism of how the child came to have that particular temperament and so does not point us in any direction in the search for alleviation of the problem. But regardless of these difficulties it is common for parents to identify clearly different temperamental states in their children.

Thomas and Chess (Thomas *et al.* 1968; Thomas and Chess 1977), in a study of children from infancy to adolescence, interviewed mothers about their child's everyday behaviour during daily routines, their responses to any changes in these routines or environment, and their reactions to any special events or life situations and rated them in ten categories:

1 activity level
2 rhythmicity
3 approach/withdrawal
4 adaptability
5 intensity of reaction
6 threshold of responsiveness
7 quality of mood
8 distractibility
9 attention span
10 persistence.

They found clusters of temperamental characteristics in some children and suggested that several groups existed with defined characteristics.

1 Difficult temperament children are negative in mood, avoid/withdraw, are non-rhythmical as babies, and settle slowly. This accounts for 10 per cent of children who are identified as the criers, poor sleepers, and poor feeders as babies.

2 Easy temperament children are positive in mood, approach new events and people, are rhythmical in their schedules, and adjust quickly to new surroundings. These account for about 40 per cent of children, who are delightful to be with.

These two groups include about a half of all children but there are a variety of other smaller identifiable groups, the most commonly known one being 'slow to warm up' children who behave as the label implies. Thomas *et al.* (1983) claim that these clusters are predictive of whether the child will develop a behaviour disorder and if so, the type of disorder (Graham *et al.* 1973).

This work has come under criticism in recent years as the amount of detectable continuity in temperamental characteristics is often only slight. The alternative view proposed is that temperament is a social perception and that the concept of difficult temperament can be justified only as a parent perception rather than as a characteristic of the child (Bates 1980). One study suggests that a child's temperament can be predicted before the child is born by asking the mother her attitudes during pregnancy (Vaughn *et al.* 1980). The problem of separating the mother's perception of the child's behaviour from the actual occurrence of the behaviour has confused many research findings. Wolkind and DeSalis (1982) found that mothers' descriptions of high levels of difficult behaviour in 4-month-old babies predicted relatively high levels of behaviour problems at 42 months. Similarly Bates (1980) found that mothers' perceptions of difficult temperament in their babies at 6, 13, and 24 months of age predicted behaviour problem ratings at 3 years. The major problem for this field of research is attempting to determine whether the temperamental difficulty is the precursor to the later problems and that it is part of the genetic make-up of the child (Thomas *et al.* 1983) or whether a self-fulfilling prophecy is occurring with parental attitudes being the most important determining factor.

Lee and Bates (1985) examined the style of interaction between mother and child and found that 2-year-old children described as

5

having extremely difficult temperaments tended to resist their mothers' attempts at control. They were often more negative and so their mothers used more intrusive control methods. The level of conflict between mother and child was much higher than with the easy child. The researchers see this as the process by which difficult temperament is linked with the development of later behaviour problems. The importance of the effect of the child's mood and personality on the parents' mode of interaction cannot be denied. A parent who has managed to rear other children perfectly well with few problems may suddenly find that their strategies do not work with the next child. Whether we can postulate a clash of personalities is difficult to say but it is very evident that some children do tax their parents' good will, control, and care to the utmost.

Temperament seems to have a part to play in the evolution of behaviour problems in later childhood, and may be linked via the parents' reactions and management style to an enduring and persisting problem.

Language delay Many studies have identified the association between language delay and behaviour problems in young children (Cantwell *et al.* 1980; Stevenson and Richman 1976; 1978). Stevenson and his colleagues (1985) found that children with low language structure at 3 years showed higher rates of neurotic behaviour problems at 8 years. This applied whether or not they had behaviour problems at 3 years, and reveals a specific association between early language development and later behaviour problems. The poor language structure that these children showed were immaturities in sentence construction using only nouns and verbs, not having three-word phrases, and indicating questions only by intonation.

There is no reason given for the language delay in these children and it seems important to ascertain whether medical difficulties with intermittent hearing loss were present or whether these children were demonstrating poor language development due to low levels of language stimulation and adult interaction at home. Several studies have demonstrated an association between social disadvantage and language delay (Starte 1975; Richman *et al.* 1982).

In work with pre-school children with behaviour problems the issue of hearing loss and language delay is often raised. Children cannot function appropriately if they cannot hear what is being said by their parents. The frustration in communication that these children experience is evident in their behaviour. Toys are frequently thrown when children cannot make themselves understood; social skills develop slowly as they snatch instead of asking for what they want. Poor social relationships with other children as well as adults are common.

Developmental delay The problems associated with children who have severe developmental delay are outside the scope of this book, although the principles of behaviour management are equally appropriate (Carr 1980). But many children with mild developmental difficulties will come to the notice of professionals when behaviour problems are reported by the parents. Parents may complain that their child is not toilet trained, shows immature behaviour, or doesn't appear to listen to them. The child may not be making adequate developmental progress and the parents interpret the behaviour as a problem rather than recognizing it as appropriate behaviour for the child's developmental status. The parents' expectations and the child's ability need to correspond. Parental anxiety and pressure on the child can create additional problems in the child and exacerbate the situation. Counselling about the child's difficulties will help parents recognize more appropriate ways of playing with and helping their child maximize their potential. Toys that are more suited to the child's intellectual level can be suggested plus indications of the behaviour that can be expected in a child with a mental age younger than their chronological age.

Overactivity A high level of activity is an important feature of a child's behaviour as it disrupts the development of normal parenting patterns. The overactive child is frequently described as non-compliant or conduct disordered by parents (Barkley 1981), who do not understand why the child is disobedient. Children who are never still, climb on furniture, lean out of windows, climb fences in the garden, and run wildly in the park will exhaust parents. They need to be monitored continually to avoid danger and require a lot of activities to keep them occupied and amused. They often have difficulty entertaining or playing by themselves and so the parents feel that there is no time in the day that is private or for relaxing. Parents often need help in creating a safe environment for the child to play in and so reduce the strain of continual supervision. The issues related to management of the overactive child are discussed in full in Chapter 9, but it is clearly one aspect of the child's characteristics that will markedly affect how parents and other adults will respond to the child.

Babies vary markedly in their attention span: some are content to gaze at pictures for several minutes while others' interest lasts only a few seconds. The demands that a short-attention-span baby makes will surprise new parents who expected their baby to be able to amuse him or herself for reasonable periods of time. Matching the level of stimulation to the needs of the baby is a very fine art and takes skill, patience, and good observation.

Environmental factors

These encompass the range of social and emotional pressures and reactions that affect the child. These factors on their own do not cause behaviour problems in young children and in many instances children develop and grow with no identifiable problems despite appalling environmental stresses and circumstances (Garmezy 1985).

Maternal depression Maternal depression is a very significant factor in the family life of very many young children. Researchers have found a disturbingly high rate of 30 per cent of mothers with young children showing marked depressive symptoms (Brown and Harris 1978; Richman 1978; Richman *et al.* 1982). There is a very strong association between maternal depression and behaviour difficulties in young children. Pound and her colleagues (1985) looked at the interaction between depressed mothers and their children and found that the rate of marked behaviour problems was related to extensive bouts of depression and poor quality of parental marriage. The depressed mothers tended to have had difficult relationships with their own parents and all had poor marriages with husbands who had a long history of personality disturbance, were aggressive and anti-social. In some cases the couple had developed a vicious circle of poor communication and minimal co-operation so that they both felt unsupported.

8

Brown and his colleagues (1978) examined a group of mothers in Camberwell and were able to isolate four vulnerability factors related to depression:

1 loss of own mother before age 11 years
2 lack of a confiding relationship with husband or boyfriend
3 not going out to work
4 having three or more children all under the age of 14 years.

He found a 42 per cent depression rate where there was a child under the age of 6 years.

Richman (1978) also found a significant association between poor marriage and maternal depression, but did not find an association with the extent of support from relatives or friends. Neither was there an association with mother working or not, nor with social class. These mothers may not in fact be very socially isolated as they often have their mother, sisters, or friends who live close by (Pound *et al.* 1985). But the reality of everyday life is that they are alone with their children for most of the day each week.

All of the researchers agree that the best antidote to depression is a good marriage but very few families had ever been offered marriage guidance. The present orientation towards family therapy and helping parents jointly in the management of their children is starting to emphasize the importance of the marital relationship (McLean 1976).

Environmental stress Problems with housing and poverty are specific factors that have been linked with the development of behaviour problems. Richman (1978) found a higher rate of behaviour problems in children living in tower blocks. But it was significant that depression was particularly high in mothers living on the fourth floor or above. Damp housing conditions, lack of electricity or hot water, and overcrowding are all additional stresses to the family. The large proportion of homeless families with young children and unsupported mothers living with pre-school children in single bedsits is an immense area of deprivation and distress.

The effects of this type of stress appear to be mediated through the parents' emotional reactions to their situation. Richman *et al.*

9

(1982) have commented that it is unclear whether the parents' perception of deprivation or the real level of deprivation is important. Demoralized parents who feel helpless and trapped by unemployment and council housing conditions will generate feelings of anger and depression that will in turn influence care of their children. Being preoccupied with stress will effectively cut parents off from children. They may feel unable to affect their environment or the 'system' and so give up actively participating and generating enthusiasm in their play and interaction with their children. Young children demand a great amount of energy and resourcefulness from parents, plus endless patience and a sense of humour. Once a parent loses sight of the child's needs and becomes involved in his or her own problems control and discipline difficulties will arise as the parent becomes emotionally erratic and inconsistent in reacting to the child.

Many families living in cramped housing conditions and with a low income rear their children very well. The difference may be the parents' mental attitude towards their role and their children. Some community work with such families is now tending towards fostering and encouraging a sense of independence, self-reliance, and initiative in the parents. The *Child Development Project* (1987), which is a collaborative health-visiting programme offering parents support and guidance in bringing up their pre-school children in areas of social stress, specifies the importance of the health visitor's developing the parents' self-reliance and working collaboratively with them rather than in an 'expert' role of advice-giving.

Parental management techniques In looking at all of the factors related to the development of behaviour problems in young children we have repeatedly come back to the way in which environmental influences are mediated by the parents. The manner in which parents manage their children's behaviour is probably one of the most important factors in the development of behavioural difficulties. Sometimes it is possible to help parents with direct information that they require about how to cope with a problem, but in other instances a wider approach of providing emotional support to the parents before even considering intervening at a management level is required. A poor marital relationship, adverse early experiences of being cared for in their own family as a child, or emotional and personality disturbance will probably require extensive help before these parents can provide the emotional warmth and care that the developing child requires.

Patterson and his colleagues working in the USA have carried out extensive parent-training programmes with parents of anti-social children. They have developed detailed observational techniques to monitor changes in the parents' style of management and have identified four key family management practices that are related to the development of problem behaviour in the children:

1 failure to provide consistent and effective discipline related to the child's anti-social behaviour

2 poor monitoring of the whereabouts of the child

3 a low level of positive response when the child was showing sociable behaviour

4 poor problem-solving as a family (Patterson 1982).

Methods of helping families change their management style has been a significant area of research and clinical practice and will constitute most of the rest of this book.

Parental history The complexity and stress of bringing up children and meeting their emotional demands means that parents need a huge reservoir of compassion, love, and knowledge that they can draw on. How does this develop? How do parents learn to be good parents? The general assumption is that this is learned from childhood experiences of being loved and cared for. Rutter and Madge (1976) have found that although there is no direct link between a parent's childhood experiences and their ability to provide good parenting, there is an indirect link through the acquisition of social values and attitudes and the influences on personality development. Most importantly, the ability to develop and maintain a happy marriage is linked to the parents' experience of their own parents' marriage. Stress and emotional discord in childhood is an important precursor to the development of stress and discord in emotional relationships later in adult life.

When abnormal parenting patterns are experienced, such as

physical and sexual abuse, there is a much higher intergenerational link of poor parenting experiences. A high proportion of parents who abuse their children have experienced serious neglect and abuse in their own childhood. Mothers who have been separated from their own parents during childhood have been found to have marital problems and difficulties in child-rearing (Frommer 1973). So it would appear that the intensity of the problems experienced in childhood are of significance and likely to affect later emotional relationships.

A detailed study of women brought up in care since their pre-school days showed that nearly one-third had marked problems, that is a personality disorder and severe or long-standing difficulties in sex/love relationships (Dowdney *et al.* 1985). When their parenting skills and qualities were assessed, 40 per cent were considered to be showing poor parenting, that is transient or permanent breakdown of parenting with children being cared for by someone else. The poor parenting was usually associated with overall poor psycho-social functioning, that is serious personal, social, and economic difficulties. When these women were compared to a group of women not brought up in care, the parenting problems that non-care mothers showed were in the context of general good social adaptation (Rutter *et al.* 1983). So although many mothers experience parenting problems they may be coping adequately with other areas of their lives and the child's behaviour problems may be a specific stress.

A detailed analysis of the parenting shown by ex-care mothers indicated that they were affectionate and caring but they tended to be more negative towards their children and were less skilful at picking up their children's cues or responding in ways that anticipated or avoided problems. This subtle difference in discipline and control methods indicates the importance of anticipating confrontation with children rather than just reacting negatively once the problem has occurred (Radke-Yarrow and Kuczynski 1983).

The finding that one in ten of the general population shows poor parenting skills, while almost half of the mothers who are depressed or have been brought up in care show poor parenting skills, is important in considering how help can be offered. The poor level of anticipation and responsivity that these mothers show affects many areas of parenting. Specific help and advice may be able to forestall the development of problems between parent and child. The protective factor of a good marriage is crucial here, but unfortunately women who were brought up in care or lived in tense, discordant homes as children tend to have poor marriages. David Skuse and Antony Cox (1985) have posed a progressive model of each disadvantage raising the risk of entering the next stage of disadvantage in the next stage of life. They also pose that certain early disadvantages mean that the adult is less able to cope with new stresses and difficulties, so a pattern of maladaptive responding and increasing maladjustment can develop.

Protective factors

This chapter has mostly considered factors that are related to the development of behaviour problems in young children, but a field of research is developing that is trying to identify the factors that protect certain children from the stresses and disturbance within their families. As we have seen, the research studies demonstrate trends but no direct causal links in the development of behavioural problems. Within all of the findings there are large percentages of children who are unaffected by the various stress factors. We can identify children at risk for developing behaviour problems but we cannot identify the 'at risk' children who show good coping abilities.

Rutter and his colleagues have identified a number of risk reducers:

1 Positive temperament

2 Gender (girls are less vulnerable than boys)

3 The presence of an adult who has a warm, supportive, and affectionate relationship with the child and who does not show severe criticism

4 The socializing influence of a positive school atmosphere (Rutter 1979).

These fit into the three broader categories of protective factors that have been identified by other workers in this field:

1 The personality disposition of the child

2 A supportive family milieu

3 An external support system that encourages and reinforces a child's coping efforts and strengthens them.

Studies of black children from socially disadvantaged backgrounds in the USA supports this triad of factors (Garmezy 1985). Also research by Wallerstein and Kelly (1980) into the effect of divorce on young children similarly identified these patterns as helping the child cope with the breakup of family life.

Investigation into this area is vital as it could pave the way for the development of preventive work in families and children. But before this can happen we need to know the mechanisms that underlie these protective factors. Why can a single close relationship with an adult help offset the stressful surroundings and marital conflict that the young child experiences?

Mia Pringle (1975) has suggested that children have four basic emotional needs which have to be met if they are to grow into mature adulthood. The need for:

1 love and security
2 new experiences
3 praise and recognition
4 responsibility.

For some children who face the world with mentally ill, drug-dependent, or inadequate parents, the fact that they have a role of protector, helper, or substitute parent for siblings can offset the calamity of their own childhood (Garmezy 1985). The concept of 'required helpfulness' as a technique for enhancing the strengths of children at risk could be important in the development of therapeutic strategies (Rachman 1979). If the stressed child can be presented with an important task that meets the needs of others, it can add a counter force of predictability and controllability that may not be present in any other part of the child's life and so strengthens the child's resilience to the stress. Responsibility may be a key factor that our present cult of childhood tends to avoid.

Summary

Behaviour problems occur in about one-quarter of all young

children. These show persistence into later childhood particularly when the problems are severe and the child has difficulties in social relationships.

Several factors have been linked to the development of behaviour problems. The interaction between environmental and social conditions and the characteristics of the child can combine to cause significant problems. Certain children seem to develop no behavioural difficulties despite very poor parenting experiences and various protective factors have been proposed.

Chapter two

Assessment of the problem

Effective intervention and treatment is based on an accurate assessment of the presenting problem. The fault of the keen therapist is to start to intervene during the assessment phase of work with a new family. It is easy to develop short cuts in thinking and analysis of problems as more experience is gained in an area of work. This leads to several traps:

1 lack of interest in and boredom with the problem and consequent poor empathy with the parents and child

2 professional distancing by prescribing change rather than working through the problem with the family

3 giving inaccurate advice based on previous experience rather than listening to the family

4 feelings of helplessness either because of previous experience of failure or prediction of no change

5 belittling the problem as defined by the parents and labelling them as over-anxious

6 limitations in developing therapeutic skills and finding new ways of working.

Most therapists are probably guilty of at least one of these faults at some point in their career.

The assessment phase is critical at the beginning of contact with a new family but will also continue throughout contact with them. It is often a dynamic and developing process. The aim of assessment is to:

1 gain detailed information about the behaviour problem

2 listen to the worries and concerns of the parents and child

3 assess the emotional functioning of the family

4 check the developmental progress of the child

5 formulate a hypothesis about the presenting problem

6 create a relationship with the family and engage them in treatment if appropriate

7 determine whether any further information or tests are required for the intervention to be effective.

Listening to parents

The critical feature is for parents to feel that they are being listened to and that their problems are being appreciated and understood. They should be taken seriously and be given due consideration. Parents will often pace what they reveal initially, giving only information that they feel is required. This may not be what is required at all and so careful and gentle questioning will be needed. The anxiety of talking to a professional should not be underestimated. Quite often all the things that parents want to say go out of their heads and it takes time and confidence in their listener to start to explore the greater areas of concern. There may be a lot of anxiety, guilt, anger, or desperation locked away and although this is often painful to expose, therapeutic progress is unlikely to be made until openness is achieved. No parent is going to bare their soul to an uninterested, cool, busy professional. A relationship needs to develop with the professional showing genuineness, warmth, and empathy with the parents and child (Truax and Carkhuff 1967).

Cunningham and Davis (1985) have identified three models of consultation in current practice:

1 The expert model
The professional takes control, makes all of the decisions, selects the information he or she thinks is relevant to the parents, and elicits only certain information that the professional feels is important. Consideration of parental views and feelings, the

need for a mutual relationship and negotiation, the sharing of information are all given low priority. This approach can foster dependency and feelings of incompetence on the part of the parents. But often parents won't ask questions or indicate misunderstanding and so start to feel dissatisfied and fail to carry out therapeutic decisions.

2 The transplant model
The professional transplants his or her skills to the parents but still retains control of the decision-making process. This is a very commonly used model of intervention with parents and children as it recognizes the competency of the parents to effect change in their child. It requires the professional to maintain an ongoing positive relationship with the parents and so improves communication and parental satisfaction. A problem arises if the professional ignores the individuality of the families and fails to tailor the methods specifically to the family.

3 The consumer model
The role of the professional is to listen and understand the parents' views, aims, and expectations and to provide the parents with a range of suitable options and the necessary information from which to select. The professional respects the parents and acknowledges their competence and expertise in knowing more about the total situation than anyone else. Negotiation is the core of the process with clear and honest information exchange. One implication is that professional power is not just determined by professional status but by effectiveness in establishing the negotiating processes and helping to find solutions.

This collaborative approach has been described as 'partnership' (McConkey 1985; Mittler and Mittler 1982; De'Ath and Pugh 1986) and acknowledges the sharing of expertise.

The initial interview

Settling into the first interview is usually quite a tense period. The parents do not know what to expect of you and you don't know what to expect of them. Introductions are important: you must say your name clearly and indicate your profession to the parents. Many parents become very confused by the range of professionals that they see and will call everyone doctor. When the whole family is in the room ask everyone's name individually including the children as this helps everyone feel acknowledged and important. Some small children are initially very shy and won't speak, so asking an older sibling or the parents to prompt can help. Knowing the ages of the children is also crucial in quickly planning toys and activities for them to do during the session. This forestalls any wrong assumptions about immature behaviour for the child's age or a small child being older than appearance suggests. A quick check on the relationships can also avoid some embarrassing assumptions when there are now so many reconstituted families.

The parents should be encouraged to describe their concerns in their own words. When referrals have come from other professionals it is important to get back to the parents' view rather than working from the information in the referral letter. Open-ended questions are useful in encouraging parents to talk, for example 'Would you like to tell me what you have been concerned about? Would you give me your view of the problem?'

When the whole family attends the initial interview the professional can meet all of the family members and the reason for the session can be clarified. All of the family members should be encouraged to put forward their viewpoint even if it differs from that expressed by others. Parents sometimes feel embarrassed about describing their child's problems in front of the child, so asking the child first why he or she thinks they have come to the clinic can open the discussion. If the child does not know or is too shy to talk a suggestion that 'Perhaps mum or dad can remind you?' and encouraging the parents to talk is one way around the problem.

Children who are showing behaviour difficulties are already very aware of the problems. They will have heard repeated discussions with other people previously, or comments from their parents that they are 'bad and naughty'. Reassurance that the child is already fully aware that something is wrong can give parents confidence to talk. Often it can be a great relief to a young child that issues are being brought out into the open and talked about. Parents may be able to express their concern in the clinic while they just get angry and irritated at home. Later sessions with the parents can be held in private if necessary if there is significant information that cannot be discussed in front of the child, but usually this applies only to specific marital problems or sexual difficulties. Other concerns about loss, bereavement, illness, separation, adoption, and the myriad other 'sensitive' areas need to be dealt with in the family sessions. The fact that parents are trying to keep an emotional secret from the child can often be the root cause of the problem. A lack of trust in the parents because of a worrying secret can undermine the child's sense of security at home. Parents may have carried around concerns about a past event that they feel might harm the child but often it is not as serious as they think and the subject can be raised in later sessions with the child present.

During the first session it is important for all family members to have their say. There is often a spokesperson for the family, but the views and opinions should be checked out with their partner and the children. Sometimes you need to guide the conversation so that others can talk. Cunningham and Davis (1985) have succinctly listed several ways of doing this:

1 Questions: these should be open ended and not answerable with a simple single reply.

2 Statements: these reflect the professional's interest or empathy with the problem, e.g. 'That sounds terrible' or 'I suppose that makes you angry'.

3 Prompts: nodding, saying 'yes' or 'mmm', or asking for clarification 'What happened next?' will all encourage the speaker to continue.

4 Silence: allow parents to think and formulate what they want to say.

5 Requests: 'Can you tell me more about that?' or 'Yes, go on' will encourage further expansion.

To include all of the family members it may be necessary to ask explicitly for one member's opinion. 'How do you feel about what has been said?' 'Can you tell me your views?' 'Is that how you feel?' are all questions that suggest another family member contributes to the discussion. Some parents do not like disagreeing in front of an outsider and may need permission to do this. So a statement such as 'Lots of parents have different views about their children' or 'I wonder if there are times when you don't totally agree with each other?' may enable this to happen. Checking with the child can also be helpful. 'Who's cuddly? Who gets cross? Who's soft? Who shouts?' can be a game to include all of the children in describing their parents. Checking back replies with the parents can confirm these family views and allow the parents to talk further and explain what it means.

Depending on how long your first session lasts, you can move into the main areas of assessment and gain a fuller picture of the child and family history. You need to know who they have been to see, what advice they have already tried and what they thought about it. Sometimes there are significant factors that are affecting life at home, for example maternal grandmother living with them, difficult neighbours, a child living away from home.

Developmental assessment

Is the child's behaviour age appropriate?

Children's behaviour problems become a focus of concern when the child is behaving inappropriately or excessively for their age. Tantrums are common in the 18 months to 3 years age range but regular occurrence in a 5-year-old would be cause for concern. Most 2-year-olds have a short concentration span and will flit between activities like Playdoh, Lego, or playing with cars and dolls while a 5-year-old can settle to play table games and puzzles. Some parents have inappropriate expectations for their child's level of development and may just require some help in understanding and acknowledging what their child is able to do and how appropriate this is for their age. In other cases the parents' view of what their child should be able to do is appropriate but the child is showing a delay in his or her development and needs more detailed assessment of the level of progress.

Maria's (3.5 years) parents were concerned because of her severe headbanging at home. They felt that she was out of their control. On observation it was clear that she had a marked language delay and could say only two or three clear single words. Her play centred on simple covering of dolls or putting objects in and out of containers. Her parents felt that she was being difficult and kept presenting her with toys and activities

21

that she could not do. Her elder sister (8 years) had a much more accurate view of what Maria liked to play with. On detailed assessment of her developmental level and language skills, Maria was identified as showing a marked developmental delay. In general she was functioning at an 18-month to 2-year level. Her parents required extensive help with accepting this and finding suitable ways of managing and playing with her. As their expectations of her ability began to match her developmental level they stopped being so irritable and anxious with her.

Keeping an eye on the child's play while talking to parents can provide a lot of basic information about the child's developmental level (Lowe 1975). Simple developmental guides like Sheridan's scales can be very helpful indicators during the session (Sheridan 1973; 1977). A knowledge of normal language development is an important observational tool (Eisenson 1986) plus having a variety of toys available allows observation of a wide range of play (Newson and Newson 1979; Garvey 1977; Matterson 1975; Singer 1973):

1 Cars demonstrate whether the child understands their symbolic use and they are not just things with wheels that can be spun. Cars also demonstrate whether imaginative play can develop or whether the child is showing repetitive and uncreative play pushing the car backwards and forwards on the same spot.

2 Dolls and covers demonstrate symbolic doll play and caring reactions.

3 Bricks demonstrate simple constructive play and eye/hand co-ordination skills.

4 Crayons and paper give the child a chance to doodle and draw, pencil control, and the ability to imitate simple geometric shapes or draw people can be observed.

During the session the demands that the child makes on the parents for help and how they respond to deal with the interruption is useful information. They may be very irritable with the child, have difficulty distracting the child, or be very responsive and encourage repeated interruptions. The sharing of child care in the session is also evident. The child may automatically gravitate towards one parent, may touch and climb on one and not the other. Some parents naturally take turns in distracting or managing the child. The family interaction that takes place provides important insights into family functioning.

The length of time that the child stays with any one activity indicates the attention span and restlessness that the child shows at home. Sharing and co-operation between siblings can be observed, and if fights break out the method of handling by the parents provides on-the-spot evidence of management skills. To observe the parental handling of the situation it must be made clear that the parents are expected to control their children during the session and do what they would do at home. In other instances the parents will need help or the session may become completely disrupted. The professional will need to take control and demonstrate how to set limits. Most young children luckily will respond to the authority of a stranger and so the task is not as daunting as it sounds.

A general developmental history of the child is always useful and the simple developmental milestones should be checked with the parents. The generally accepted norms for these are:

1 Sitting (around 6 months)
2 Walking (around 1 year)
3 First words (around 1 year)
4 Using phrases and short sentences (around 2 years)
5 Toilet training (around 2 years).

Any marked deviations from these should be queried. A brief medical history of:

1 complications of pregnancy or birth
2 any serious illnesses or accidents
3 any hospitalizations

should cover most aspects that could affect the child's development.

Is further developmental assessment necessary?

If you suspect that the child is showing a delay in development then a more formal assessment may be required; this should be discussed fully with the parents and their permission sought. Up to the age of 2 years the developmental screening tests (Griffiths 1954; Bayley 1969) provide a profile of the child's skills. This includes identification of motor, expressive language, eye/hand co-ordination, cognitive and social skills. There have been extensive criticisms of these tests as they are not predictive of later ability but they provide a rough guideline to any inequalities across the range of developmental areas. They can also clearly indicate marked levels of delay and so enable the professional to plan a course of intervention and further investigation. Sometimes the delays can be psycho-social in origin, parents may be under-stimulating or neglecting the child, but this can be verified only by demonstrating a change in the child's rate of progress once intervention has occurred.

Psychologists use tests that examine the cognitive skills of the child. There are difficulties assessing the child between the age of 2 and 4 years and so a range of different tests is used in an attempt to tap a wide range of the child's skills and maintain the child's interest and motivation to co-operate. They include tests of concepts (size, colour, number), spatial skills (jigsaws, puzzles), fine motor co-ordination (drawing and mazes), verbal reasoning and vocabulary (Wechsler 1967; McCarthy 1970).

Language delay is one of the most important areas to check as it is highly correlated with behaviour problems and later reading difficulties at school (Stevenson 1985). Parents who do not detect an intermittent hearing loss can become irritable and controlling and label their child as disobedient and unresponsive. The fact that at times the child seems well able to respond to them reinforces their view that their child is being naughty. A survey has shown that children who suffer upper-respiratory-tract infections and middle-ear infections are more likely to present with management problems and temper tantrums than children who have not suffered these illnesses (Bax *et al.* 1983). Similarly a study of 5-year-olds with a mean conduction loss of 20.2 decibels showed a higher incidence of maladjusted behaviour, short attention span, dependency, and poor motivation than normal hearing children (Silva *et al.* 1983).

Mark (5 years) is the middle of three children. His mother complained that he was completely out of her control. He fought with his siblings and was continually into mischief. He had destroyed bedroom furniture, tipped Coca-Cola into the video recorder, broken mirrors, and had lit some small fires. His mother had wanted him to be put into care and felt that she was unable to relate to him. On assessment he was found to show moderate learning difficulties and a marked language delay both in comprehension and expressive language. Referral for hearing tests revealed that he had recurrent otitis media and consequently had intermittent hearing loss. He was put on the waiting list for insertion of grommets. Once his mother realized that he had these additional problems she was able to understand how frustrated he had been and also how irritable she had been when he did not respond to her. Help with management skills, communication skills and language games improved their relationship and he started to make good progress in his language and his general behaviour.

A speech therapist will carry out formal and informal assessments of the child's verbal expression and comprehension as well as advise on language activities parents can carry out at home (Bishop 1984; Reynell 1977; Wheldall *et al*. 1979). Hearing checks are essential as conductive hearing impairment is very frequent in young children. The critical time for an adverse effect on language development is during the first three years of life (Sak and Ruben 1981; Zinkus *et al*. 1978; Paradise 1981). Delay rather than a deviant pattern to language development is reported and 3-year-olds have been found to be 5–8 months behind in their language norms (Jerger *et al*. 1983) while 5-year-olds can be one year behind (Ling 1972). Thirty per cent of children under 2 years of age have been found to have middle-ear disorders (Reichman and Healey 1983) while in a survey of London nursery children Shah (1981) found evidence of unsuspected middle-ear infection in 35 per cent of the children. It seems likely that there are many children with conductive hearing impairment who have listening and comprehension difficulties but pass standard audiometric screening (Bamford and Saunders 1985). Middle-ear infections are frequently treated with antibiotics and this may be the reason for the increase in non-infected glue ear (Smyth 1984). Consequently parents may not suspect that their child has any hearing problem as there is no ear infection.

The reasons why this type of hearing loss affects language development is not yet clear. Part of the difficulty is that the same environmental factors which predispose children to middle-ear infections may contribute independently to developmental delay. Low socio-economic status, poor quality of parenting, adverse environmental conditions have all been associated with otitis media and developmental delay (Webster *et al.* 1984; Webster 1986).

Family assessment

Many models exist for assessing family functioning (Barker 1986) and the following ideas are extracted from a variety of theories of family therapy that I have found to be particularly useful (Burnham 1986; Gorell-Barnes 1984; Mason and O'Byrne 1984). Information is gained from observing the family in the session as well as asking questions that probe into the relationships with the family. Families are usually unable to describe how they function to an outsider and so questions that enquire about this directly are likely to be unhelpful. Indirect methods are the most useful. The pattern of relationships between different family members and habitual ways of interacting need to be kept in mind to see how the family works as a system. Asking one member of the family to describe interactions between other members is one way in and forms a 'triadic' analysis (Bowen 1978; Coppersmith 1985).

Is there a scapegoat?

One child can be given the label of being the naughty one which lets the other children in the family off the hook. Many parents describe their children as being as different as 'chalk and cheese'. They can often be blind to the fact that the good child may be stirring up the problem and letting the naughty one get the blame. The process of 'scapegoating' can make therapeutic intervention difficult unless the parents acknowledge what is happening. To allow the naughty child to be seen as good, the good child also needs to be seen as being naughty. This change in balance and role for the children may be studiously opposed by the 'good' child.

Tom (4 years old) was described as disruptive and disobedient at home. His sister, aged 7 years, was an angel in comparison. She helped her mother and always did as she was told. Watching the two of them play together during the session it was easy to see that Tom was active and restless while Sue would sit quietly and watch what was happening. They played together co-operatively with a set of cars but once Tom decided that one of the cars was his favourite Sue quietly took it when he wasn't looking. Tom then howled and snatched it back and the parents intervened to tell him off for making a noise and for snatching. Sue sat quietly and smiled while this was happening as if she had nothing to do with the incident.

The 'good' child will often tell tales on the naughty one under the guise of helping the parents know what is going on. They are referred to in disputes to tell the parents what happened and are believed in preference to the 'naughty' child. Parents caught in this situation need the opportunity to balance their views about what is happening and watch more carefully for the trigger to the behaviour problems. More equal blame is necessary and the parents need to be wary of automatically labelling the instigator. No child should be put in the powerful position of having to tell tales on another child. If the parents do not know what has happened they should either not interfere in the upset or equally attribute blame knowing that a row cannot happen without two parties being involved.

One mother surprised herself one morning when she awoke early to hear her two children whispering downstairs in the kitchen. She crept quietly down to find out what was happening and heard her 5-year-old girl tell her 3-year-old brother to open the fridge and get out some chocolate. The sister stood back while the little boy did as he was told. He had to reach up high to get the chocolate and accidentally knocked over a bottle of milk. When the mother went in, cross that they were in the kitchen alone, the girl immediately blamed her brother saying 'He did it, he opened the fridge, I didn't touch it!'

Is there parental conflict?

When recounting the problems they have with their children, parents will often appear to put all the blame on their children. But when the therapist starts to enquire how they react to the

27

problems at home a difference in opinion may be revealed. The child may gravitate to the parent that is easier to manipulate or try to play one parent off against the other. Differences in opinion can be accentuated by this process so that the parents start to argue with each other rather than dealing jointly with the child. Parents need to present a combined front to the children which is firm and united.

The role of disciplinarian in the family is an unpleasant task. Mothers may threaten with 'Wait until I tell your father' and then load the father with tales of woe as he walks through the door in the evening. In other families the mother may be responsible for the discipline and management of the house and feel she can never have fun with the child and that father seems to have all the nice times.

Mrs S. complained that her husband never backed her up in her control of the children. He did not contradict her but just said nothing and so she felt that this was criticism of her handling of the problem. If she didn't discipline the children he still would not intervene and would just say 'Well, they're only children once'. She was upset at always seeming to be cross and doing all of the shouting. She felt that the children did not like her because of this and seemed to be taking less and less notice of her. They had lots of fun with their father and she resented their good times together.

In cases where there is marked marital conflict and the parents are failing to achieve a satisfactory relationship, the children frequently play a significant part in the problem. It may be that the only times the parents show joint concern is when the child misbehaves and so the child continues to be difficult as it keeps the family together. Alternatively the parents may use the child as a pawn in their battles and try to gain allegiance from the child (Minuchin 1974; Barker 1986).

A specific focus on the marital relationship apart from management of the child may be indicated. Not recognizing the need for this will undermine the implementation of therapeutic advice and the child's behaviour problems are likely to continue or get worse. Focusing on a disagreement about the child is often the first step to admitting that there is a significant marital problem. This unthreatening introduction into discussing a marital difficulty and an explanation that a combination of therapy approaches, that is managing the child and facing up to the marital disagreements, is likely to be most effective and help the parents understand the link. Some parents get upset when they come for help with their child when a therapist starts to investigate their marital relationship, particularly if the child's problems are all attributed to the marriage. Some parents will terminate contact with the therapist because they do not understand why certain questions are being asked. They feel threatened that it is prying into their own personal affairs. The therapist should explain fully why certain areas of questioning are being broached so that parents feel part of the assessment procedure. Parents need time to understand how their problems affect their children and that it is possible to help them with management issues if they work together and support each other. If parents continue to be resistant to discussing their difficulties, this should not be pursued. As they gain confidence in the therapist opportunities will arise again for these issues to be discussed.

David (3.5 years) was refusing to pass a motion in the toilet and had become very constipated. He periodically became very bloated and had severe abdominal pain due to retention of faeces and then would pass very large amounts in extreme pain. His mother felt helpless about the problem and that it reflected on her capability as a mother. At home she was becoming progressively more disorganized and dissatisfied with her role as wife and mother as she felt that all her attempts to exert control were undermined by her husband. She had recently spent a lot of time finding out information about schools and playgroups, then her husband had completely overridden any opinion she had started to form. This was just one example of a repetitive pattern of interaction they had. She expressed intense feelings of irritation and anger at this which were denied by her husband.

On examining the pattern of soiling it was possible to see a correlation between the times the parents had a build-up of tension about a difference of opinion and the times David began to retain his faeces. Marital work was accepted by these parents in an effort to solve the problem, and progress was made once the father finally admitted that he had been told at work that he was too domineering and was unable to delegate responsibility to his juniors.

What are the parents' childhood experiences?

Therapists vary in the importance they attach to background and childhood experiences of the parents. Some feel that it is crucial in their understanding of how the parents react now, while others will concentrate only on the 'here and now', observe parental reactions, and intervene directly at that level. When a parent is very resistant to changing their reactions to their children it is helpful to unearth why they feel so strongly and often this is because of childhood experience. Their view on discipline may be highly related to experiences of a strict and authoritarian father. The parent may either emulate this approach or completely refute it and feel that they never want to be like their parents.

A very common reaction is when parents felt emotionally deprived as a child and try to over-compensate for this by providing material possessions for their children as proof of their love and care. The children become spoiled and materialistic in their attitudes and parents complain that they are so demanding and never satisfied. 'We give them everything they want and yet they behave so badly' is a frequent complaint.

What is the quality of interaction between parent and child?

There is a continuum in family disturbance and the level of therapeutic input that is required. Some families who ask for help have a basically good relationship with their children. They provide good care, love, and stimulation but may have difficulty with one or two specific areas of behaviour problem, for example sleep problems, toilet training. These families will usually benefit from therapeutic advice very quickly and will implement ideas effectively to make a good improvement. But there are other families from deprived and stressful environments who face difficulties in all areas of their lives and the children's problems are yet another stress. These parents may not be providing a good quality of interaction with their child and so demand a much higher level of therapeutic input. Similarly families where the emotional relationships are very fraught and show long-term conflict require extensive help and referral to specialist agencies.

The style of family interaction is important as it reflects on the rearing pattern adopted. Some parents may be very authoritarian and strict, others may be lax and give in easily, while others may be inconsistent and chaotic. Children's behaviour problems can arise in all of these contexts and so the advice needs to be specifically tailored to the individual family's requirements.

Cross-cultural issues can arise when expectations of child-rearing patterns may differ across cultural groups. Expectations of parental roles and responsibility may differ from western views and the techniques that parents use may appear inappropriate for our cultural viewpoint. Differences in reactions to different-sexed children is often a noticeable area of variation. The therapist's task is to be sensitive to these differences and work with the parents to devise strategies of change that fit in with their cultural viewpoint. If a child is showing emotional distress and behaviour problems no matter what the ethnic group the relationship problems in the family are still critical.

> Sayeed (2 years) was showing severe behaviour and eating problems. He was the only child of an Asian couple who were living with the father's parents. The mother was very distressed at the living arrangements as she was the housemaid for the whole extended family and had very little time to spend with her son. The grandparents completely dominated the boy and gave him high levels of attention for his difficult behaviour. The only time the mother spent with the boy was during meal-times and she had become so anxious about him eating sufficient quantities that she hovered over him and interfered with his eating pattern. Gradually he had started to reject food which had increased her level of anxiety and gained him more attention. The cultural pattern of the son's wife being subservient to his parents had created immense difficulties for this mother as she was unable to counter any of their behaviour directly.

Behavioural assessment

Parents often arrive at a session with a large number of complaints and generalizations about their child's behaviour. 'He's disobedient, naughty and has a terrible temper' describes a range of behaviour that has different meaning according to the parent's expectations of how the child should behave. What does disobedient mean? What does the child do when he or she is naughty? Helping parents clarify the definition of the problem is the first step in assessment.

What is the child doing?

Parents may need help in giving a detailed description without generalizing and blaming the child. Asking them to recount the last incidence of the problem behaviour often helps. The therapist needs to find out how often the problems are occurring and how extreme the behaviour is in order to assess the severity of the problem. A tantrum can be a simple process of children losing their temper, lying on the kitchen floor, and screaming in anger for two minutes. It can also involve destruction of furniture, hitting people, hurting themselves, and screaming for half an hour or more. It may happen once every couple of weeks, or four times a day.

Sometimes parents cannot answer the questions clearly because they have never thought of observing their child's behaviour so closely. Showing them how to record instances of the problem for discussion can be helpful. Simple charts of how often certain behaviours occur can start to illuminate the picture of what happens at home (Herbert 1981; McAuley and McAuley 1977). The day can be broken up into sections for recording purposes. The length of those sections will depend on the information required and the type of problem being recorded.

Behaviour	7.00–9.00	9.00–11.00	11.00–1.00	1.00–3.00
Tantrum	11	1	—	—
Swearing	11111	111	—	—
Hitting	11	1	—	—

Parents can record the intensity of the problem, for example whining and moaning as opposed to screaming, on the same chart by colouring the tick or making it bigger. Charts should be designed to show the information that is required and so they can be creative. The aim is for the parents to fill them in as accurately as possible, so they should be simple to fill in and placed in an easily accessible place in the home. The fridge door is often a central position. By completing the observations parents may redefine the problem. The child's refusal to comply may not seem as bad as the child's habit of answering back. The parents will begin to identify what it is that irritates them so much. The chart may also help parents recognize that the problem is not as bad as they thought or that finally they can demonstrate the seriousness of the problem.

How are the parents reacting to the problem?

The next stage of analysis is to define the context in which the problem behaviour occurs and how the parents react to it. Parents will have learned how to observe the child, but they also need to learn how to observe themselves. What do they do when their child refuses to get dressed in the morning? The parents need to recognize the link between how they try to manage the behaviour and the occurrence of the behaviour, so reactions like smacking, shouting, nagging, sulking, giving in, or ignoring need to be identified.

There is often a trigger that starts the problem. This can be a request by the parent or the child, a nag, a refusal to let the children do what they want. A repeated pattern of interaction between the parent and child can develop. The parents may continually make requests that the child ignores and the parents lose their temper. The mother at the end of such an interchange may feel angry, depressed, not valued, or negated by her child. These feelings can build up into the next repeat of the same interchange. Parents may generally feel irritable with the child and expect not to be obeyed. They may give up and try to avoid asking the child anything or feel angry before they even start to ask the child. Identifying these patterns helps the parents recognize that the methods they are using to control their children are not working.

Another type of chart helps parents begin to stand back from the emotional reactions they have and see what is happening with their child. Beginning to think about how their reactions affect the child can be an important step. Most parents can identify the first phase of interaction with their child, that is they can see what the child is doing that is irritating and they see how they react, but rarely do they then follow through the interaction to see what happens at the end. Quite often a series of progressively unpleasant interchanges will take place with the child becoming more obstinate and the parent more angry. The end point can vary between the parent just giving in for a peaceful life, the whole event fizzling out with the child still not having done what was asked or the parent having smacked the child and walked away. Many parents cannot identify who wins these battles and when they think about it carefully admit that in reality the child mostly wins.

A chart that can help detect these patterns is called an ABC chart (Gelfand and Hartman 1984; Herbert 1981). The A stands for antecedents (trigger events), the B for behaviour (the problem), and C for consequences (what the parents do).

Antecedents	Behaviour	Consequences
called him to get up	ignored me	I shouted 5 times, lost my temper

Once the observations are completed the parents can devise a hypothesis about what is maintaining the problem behaviour. This will provide the guidelines for change. The parents can pinpoint the problems that they do not know how to cope with and a discussion about different strategies of management can develop. The parents should feel an integral part of this process as it is pointless to give out a piece of advice on how to change their reactions unless they understand the rationale behind it. They need to share in the investigation and think through what they feel they can and cannot do. A plan that works for that particular family is achieved through a joint decision-making process.

Some parents need help in identifying how they are reacting to their child and so professional observation of their interaction may be required. Attendance at a day centre where the parents and child attend together can be very valuable or the professional's going to the parents' home to watch a play session will enable sharing of the observations.

Summary

Assessment is a vital part of effective intervention. As full a picture as possible of the family and the child is required before therapeutic hypotheses can be made. Professionals often intervene before they understand the problem in full and so fail. It is all too easy to feel that we know the answer to the problems presented and so precipitously give advice. The model presented here of working with parents enables the clinician to progress at the parents' rate of change and understanding.

The clinician's role is to bring into focus some areas that parents may not have thought affected the problem. Sensitive questioning will reveal aspects within the family and about the child that may have been ignored previously. The professional therefore needs to keep an open mind to check on relevant information. Certain areas of consideration are of particular value:

1 the developmental level of the child
2 family functioning
3 parental management style of the child.

Chapter three

Positive parenting

When children are disobedient and demanding, it can be difficult for parents to recognize good qualities in them. The day can be one long confrontation and by the evening both parent and child feel distressed and disturbed by the battles and arguments that have taken place. Parents can start to hate their children and progressively withdraw from any pleasant and enjoyable contact with them. Some parents describe feeling so frustrated and angry that they want to hit and hit their child. Others who are aware of these feelings dare not touch their children for fear of going too far and seriously hurting them. Others step over the line and physically batter their children.

> Mary, mother of two boys aged 4 and 6 years, described how desperate she would feel. She lived in a one-bedroomed flat, four floors up in a tower block. The boys, both lively and active, were up to mischief all day long. They climbed on the furniture, threw toys around, never did as they were told, and Mary felt that she was screaming at them all day to be quiet and leave her alone. She acknowledged that she had a bad temper but recently she had felt so angry that she had hit the younger child repeatedly around the head and shoulders, bruising him. She had felt herself wanting to hit harder and harder venting all of her pent-up anger against him. Finally she had collapsed on the floor sobbing and at that point realized that she needed help. She asked for her boys to be taken into care because she was terrified that she would do it again. She was referred for therapy and management help and within four months had improved dramatically in her relationship with her sons.

Parents at this point of desperation often cannot identify any good characteristics in their children. They still love them but feel so undermined and out of control that they become more aggressive and violent in an attempt to finally gain power.

Other parents start to withdraw emotionally from their children instead of becoming violent. All interactions are curt, negative in quality, and show irritation and poor tolerance. The child receives no interest from the parent and so starts to behave in a way to gain more attention regardless of the fact that it is negative and unpleasant. The maxim that 'negative attention is better than no attention at all' seems to be an important governing factor in children's behaviour.

Looking on the bright side

The first step in treatment is to help parents try to identify what are the good characteristics of their child. Some will say 'He's cuddly and can be very sensitive at times' or 'She is lovable some of the time and is good when we go out'. Most parents will readily describe these features but they say that the problem behaviours get in the way of appreciating their child's good qualities. The day is taken up with trying to control the child rather than having fun. If the child is behaving well or playing quietly the typical parental attitude is 'let sleeping dogs lie'. They do not want to disturb their child by commenting on how good he or she is in case the child starts to demand attention again. In many instances the parents may not realize that their child is well occupied and has not interfered with them until it is too late and the child has started to demand attention.

Parents can often be experts at telling their children what is naughty behaviour but not necessarily at telling them what is good behaviour. Children are expected to know it or extrapolate from the reprimands. Forehand and McMahon (1981) have written a very helpful and detailed therapeutic account of how to help parents with non-compliant children, and they have developed a method of helping these parents through an activity they call the 'Child's Game'. This is an exercise teaching parents how to build up a more positive relationship with their child by attending to good behaviour. As the parent starts to show interest in the child's activities and play, the child begins to experience an enjoyable interaction with the parent. This first step of improving the quality of the relationship is essential for the development of discipline. Expression of displeasure or withdrawal of attention becomes a much more potent force for managing misdemeanours once the child realizes that the parents can be very pleasant and loving. If a parent is irritable and unhappy, whether the child is behaving or misbehaving, emotional control methods are ineffective.

The rationale for this approach is to develop a warm and caring relationship between the parent and child with clear and identifiable limits set by the parent about the child's behaviour. These limits will be flexible and change as the child grows but the aim is to help the child learn the appropriate social and emotional behaviours to help him survive in society. This is not bargaining with feelings or providing conditional love contingent on good behaviour. It is helping the child and parent recognize the intensity of positive feeling that can exist between them and that their love is unconditional. They both need to recognize that displeasure and anger can be shown openly without their relationship being destroyed. Not only should the parent feel able to express upset at the child's behaviour but equally the child needs to be able to do this towards the parent.

The Child's Game is basically a free play situation where the child chooses any series of activities for 10–15 minutes during which the parent will join in under the child's direction. During this period the parent is taught two types of positive interaction skills: attending and rewarding. Attending is simply describing what the child is doing, rather like a running commentary on the activity. This provides a constant source of attention and makes sure that the child realizes that the parent is fully participating. The commentary can be just descriptive: 'Oh, you're putting the clothes on the dolly. Where's the skirt? Oh, yes there it is. That's a bit tight to put on. Oh, what a squeeze. Poor dolly's legs. Where are her pants? I wonder if they're in the basket? Oh, there they are.' This could be the observation of a mother about her daughter's play which does not demand any interaction from the child but is verbalizing what perhaps the child is thinking. Another example could be: 'That's a big car. It goes brmm, brmm all over the room. It's going very fast, over the carpet, on to the chair, and now on to the table. Oh, dear it's fallen over. Let's pick it up. I wonder where it is going now? Under the chair, ooh, that's a bit low, you can't get under there. Let's try the other way.'

This can be difficult initially for parents when they are not used to doing it, but after a little practice and getting over their embarrassment it starts to flow more easily. The commentary should not interrupt or structure the child's play and the parent needs to resist the temptation to turn it into a teaching session. The parent can join in but playing in parallel alongside the child may help the parent not take over what the child is doing. If the child starts to be deliberately naughty, throwing toys or destroying the activity the parent should stop talking. Interestingly, parents find this particularly hard as it is often the complete opposite of what they normally do. They may sit around watching their child play but only say something when the child starts to misbehave; injunctions not to do something or to be careful or not to make so much noise focus on control issues only.

The second type of positive interaction that parents can be taught is how to reward good behaviour. This can be a physical demonstration of affection, a hug, a kiss, or a pat, or it can be a statement. General statements like 'You are a good boy', 'That's really nice', 'That's right' can comment on what the child has just done. At other times more precise feedback is valuable 'Thank you for putting your toys away', 'What a good boy for coming when I called'. The precise statements are particularly useful as they teach the child clearly what the parent wants and identifies both to the parent and the child what is 'good' behaviour.

Parents are delighted with what they learn about their child during these sessions. They may never have closely observed the play, perhaps thinking it was boring or just something to keep the children out of their way. The child comes to know when the special time is and guards it. If there is more than one child in the family then a special time each is valuable. Using the time after one has gone to bed can avoid interruptions; 10–15 minutes per child is only a small time out of the whole day and it needs to be given high priority.

Setting goals of treatment

Once the relationship between the parent and child is starting to improve the parent will be able to think more clearly about the goals of treatment. Planning which behaviours they would like to see changed can be difficult when everything looks bad (Birnbrauer 1978). In families where they are able to identify good characteristics at the beginning of treatment the parents and child may have a sufficiently positive relationship to move directly into this phase.

It is usually much easier to identify bad behaviour but the process of behaviour change has two sides. If a parent wants behaviour to stop there should be something to take its place. If children are to stop breaking their toys what should they be doing instead? Once parents begin to think about what they want to see their child doing rather than what they don't want to see, their whole orientation to management starts to change.

It is possible to help parents draw up two lists. One of behaviours they want to decrease and the other of alternative behaviours that need to increase.

Behaviour to decrease	Behaviour to increase
Hurting the cat	Stroking the cat
Hitting his sister	Sharing with sister
Refusing to get dressed	Get dressed on first request
Screaming when put in buggy	Get into buggy quietly
Throwing food	Eating cleanly
Screaming for biscuits	Asking quietly for biscuits

Helping parents draw up these lists builds on the information they have gained from the assessment phase where they have already learned to specify the problem areas. Once they have realized what they want to achieve they can talk about this to their child. For example

'I've been doing lots of shouting recently and we've both been unhappy. Let's try and be happy again. I want to try and stop shouting at you in the morning so I'm going to put out your clothes for you to get dressed. When I come into get you dressed let's try and be friendly and get it done quickly without fighting, then we'll both be happy.'

A simple start like this can be the first goal of change. The parents may need some help in learning to say positive statements to their child and in identifying the times at which to say them. Learning to explain their feelings to the child also helps the child realize the impact of his or her behaviour on the parent. A statement such as 'That makes me feel very angry/unhappy/sad/upset when you do that' rather than immediately shouting at the child enables parents to stand back from their immediate emotional reactions and also teach the child awareness of other people's feelings.

The complementary skill to positive attending is ignoring. Using the two together is an effective and calm method of achieving behaviour control. Ignoring does not evoke the same intense emotional reaction as punishment in either the child or the parent. Consequently it can be much easier to use and the parent does not finish the day feeling exhausted after shouting and nagging. Parents may have tried this method in the past and failed. When children have not been warned that their parent is going to ignore them rather than shout at them the rate of their difficult behaviour may temporarily increase (Sajwaj and Dillon 1976). This is because they have not yet learned the new rules and are still trying old techniques of gaining reactions from their parents. They will try harder for a period until they realize that this strategy no longer works. Parents can give up during this process feeling that the plan is not working or even making the problem worse. Sometimes they feel so goaded by their child that they lapse into hitting and shouting. Parents can benefit from some guidance in persevering with the ignoring method and in recognizing the differences in their child's behaviour. The general irritable tone in the family will also reduce and become more relaxed.

For ignoring to work parents need to learn how to avoid all contact with their child for a short period but remain completely calm and uninterested. Turning away to avoid eye contact, not talking or commenting on the behaviour, and not touching or allowing the child to climb on to their lap are essential characteristics. As soon as the child stops misbehaving the parent can attend to him or her again. These phases should be short and not involve the parent being sulky for half a day. The message that the parent is giving should be very clear to the child. It is a method of behaviour control that can be used for most forms of behaviour management except where the children are being destructive or likely to hurt someone else or themselves.

Young children have very different temperaments and so the

style of management of one child may not suit another. Parents may be confronting their children repeatedly demanding them to do what is asked and find that this produces immense negative emotional reactions: temper tantrums or complete refusal to co-operate are common. Some children may be submissive to this approach while others fight back and will not have their willpower broken. Continual clashes of this type should alert parents to the fact that this approach is not useful with their child. Children go through defined periods of oppositional behaviour and may need humouring out of them. Many parents comment that their child did the complete opposite of what was asked for several months and so the parents learned to say the opposite of what they wanted, for example, 'I really don't want you to put your pyjamas on now', or 'I don't think you can eat all of that food'. Similarly a sense of competition will often overcome the resistance. Turning the request into a race invokes the child's sense of competition. The problem is that when a parent is feeling depressed or overwrought it is difficult for them to think of alternative strategies. They just want the child to do what is asked quickly and dread a battle. The parents want to achieve a minimum of emotional involvement because they have no energy to think and no patience but the result is often a greater investment of time and effort through forcing the child via threats, smacks, and shouts.

Using specific rewards

Occasionally children require some additional recognition that they are behaving well apart from their parent telling them that they are good. This is common at the beginning of a behaviour change programme to enhance the process and speed up the initial rate of change. Both the parent and the child want to experience success. Giving children specific feedback about their behaviour is crucial for behaviour change and one method is to use a more 'concrete' form of reward together with attention and praise. There are several ways of doing this, but the most common is a behaviour chart (Herbert 1981). It can be tailored specifically to the needs of the child and parents and its design can vary widely. Children with a mental age of 3 years and above can understand the principle and benefit from its use.

Emma (3½ years) was very strong willed at home, refusing to do what her mother asked throughout the day. Her mother identified three problem areas in which she wanted to see change:

1 getting dressed in the morning without a fuss
2 coming to the table for lunch when called
3 putting her toys away into the box at bedtime.

She planned a chart where Emma would receive an animal sticker to stick on a wall chart when she had completed any of these required tasks. She talked with Emma about the chart and what it was for and put it in the kitchen where Emma could see it clearly. Each morning her mother drew Emma's attention to the chart and gave her a lot of praise and attention while she selected a sticker for her good behaviour. The easiest task for Emma was learning to come to the table for lunch when called and once she had started to receive stickers for this she became aware of how to earn them. She was very excited by the stickers and would tell her father when he came home from work.

A readily visible chart gives children the opportunity to see how good they have been. Stickers can be used or the child can tick the chart, colour in a square, draw a happy face or whatever they like. The important feature is that the parents demonstrate their recognition of the good behaviour and praise the child while the chart is being filled in. No child will gain pleasure or motivation from a chart if a parent is half-hearted in giving out a sticker or says, 'I haven't got time to think about that now'.

Charts can be used for all types of behaviour problems from encouraging children to sleep in their own beds, to passing a motion in the lavatory, having a dry bed, or behaving well while out shopping. It is essential that parents understand that stickers cannot be removed once they have been earned, no matter how badly behaved the child is. The contract with the child must hold firm and the parent cannot deny that the child did behave well for that one item of behaviour.

A mother of three children aged 3, 5, and 6 years found meal-times unbearable. They would kick each other under the table, take food off one another's plates, throw food on the table, shout and scream at each other. She had tried separating them to eat in different places but it had not worked as they tried to run around while eating. She agreed to try a behaviour chart and identified that each of them should sit in their own chairs, eat their own food quietly, and not interfere with each other. If they were able to do this over the course of the whole meal-time they received a sticker on the chart. Each child was able to earn a sticker so that they would all be motivated to behave. It worked on the first day of application. Each child was proud of how good they had been, each of them earning three stickers for the three meals.

Some therapists express concern that a child may become addicted to earning stickers and that it may be difficult to wean them off charts. In reality children usually start to lose interest after about two weeks once they realize that they can earn them relatively easily. The social recognition of their good behaviour is then more important to them. When a child appears to be losing interest it is important to check carefully with the parents how much social back-up is being given. Children may be feeling that this is the only safe way they have of proving how good they can be. If a weaning process is required, the parent can progressively increase the requirements for earning a sticker, for example two nights, then three, and then a week of dry beds before a sticker is allocated. Alternatively it is possible to reduce the value of the sticker by asking the children how many they would like. Once the children realize that they can have as many as they want they stop wanting them.

Some parents find the change in approach to positive rewarding very difficult. They feel that it is not appropriate for their naughty child to receive special treatment or they feel that they should not reward the child for doing something that other children do naturally. These are often parents who are very strict, have high standards, or are punitive in their approach to management. Such attitudes are often very difficult to shift and the therapist who forces an alternative view of management is doomed to failure. It may take a long time discussing the parents' child-rearing philosophy and even discussing their own childhood experiences of discipline to unearth the cause of these deep-seated feelings. A gradual recognition by the parents that their approach does not appear to work is necessary before they will try another approach.

Recognizing the fact that they do not seem to be enjoying their children and are missing the fun of childhood can be one way into helping them realize the value of a positive approach. Empathy with the sadness they must feel about the problems they are facing with their child, particularly stressing the lack of a happy relationship, can facilitate a change in attitude.

Developing parents' confidence

The fact that such apparently simple management methods work is astonishing to some parents. The years of battles and punishment that have not worked help them realize that keeping calm, ignoring slight misbehaviour, and rewarding appropriate behaviour are more effective ways of controlling their children and of having a more pleasant life. Their confidence in themselves as parents increases and their relationship with their child improves. The attribution of the positive changes to their own efforts is important so that they feel confident in managing without the help of a professional. It is the therapist's task to emphasize how capable the parent has become and encourage them to continue.

Learning to anticipate

The child

Parents of well-behaved children use consistent and effective management methods and so are predictable in their reactions. The child learns what to expect. Some parents achieve this by being consistently very strict while others are very caring and child-centred but establish clear boundaries for the child's behaviour. In both cases the child understands what is expected and can choose or not choose to comply, being fully aware of the consequences.

Most behaviour problems are triggered by situations where children have learned that if they try hard enough they can get their own way (Bijou and Baer 1976). If the parents' reactions are inconsistent or uncertain the child will start to make more and more demands until the predictable success occurs. For example some mothers feel very embarrassed about reprimanding their child or dealing with a tantrum in public and so the child rapidly learns that a tantrum could produce sweets if enough fuss is created (McAuley and McAuley 1977). If screaming for sweets in the supermarket can occasionally be successful the child learns that it is worth having a go every time they pass the supermarket checkout. Similarly when children have been ill, parental expectations of their behaviour changes, and sometimes it is difficult to re-establish previous patterns of sleep and feeding when a parent is unsure whether the child is fully recovered.

Children can behave quite differently in different settings or with different people. Some fathers say that their child does as he's told while the mother complains that she has no control. Children learn to discriminate between places and people very easily.

The parent

Parents can also learn to anticipate which situations are likely to cause problems. Being prepared and firm about their views will help forestall a problem. Many parents use avoidance strategies either by alternating the environment in some way, for example removing ornaments from low shelving, or by setting rules like banning felt tips except when an adult is supervising. Distracting techniques are frequently used with pre-school children either before a problem arises or as a palliative once the problem is occurring, for example pointing to an aeroplane flying in the sky to help the child forget that the ice cream van is parked outside the playground.

Holden (1983) followed mothers and their toddlers around supermarkets to see how mothers use different strategies to avoid behaviour problems. Some mothers would avoid problems, distracting their child by talking to them and involving them in the shopping, while others would distract their child once they had started to be difficult. Another group shouted and were negative when their children began to misbehave. When the mother was able to anticipate a problem the children made fewer demands and there was less need to control the child. The latter group had the most difficulties and the greatest number of demands from the children.

Similarly some parents anticipate problems in car journeys by preparing toys, books, and songs to amuse their children and avoid squabbles and boredom. This ability to be aware and think ahead is another aspect of parenting that can be discussed and planned with parents. They may have anticipated to the extent that they dread doing certain activities like going shopping with the children but have not developed their thinking to see how to avoid the problems. This process links back to the idea of positively tracking the child's behaviour. If children are being quiet and good while out shopping many mothers ignore them and only respond once they are difficult. If the mother learns how to gain positive interaction from her child during shopping many of the behaviour problems will resolve immediately.

Another form of anticipation was demonstrated by Shaffer and Crook (1980), who showed that mothers who are careful in the timing of their control methods are much more likely to gain compliance from toddlers. There needs to be a sequential strategy in which the mother makes sure that the child is correctly oriented. A sudden request is doomed to failure but if the mother has gained the child's attention first she is more likely to achieve compliance. So parents need to take into account the attentional state of the child before making a demand and by being aware of the need to gain attention they can avoid a clash of wills (Stayton *et al.* 1971).

Summary

Positive parenting is an approach to child management that emphasizes the good qualities of the child's behaviour and helps the parent to become aware of them. Often the good qualities can be hidden by the problems and parents need help in changing their emphasis on bad behaviour to good behaviour. Intervention is geared towards improving the parent–child relationship by learning how to play with the child, experiencing happy play sessions together, identifying the child's good characteristics, planning on increasing certain good behaviour, and using reward techniques. Parents can learn to anticipate difficulties and develop avoidance strategies as part of a positive parenting approach. Building up parental confidence in these techniques can sometimes present a problem as they may be contradictory to the parents' viewpoint.

Chapter four

Setting limits

Aggressive and disruptive behaviour

Aggressive and destructive children usually cannot be contained purely by the ignoring and rewarding methods described in the previous chapter, so parents need to learn alternative management methods that will enable them to gain rapid and effective control. It is not possible nor is it appropriate to ignore behaviour that involves breaking toys, destroying furniture, or hurting others. Children need to understand and learn where the limit is for their behaviour. They need to be taught the consequences of their behaviour and that it is not acceptable. Violent actions are often the result of experimentation, anger and frustration, or lack of self-control. They are easily imitated and winning provides the child with a sense of satisfaction and power. This pattern of behaving can become habitual as the child either learns to vent angry feelings or uses aggression and violence to control others.

In some families with aggressive children the boundaries and limits on the child's behaviour may not be clear and a struggle for power can take place between the parents and child which rapidly escalates into violence. Patterson and his colleagues (1975) have worked extensively with aggressive children and their families and have tried to explain how the interaction becomes progressively more violent. They call this the 'coercive hypothesis' when both the parent and the child learn that they can occasionally win a battle by shouting louder or hitting harder. There are two paths of escalation, one in which the parent gives in and one in which the child gives in (Wells and Forehand 1981).

a) mother gives a command

    ⇔

child screams and refuses to comply

    ⇔

mother gives up to avoid having a screaming child

b) mother gives a command

    ⇔

child screams and refuses to comply

    ⇔

mother shouts and repeats command

    ⇔

child screams louder and still refuses

    ⇔

mother shouts louder/hits and repeats command

    ⇔

child complies

A spiral of anger and aggression develops with the parent and child becoming progressively more unpleasant to each other (Patterson 1980; Reid *et al.* 1981). The parent is also demonstrating to the child how to behave in an aggressive and anti-social manner (Patterson *et al.* 1975) and is likely to be copied in the future. Either the parent or the child can initiate the interchange by making a demand. The number of demands that a parent or child will make can depend on their past experience of those demands having been met or be the result of a pattern of behaviour that has evolved due to other problems, that is child's poor concentration span, or mother's irritability due to depression or an unhappy marriage.

a) child makes a demand

    ⇔

mother refuses to comply

    ⇔

child screams and further demands

    ⇔

mother complies

b) child makes a demand

      ⟱

mother refuses to comply

      ⟱

child screams and demands more

      ⟱

mother shouts and refuses

      ⟱

child screams louder and demands more

      ⟱

mother shouts/hits and refuses

      ⟱

child gives up

Parents often feel that their children should not have everything that they ask for and try to provide some restraint. But unfortunately unless this restraint is very clear and firmly upheld children will rapidly learn, by making a great scene, particularly in public, that they can get their own way. Some parents cannot bear to see children cry and try to avoid this at all events, others may be erratic and inconsistent in their controls. This can happen in the closest of relationships when the parent is wanting to be caring and kind but realizes that some limits need to be set. They find difficulty in confronting their child and want to avoid tears and battles but feel angry about the child's constant and insistent demands (Douglas and Richman 1984).

When parents are overstressed and have little energy or patience they may give in quickly to be left alone. The child will then begin to make even more demands and the parent may become punitive in order to stop the demands. The anger that builds up characterizes the general pattern of interaction between the parent and child with the parent being erratic and inconsistent in reaction and the child being aggressive and difficult in order to gain attention and have his or her own way.

Naturalistic studies of parent–child interaction in the home (Patterson 1976) have demonstrated that in families with a difficult, aggressive child there are high rates of aggression, particularly towards the mother. These children are often nagged and reprimanded by their mothers even when they are behaving well. This may be due to the 'halo effect' of expecting bad behaviour from a child labelled as naughty. Events that occur out of sight are automatically blamed on the child, or the mother may anticipate problems and keep warning or threatening the child in order to forestall a problem. Parents are often heard warning their child at the door to the nursery 'Now don't be naughty today' as a farewell rather than 'Have a lovely time'.

Snyder (1977) found that an indiscriminate use of attention was more frequent in clinic-referred families than in normal families. The mother's behaviour was often related to how the child had behaved, but there were long aggressive interchanges which were often the only predictable interaction that the mother and child demonstrated (Wahler *et al.* 1981). Once these mothers and children started an argument they were likely to last twice as long as in non-clinic families. Neither the parent nor the child was able to let go of the argument. These parents appear to have difficulty in saying 'no' firmly and then ignoring the child's behaviour. Every time the child makes demands the parent provides a retort and opens up the possibility of more interaction about the demand. Once an argument is in progression the child may feel that there is an increased likelihood of the parent's giving in.

Wahler has tried to identify in which families these problems are more likely to occur and has suggested that 'insular' families are at greater risk for producing non-compliant and aggressive children. These families are characterized as being socio-economically disadvantaged and socially isolated. The parents have very little social contact with friends, relatives, or authority and any contact they have is often unpleasant. They reject help from outside agencies which they see as interfering and so often show a poor response to therapy and intervention.

Wahler and Dumas (1986) found that 'insular' mothers were more angry and irritable than non-insular mothers towards their children, whether the child was being naughty or good. A mother who is living in an environment where she is very isolated and whose general social contacts with neighbours, relatives, and husband are mostly unhappy or antagonistic is likely to behave differently from a mother who generally has pleasant interactions with most people but occasionally experiences some aggressive reactions from her child. When an 'insular' mother responds she is reflecting her total reaction to all the people she meets rather than that particular person (Dumas and Wahler 1983). Researchers found that on a day when an 'insular' mother reported having an argument with another adult before she was observed at home with her child, she was more likely to behave unpleasantly towards her child (Wahler and Graves 1983). So it appears that a general tendency to unhappy and aggressive social interaction spins over into mother–child management struggles.

Wahler and Dumas (1986) suggest that in these families the only predictable response that the child receives from the mother is that she behaves aggressively when he does. There is evidence that both animals and humans prefer predictable rather than unpredictable reactions even when predictability is obtained from a very unpleasant experience. Children who live in 'insular' families are therefore reinforced in their long fights with their parents as this may be the only predictable response they know their parents will provide.

Wahler and Dumas (1986) found that 90 per cent of aversive interchanges with parents are initiated by the child rather than the mother. They repeatedly demanded that their mothers played with them, gave them things, and helped them but their mothers rarely complied. As the child became more demanding in a more unpleasant manner the mother would respond negatively until a long sequence of shouting and hitting would develop. The mothers in general were detached and uninterested in their children. They were also immature in the battles they had with their children, often fighting to have the last word, calling the child names, or taunting them with statements such as 'You just dare'.

Management of aggression

Many parents manage aggression by hitting or shouting at their child. This may work or not, and if it doesn't there is a serious problem as hitting can escalate to dangerous levels, with parents' losing their tempers and losing control of their actions.

Parents in these circumstances need to learn how to stop an escalation of this behaviour by using a 'time out' method (Douglas 1988). This is an extreme form of ignoring. The child is removed to another place, usually a bedroom or into the hall, to avoid any reinforcement for the aggressive behaviour. The parent avoids responding in anger or punitively as the child is out of the way (Herbert 1981; Forehand and McMahon 1981). There are various ways in which this can be carried out depending on the age of the child and level of control of the parents. The simplest form is putting the child on a chair to one side of the room for between two and five minutes and ignoring the child while seated. The parent must stay calm and firm but show disapproval at the behaviour. The child may initially need to be held briefly on the chair, but the parent can release hand pressure as soon as the child settles on the chair. Once the tantrum or violence has calmed down and the child has stopped fighting and crying he or she can get up off the chair. If the child shows a habit of prolonged crying then instead of expecting him or her to sit there for a long period of time, the first break in crying after a few minutes should be taken by the parent as an opportunity to allow the child to get up. Ignoring should continue until the child stops crying.

If the parent finds difficulty in not reacting to the child while in 'time out' on the chair, it may be better for the child to be placed in a safe separate room for the equivalent time. Some parents use the hallway, others the bedroom. But the time should still be only a few minutes and the parent should go to collect the child and indicate when it is appropriate to join the family again.

Time out is a very effective way of controlling aggressive behaviour but it needs to be applied at the time of the problem and the parents must remain calm and firm. Short frequent periods in time out provide rapid learning experiences for the child. Some parents may already use a variation of this procedure by sending children to their rooms, but this is usually for long periods to get the children out of their way. After the first few minutes the child is not going to learn any more from the experience and will either fall asleep, start to play, or get up to mischief in the room. The purpose of the technique should be made very clear to parents so that they can also make it clear to the child what they are doing and why they are doing it.

Mary, aged 4 years, showed a lot of aggressive behaviour towards her younger sister of 2. She would not let the younger child share her toys and would often snatch toys from her. She had three or four tantrums a day and was generally very volatile in her emotional state. Her parents had been very aware of the problems of sibling rivalry when the younger child was born and had tried very appropriately to help Mary accept the situation.

Her mother had taken great care to provide a lot of love and attention to Mary, often at the neglect of the baby. They came for help at a point when Mary was starting to pull her sister's hair violently and scratch her face in anger. They needed an immediate solution for an urgent problem. The family were observed for a day and it was evident how Mary attempted to dominate her sister at all times. A time out procedure had been discussed with the parents and they had used it unsuccessfully at home.

During the observation day it was evident what was going wrong. The parents were reluctant to use the technique and gave her lots of warnings and did not carry out their threats. The one time they were encouraged to sit her on a chair, after she had scratched her sister, both parents moved over to her and fussed her, talking and explaining to her why they were putting her on the chair. She gained a great deal of parental attention during this. When prompted not to talk to Mary but just stand behind her and hold her shoulder it was evident how difficult the mother found this procedure. The mother was prompted when to let go and once Mary made a two-second break in her crying after several minutes of screaming she was told she could get up. The parents were then encouraged to go and check on the sister to let Mary see that they were concerned about her and were giving the sister attention.

Once the parents had been shown how to carry out the technique they became more confident in using it and over the course of the next two weeks Mary stopped physically attacking her sister.

Temper tantrums

Temper tantrums are commonly reported from the age of 2 years old. Jenkins *et al.* (1984) found that 19 per cent of 2-year-olds, 18 per cent of 3-year-olds, and 11 per cent of 4½-year-olds had tantrums at least daily. A quarter of these children were also reported to be difficult to manage and demanding attention. The toddler age group is particularly prone to this type of behaviour problem and parents may seek help from GPs and paediatricians who may just say that the child will grow out of it (Christopherson 1986).

Learning how to cope with this behaviour can often set the scene for later management skills, particularly in parents who are uncertain and lacking in confidence. Parents who give in to a toddler's temper will increase the likelihood of tantrums recurring and find themselves becoming more angry. Parents use a variety of techniques, from reasoning and explaining to threatening and slapping, when a child is having a tantrum, all of which have little or no effect. The child is usually too emotionally overwrought to listen to reason. A slap often makes the situation worse and the child's cries louder while parents' shouting only increases the general noise level.

Tantrums occur frequently when children are trying to get their own way and several explanations have been proposed:

1 The child has learned that tantrums effectively help him or her to get his or her own way.

2 The child may have a low tolerance to frustration and his or her emotional reaction may erupt out of control.

3 The child has learned that tantrums gain parental attention.

4 The child has learned that tantrums gain a predictable response (even if it is aggressive) from the parents.

5 Immature speech in the very young child or delayed speech can interfere with the child's ability to express needs and desires and create a sense of frustration.

Management of temper tantrums

The first step in helping parents cope with tantrums is to encourage them to identify the triggers for the behaviour. Is the child showing frustration with immature skills? During the toddler period some children's awareness and motivation outstrips their co-ordination and so anger at not being able to get the doll's arm into the jumper or the man into the fire engine can suddenly cause the child to scream in frustration and throw the toy across the room. Similarly young children resort to screaming because they cannot use words to describe what they want. Parents may be too busy to attend to them or not fast enough in their reactions and understanding of what is required and so the child tantrums in desperation and anger. In both of these instances children need prompt attention and help to teach them to cope with the problem. Understanding and compassion will defuse the situation with the parents showing them what to do and helping the children with the task. Indicating understanding of poor language skills does not necessarily mean that children receive what they are asking for but the fact that poor language has not interfered with the process of communication needs to be made clear to children. Noises and gestures are very easily understood even if the child cannot talk.

In other instances the temper tantrum is a bid for control of other people. This can be with parents, siblings, peers, or other care-takers. Once this is recognized, the parents can learn how to counteract it. They should decide if there is any behaviour that they would like to see in its place. For example asking with 'please' may gain compliance from the parent while asking without it won't. Asking for a biscuit after a meal will be acceptable but not before. The child needs the opportunity to find out what is an acceptable demand that might be met. The most important lesson to be learned by both the parents and the child is that when mother says 'no' she means 'no' and not 'well if you make a louder fuss I might give in'. Setting the limit and sticking to it is the key factor in behaviour control.

Sometimes the problem is triggered by the parent. Expectations that the child should hold the parent's hand while crossing the road, or sit in the safety seat in the car, can be met by great outbursts of temper in the confident 2-year-old who wants to be totally independent. Parents' giving in to avoid a fight reinforces the child's difficult behaviour next time this same situation occurs and can also be dangerous: 2-year-olds don't forget and so parents cannot hope that their child will not remember their giving in. The child has no awareness of danger and must not be allowed to make the decision about levels of independence. Dangerous circumstances as in these two examples are often easier for parents to understand and realize that in fact they do exert effective control at some times. When parents recognize that a particular issue is important they can and will take control and set limits. But some children, either through their experience of using tantrums to get their own way or through general strong will and temperament, will take a lot of teaching and repeated experiences to realize finally that they cannot always get their own way. Some children may be forced three or four times into a car safety seat to learn the rule but others may take twenty or thirty confrontations over the course of several weeks before they give in.

Parents should try to list a series of daily confrontations that evoke tantrums. They need to describe initially what issues they want to stand firm on and what issues they can give way to. It is helpful for them to recognize that if they intend to carry through what they say, they may need to reduce the number of demands that they make on the child. An environmental change can ease this: it is much easier to say that you don't have any sweets in the house than to say 'no' to a child who knows that they are in the cupboard.

Most tantrums are best left to blow themselves out. Children may headbang, throw themselves on the floor, kick furniture, scream, and cry but as long as they are safe and are not escalating into aggressive or destructive behaviour they should be quietly ignored. If the parent walks away or shuts the door on the child, the child may get up and follow and just start all over again. So just turning away and getting on with a job is the most effective response. Once the child has calmed down the parent can make a brief comment about it all being over now and then continue as if the tantrum had not occurred. Some children will want a cuddle as they will have become very upset; others may want a little sleep as they will have exhausted themselves. The parents should react calmly and lovingly as normal but under no circumstances should children gain their demands through deliberately having a tantrum. A simple explanation to the child about how mummy is not going to give in to tempers can help the child learn more quickly.

Some children are selective about where they have tantrums especially when parents become distressed by difficult behaviour in public places: on the bus or in the shops are prime target areas. Mothers often recount how embarrassed they feel and that if they try to ignore their child's screams in town then other shoppers make comments like 'Oh, give him a sweet, he's only small'. If this is an important problem to the parent, they should practise at home saying 'no' before they do it in public. They need to gain confidence and the child needs the opportunity to learn how the parent can establish limits. The next stage is to set small targets like going past or in the local sweet shop, without buying sweets, before the major trial of waiting in a supermarket queue beside the sweet shelves. If the child has been told in advance that sweets and toys are not going to be bought this warns the child that tantrums will not work. Parents also need to be aware when their child has behaved well and make a comment about this so that the child receives praise and recognition for good behaviour.

Setting a simple structure to the day can also help manage the toddler. Being aware of their limitations of ability and attention will prevent the parents' feeling irritated. A mother may set out some crayons and paper or plasticene while she gets on with the ironing but she should expect to be interrupted and asked for help.

Non-compliance

One of the most common complaints of parents is that their child will not obey them. Parents will shout, hit, nag, and lose their tempers in order to gain control of their children but find that nothing works. Sometimes their demands and requests invoke an aggressive response from the child while in other families the child just ignores the request or blatantly refuses to comply. Mothers often say that they say the same things over and over again and end up losing their tempers in order to get a response.

Gaining obedience from children will partly depend on their developmental level and whether they understand and can carry out what is expected. A 3-year-old should be able to put toys away in a big box but cannot sort out clothes for a cupboard. Similarly some attempts at self-dressing are possible at this age (excluding buttons and fastenings) while a 5-year-old should be able to manage all aspects of getting dressed. The majority of children throughout most of junior school life have no concept of time and rushing.

The way the parent asks is also important in determining whether the child will comply. Forehand and McMahon (1981) outlined four types of commands that reduce the likelihood of a child's complying:

1 A chain command where a series of requests is made altogether so that the child gets information overload, e.g. 'Put your toys away, tidy up your bed, and put those shoes in the box'.

2 A vague command where the child does not understand the

meaning behind the statement, e.g. 'Be careful' instead of 'Please come down off that wall'.

3 Question commands where the parent appears to join in the activity but in fact does not intend to do it, e.g. 'Let's pick up the toys' rather than 'Please, pick up your toys'.

4 A rationale after a command which can obscure what is required and encourage the child to ask questions and side track, e.g. 'Please pick up your toys, you've got a friend coming and I want your room to look tidy'. If a rationale is used it should be before the command so that the command itself is clear and the last thing in the child's mind.

Management of non-compliance

Parents may need help in learning how to ask their child to do what is required. They need to learn to

1 be specific and direct
2 give one command at a time
3 wait five seconds to check whether it has been carried out.

It is common for some mothers to ask their child to do something and then walk away expecting it to be done. But when the parent is teaching the child to do what is asked, the parent needs to wait and check. This is the process of carrying through what is said so that the child learns that parents mean what they say.

Forehand and McMahon (1981) have devised a Parent's Game which continues on from the Child's Game described in the previous chapter. This is a training exercise during which the parent learns to use appropriate commands and follow through after five seconds either by rewarding and attending to the child if he or she has complied or by using time out if not. The parent warns the child that time out will be used if he or she does not do as he or she is told. This is a deliberate training strategy that is used in the clinic and observed so that the parent learns how to do it at home.

Most therapists just ask the parents what is happening at home and suggest that the parents keep diaries of events to discuss in detail during a therapy session. Two or three specific problem areas can be identified with the parents that they would like to work on first. Once specified, these problem behaviours can be talked about to the child and clear guidelines given about what is expected and what is going to happen if the child continues to misbehave. Parents can use a repertoire of techniques for behaviour change which build on each other.

1 Try to ignore the non-targeted behaviour problems during the day.

2 Make simple commands when the child is paying attention.

3 Carry through any requests or commands.

4 Persevere in getting the child to comply without losing their temper.

5 Use 'time out' if the child becomes aggressive or loses his or her temper.

6 Reward with attention and praise all instances of the child's complying with requests.

Setting clear boundaries for the child's behaviour is essential as once the child realizes that the parents are being consistent and firm in their reactions the problem behaviour will disappear. The speed of behaviour change will vary from child to child depending on their temperamental state, their past learning history, and the ability of the parents to be consistent. Some parents find the use of reward charts a helpful addition in the early stages of behaviour change. Children can start to earn stickers for the chart every time they comply with the first request. Most parents graduate to giving one warning after the initial command so that the child has a little time in which to respond but parents need to be very careful that they don't lapse into nagging to get the child to comply again. Often the change in relationship that occurs as the parents work on the initial problem areas will generalize to other times of the day as the parent gains confidence and authority.

Children go through various stages of obedience and disobedience as they develop and parents need to be aware that direct confrontation may not be the best method of handling the situation. Challenging the child via an element of competition often works: 'I wonder who can get dressed first?' or 'I bet you can't put on your own shoes' will often motivate children to comply without their realizing. Other parents use humour and may even deliberately say the opposite of what is required in the knowledge that the child will then do the reverse of the request: 'I really don't think you should eat that last spoonful' will challenge children to prove their parents wrong and consequently finish their meal. Many parents report prolonged phases in early childhood when they used this technique. Children after the age of 2 are often so keen to prove their own independence and ability that they feel they know much better than their parents and so argue or ignore parents' normal requests. This is a phase of development and is not really an indication of a behaviour problem.

These techniques are used by parents who can anticipate the child's reactions. The parents need to know how to gauge the child's response and achieve their aim without anger or upset.

Sibling rivalry and aggression

During the second year of life children start to develop some understanding of what will upset and annoy a sibling. Their motivation to support or to tease siblings develops. Family views about what is naughty or good start to be absorbed as mothers begin to talk about transgression of family rules or social behaviour. From about 18 months a child will watch and show interest in naughtiness by their siblings (Dunn and Munn 1985). Other studies have also demonstrated that during the second year most children become responsive to the distress and anger of other family members (Cummings *et al.* 1981; Kagan 1982).

The hostility that siblings show can therefore commence at a very young age: 2-year-olds become increasingly adept at asking for mother's help in a sibling conflict and can be quite explicit about what the sibling has done to them. The mother is often drawn into these fights and will start to influence the way in which the children will behave towards each other. The elder child may be made to give way to the demands of the younger one in order to keep the peace. During this process younger children learn that if they cry loud enough to get the parent involved they usually get their own way. When parents become involved in sibling arguments they have to be very careful not make the situation worse rather than better. Children can compete for the parent's favour and help, which obscures the real cause of the argument. Aggression and violence can escalate when jealousy and envy grow in a competitive atmosphere. Tale-telling on each other and inciting each other to be naughty are frequent problems faced by parents of young children. Siblings need to learn to cope with each other in arguments and fights and in general when left to find their own method of coping there is no real violence. Family rules and strategies of obtaining help often need to be made clear. So for example helping a school-age child find safe places for precious toys or possessions that the younger child cannot reach is important, but in addition making clear that any physical aggression from either age group is not acceptable.

Children will also split parental affection with one being favoured by one parent and the other child seeking help from the other parent. Parents may end up fighting the children's battles and undermining each other's attempts at discipline.

Jenny, aged 4 years, was her father's favourite. She mostly managed to get her own way with him. John, her brother aged 6 years, was mother's favourite and she had become concerned that her husband was undermining her authority with Jenny during the day when she was at home with her. It was evident in sessions how the children gravitated physically to their preferred parents. An incident occurred during one session when the children were drawing together. They started to fight about who had the most crayons and mother tried to intervene and tell them both off for making a noise. Father immediately suggested that Jenny go and sit on his lap and he gave her a big cuddle. He said that he felt it was unfair that his wife should reprimand Jenny as she was so young and did not know how to share properly yet. Jenny sat with a contented smile on her face during this interchange while mother repressed her irritation and anger with her husband's remarks.

Many families experience the problems of squabbles between siblings and learn to establish rules for mediating a problem. Some parents immediately separate the children and punish both when they do not know what has happened. Others will ignore the problem and let the children sort it out themselves. Most learn by trial and error that they can never really get to the bottom of the problem if they did not witness it and so emphasize the importance of sharing and co-operating in the family so everyone stays happy. Stressing the positive approach to social interaction is an important part of teaching children to be sociable.

Extreme sibling abuse by 4-year-old children has been reported although this is rare. These children have deliberately tried to hurt their brothers and sisters with knives, pushing them out of windows or down stairs (Rosenthal and Doherty 1984). In a study describing ten of these children it was possible to identify three groups of children:

1 Children who had been chronically abused by their parents.

2 Children whose parents had given unconscious, covert permission for the child's aggressive behaviour.

3 Children who were identified with a dangerous or destructive person in the parent's life and so few limits were set on their behaviour.

Inadequate limits being set on the child's behaviour, possible reinforcement of the aggression and modelling of aggression, and poor control of emotional reactions were all part of the learning history of these abusing children.

Patterson (1986) has recently started to look at the contribution siblings make to the development of aggressive behaviour. Naturalistic studies in the homes of families with an aggressive child indicate that the siblings of that child also show a high rate of aggressive behaviour but that this is directed at the sibling rather than the parent (Patterson 1982; 1984). Even when the siblings' reactions to the aggressive child were eliminated from the analysis the siblings' behaviour was much more aggressive in normal families. The poor relationships between siblings was more common in families which had little organization, poor discipline, and monitoring of the children by the parents. Patterson found that only the problem child was permitted to be out of control in interaction with the parents, while all of the children were permitted to be out of control when interacting with each other. This partly explains how in some families the removal of the problem child into care or residential school allows another child in the family to be labelled as a problem. He also found, in common with other studies (Dunn and Kendrick 1981; 1982), that mothers' depressed and irritable reactions were strong prime determinants for aggression in pre-school boys, while sibling irritable reactions became prime determinants by the age of seven to eight years.

Many siblings quarrel and fight particularly if they are of opposite sexes. The frequency of these fights is higher than for fights with peers. The Newsons (1976) reported that 29 per cent of 7-year-olds often fight with their siblings while only 7 per cent often fight with other children, 64 per cent sometimes fight with their sibs while 32 per cent sometimes fight with others. Twice as many boys than girls are likely to be aggressive with outsiders but they equally fight in the home. Sometimes it is clear that siblings do not like each other. This may be due to parental management techniques but may also be due to the temperamental state of the child. Parents cannot expect their children to get on with each other but family life is very difficult if there is continuous bickering and jealousy between children. Parental confidence in handling them, equal attention, and a sense of humour are probably the best approach to coping with such problems. Once parents start to try and rationalize the situation, over-compensate or feel guilty about their children not liking each other, the situation will only get worse. Talking to the children about each other, explaining feelings and actions and emphasizing the importance of not hurting each other will help foster harmonious relationships. Children need to know that their feelings of jealousy or anger with their brother or sister are very common and that their parents understand how they feel.

Mark, aged 5 years, showed a variety of behaviour problems at home. He often fought with his younger sister aged 3 years, he would snatch her toys, push her over and ride his car into her. If his parents bought her a present he was always comparing and felt that she had better things and more things than he did. In fact the opposite was true. The parents, in their concern about him feeling pushed out by his younger sister, had always given him much more and felt very upset when he complained. His mother would become involved in long discussions with him about how she treated them both fairly and then would end up getting angry with his unreasonable attitude.

Mark needed a chance to realize that his parents understood how he felt and that lots of other older brothers feel the same way towards their young sisters. Simple recognition of his feelings rather than continual arguments about how fair they were being was needed from his parents. They needed to stop arguing about the content of his complaints but deal with the underlying feelings behind them. Labelling his feelings for him and brief sympathy was all that was required. They also needed to stop rationalizing the problem to themselves and bending over backwards to be fair. Once they realized that no presents could ever be exactly the same and that they could help him to take pleasure in his sister's presents by pointing out the good features of one of her new toys to her they felt more confident in coping with his reactions.

Arrival of a new baby

Dunn (1983; 1984) in Cambridge has carried out extensive observations of sibling relationships and the effects of general family functioning of the arrival of a new baby. She found that 93 per cent of the first-born children showed an increase in naughtiness after the arrival of a new baby. They were not usually aggressive towards the baby, but unco-operative and demanding with their mother. Toilet training often deteriorated and also sleeping patterns became disrupted. Sometimes the behaviour was regressive, angry, and distressed, while others suddenly became more mature and independent. Most of the problems had disappeared by the time the baby was 8 months old and there was no link with the incidence of later problems in the relationship between the siblings. Anxious children showed a slightly different pattern: there were often marked increases in fears and worries during the first year of life of the sibling. As longitudinal studies have shown that fearful children can be at risk for later behaviour problems (Richman et al. 1982) this is of concern. The research also found that children who tended to withdraw following the sibling's birth were likely to be hostile during the ensuing years and their relationship was often conflictual.

In general, children under 5 years were more likely to be upset at the birth, but neither sex of the child nor separation at the birth determined the reaction. Children who tend to be irritable, moody, difficult to manage, and emotional about changes or frustrated will generally react with the most disturbance to the birth. A close relationship with the father can offset some of the problems. Mother's post-natal level of depression and exhaustion had a negative effect on the first-born. Obviously the decrease in the amount of time spent with the first-born will have an effect but many parents are aware of this and make a great effort to give attention to the older child. Breastfeeding was not found to be an area of jealousy and envy as many mothers prepare themselves with books, potties, drinks, and crayons to distract the older child while they breastfeed the baby. Being prepared for the demands and requests while caring physically for the newborn helps forestall many problems (Kitzinger 1979).

Summary

Families with aggressive children can be helped by teaching the parents to be more consistent and effective in their control methods. Using a 'time out' procedure for managing hitting, biting, and destructive behaviour is an effective way of setting limits for the child.

Tantrums occur frequently in young children. Those that are due to demands' being refused and bad temper can be ignored but others are best managed by helping the child cope with frustrating experiences.

When parents are managing a child who is disobedient and non-compliant they need to make their instructions clear and concise, and carry through their request. All co-operative and good behaviour should be commented on and praised.

Talking to the child and explaining what is naughty and what is good helps the child understand and learn what is expected. Children also need to be listened to and their point of view understood. Learning about parents' feelings is necessary for children to recognize the impact of their behaviour. Realizing that parents care about the child's feelings is an integral part of this process.

When siblings are in conflict they need consistent and caring control plus help in recognizing each other's needs and feelings. Learning pro-social behaviour is an essential part of controlling aggressive and violent reactions.

Chapter five

Eating and feeding difficulties

Prevalence

Eating and feeding problems are a very common cause of concern for parents. In one major study of 5-year-olds, over one-third of children are described as having mild or moderate eating or appetite problems. Two-thirds of these were described as faddy while the rest were considered not to eat enough (Butler and Golding 1986). The more children there are in a family the less likely it is that the younger child will have eating difficulties. Feeding problems are more prevalent among low birth-weight babies.

In another study in London 16 per cent of 3-year-olds were considered to have poor appetite while 12 per cent were thought to be faddy (Richman *et al.* 1982). No sex differences were found in the rate of problems but the difficulties were found to persist for one year in about two-thirds of these children and to persist for over five years in about one-third.

Identification of a problem

There is a wide range of different eating difficulties that are described by parents and the severity can vary through a spectrum of simple feeding problems to severe failure to thrive due to insufficient nutrition. Parents can become very worried about slight losses of appetite in their child while others will not notice that their child is not receiving sufficient nutrition. The following charts are useful for assessing the severity of a problem.

Height and weight charts

Height and weight charts are vital in determining the seriousness of the problem and are the best method of assessing whether the food intake is adequate over a certain period of time. Different clinics use differently designed weight charts but they all show the percentage of boys and girls who are at a particular height and weight at each age (Tanner and Whitehouse 1975). This is shown in percentile bands with the fiftieth percentile line shown in the middle (i.e. fifty out of one hundred children at that age will be of that weight or height). Lines indicating the third, tenth, twenty-fifth, seventy-fifth, ninetieth and ninety-seventh percentiles are also shown. Any child whose weight is on or below the third centile (i.e. only three in every hundred children will be this weight at this age) is very seriously underweight. Conversely, any child whose weight is on or over the ninety-seventh centile is seriously overweight.

Expected heights and weights depend on the sex of the child, birth-weight, and the height and weight of their parents. In general, children stay in the same percentile band they were in at birth. If they start to fall beneath their percentile band then they are not growing or gaining weight at the expected rate and it is important to try to determine why this is happening. In many cases this will be due to illness or a chronic physical problem. A child who is not feeling well will stop eating temporarily and rapidly lose weight over a short period but this will be regained equally quickly once the child has recovered. Certain chronic physical problems will have a long-term effect on the child's appetite and weight, for example renal failure, malabsorption syndromes, metabolic disorders, and immunological problems. But in other children the severe feeding disorder is caused by adverse social and emotional factors and this is a very important group to identify (Richman 1988).

Eating charts

Parents can be asked to keep a detailed record of what exactly the child eats over the course of a day or if possible a week. This should include details of the amount and type of food eaten, including all snacks and drinks, as well as the time and place. A precise account of the quantity eaten is important: the number of chips, the number of spoonfuls of ice-cream. The chart needs to be filled in at the time the child eats as retrospective memory is unreliable. It takes effort on the part of the parent but can sometimes help them see that their child is eating more than they thought or eating at the wrong times of day. Snacking rather than eating meals is a frequent difficulty as parents will offer food throughout the day to entice their child if they are concerned that they haven't eaten a meal. This can develop into a vicious circle with the child eating less and less at meal-times and more and more between meals.

Some parents respond to food fads in the media and become concerned that their child is not eating what is considered 'healthy' food. The growing emphasis on healthy as distinct from 'junk' food can upset parents when all their child seems to like is fish fingers and chips and there is complete refusal of fresh meat and vegetables. Alternatively parents may be unaware of the nutritional value of certain foods and may not understand the necessary balance in a diet. Excessive indulgence in crisps, sweets, and canned drinks and the lack of availability of fresh fruit and vegetables in the house can teach poor eating patterns.

Types of eating problems

Reluctance to give up the breast or bottle

The age at which parents want their baby to give up the breast or bottle varies markedly. Some decide that their child should be using a teacher beaker by the age of 6 months while others will happily breastfeed until the age of 3 years. Occasionally there is a strong reason for weaning from the breast as the mother may want to return to work, or may need to be separated from the child for some reason. In other cases the mother's resentment builds up as her child demands breastfeeding despite being on a diet of solids. Concerns about dehydration if the child refuses to drink from any other source keeps these mothers in a state of anxiety and so they capitulate to their child's demands to continue breastfeeding.

Reluctance to chew lumps

By the age of about 4 months a baby is able to push food to the back of the mouth and swallow it. This requires a level of co-ordination in tongue movements and swallowing. There can be a slight variation in this maturation rate with children continuing to push the food out of their mouths with their tongues. Babies start to bite and chew about half-way through their first year. There is a critical or sensitive period for the introduction of solid food between 7 and 10 months of age. Delayed introduction can result in a lot of resistance later (Illingworth and Lister 1964).

Parents usually notice that biting starts as the first teeth begin to emerge. There is a tendency to start on the second stage of commercially produced baby foods at this point. Sudden introduction of new textures and lumps in food may be resisted by the child. The commercial baby foods often have whole peas or pieces of carrot in the puréed food which the child will spit out or refuse to eat. Some children may be prepared to chew on finger foods like toast or biscuits but a lump in a spoonful of food that they expect to be mushy can upset them. Unfortunate experiences of gagging on lumps of food at this age can be frightening for children and cause them to reject solids. These children may continue on puréed foods for considerable periods of time or even start to reject all solids and revert back to a liquid diet. Young toddlers can thrive on a diet of milk but they need to drink large quantities and need vitamin and mineral supplements. Trying to introduce solids at a later age is often extremely difficult as the child has not learned how to chew and manage solid food. Also the mothers are reluctant to reduce the amount of milk in the child's diet because they know that this is the only form of nutrition that the child accepts.

Faddiness

Toddlers often show erratic preferences and dislikes of food (Hertzler 1983a). Sometimes this is related to the dietary preferences and habits of other family members (Hertzler 1983b). Children can suddenly start to refuse to eat foods they had previously enjoyed. In an attempt to give them what they like, mothers can overload the child with their favourite food until satiation is reached and the child doesn't want it any more. Children who have very clear food preferences will determine their own diet and if a parent is concerned about the nutritional balance then seeking advice from a paediatrician or general practitioner who can refer to a dietician may alleviate concern.

Faddiness is often a manipulative process of children gaining their own way. Mothers can find themselves preparing three different meals in an evening to cater for different tastes in the family or she may find herself offering three or four different menus to the child, all of which are rejected and the food thrown away. She has to decide whether she is prepared to carry on doing this.

Poor appetite

Parents vary in the quantity they expect their child to be able to eat so a food diary can help the therapist determine appropriate quantities with the parents. Sometimes a poor variety is offered and the child becomes bored and uninterested.

Children can appear not to like the taste of food and be not motivated to eat. They may start a meal looking quite hungry but after a few mouthfuls say they are full. Parents often fall into the trap of offering other food in order to tempt the child to eat so that the child appears to be faddy.

Failure to thrive

This is a very serious condition of childhood where the child fails to make sufficient weight and growth gain (Drotar 1985). Between 1 per cent and 5 per cent of paediatric admissions to hospital are showing failure to thrive (Berwick *et al.* 1982) and so it is of great concern to primary health care teams. Weight or both weight and height may be affected. It is a disorder of the first two years of life and is characterized by a marked deceleration of weight gain and a slowing of the acquisition of developmental milestones.

A dichotomy between organic and non-organic failure to thrive has developed, but this is often an oversimplification of the clinical picture. The recent trend is to de-emphasize the classical dichotomy. A mixed category is often presented (Homer and Ludwig 1981; Casey *et al.* 1984) where there is a combination of organic and non-organic factors. An interaction between organic difficulties, psychological problems and environmental problems has been posed (Goldson *et al.* 1985a; 1985b) with three categories, comprising children with neuromotor dysfunction, organic problems, and psychological disorders causing organic problems.

Children with subtle neuromotor dysfunction These children often have feeding difficulties that the parents do not understand. The parents start to react inappropriately to the child, attempt to force feed, and cause greater resistance. Such children may have suffered birth asphyxia, have oral-facial-palatal defects, pseudobulbar palsy or cerebral palsy, and so have poor co-ordination of facial and oral muscles. They may be irritable children who are generally difficult to care for as well as to feed (Powell and Low 1983). A detailed assessment of the functioning of oral musculature can reveal delayed or immature functioning or dysfunction where the child shows a deviant pattern of development. Movement of tongue, lips, and jaws can be analysed during bottle, breast, cup or spoon feeding (Jenkins and Milla 1988). Tongue position for food presentation and swallowing show a developmental change (Schwartz *et al.* 1984). A delay in the co-ordination of oral musculature and the integration of breathing and sucking can interfere with the development of good early feeding patterns. Help with breastfeeding style and position or types of teats for bottles can help the feeding pattern develop (Lewis 1982).

Children with clearly defined organic problems Congenital abnormalities of the intestinal tract requiring surgery clearly have an organic component, but the psychological management of these children can facilitate the development of good feeding later (Geertsma *et al.* 1985). Babies who for surgical reasons cannot feed orally for a period can be helped with opportunities for non-nutritive sucking on dummies (Bernbaum *et al.* 1983). Sham feeding is another technique to aid the development of later feeding skills in children who have undergone surgery to correct tracheo-oesophageal fistula (a congenital hole between the wind and food pipe). This technique involves feeding the child orally but allowing the food to pass out through a surgically produced fistula at the side of the neck. The child receives nutrition through a gastrostomy directly into the stomach (Blackman *et al.* 1985). The importance of this technique is that the young child experiences stimulation of the normal feeding and sucking patterns which prevents reluctance to eat once the operation is completed and the child has recovered. If children have had a long period without normal feeding experiences they find difficulty in accepting oral food, chewing, and swallowing. Inappropriate medical management of these cases can cause food refusal later because of inappropriate feeding experiences during early life.

Other children find eating very unpleasant due to their organic disorder. The taste of food may be aversive and they may feel nauseous every time they eat, for example those with renal failure and a variety of metabolic problems or allergic reactions may experience this. The child becomes conditioned to dislike food and even when the disorder has been treated the child will continue to avoid food because of past experience. Some ill children feel so angry, depressed, or anxious about their condition that they refuse to eat. Family stress and parental anxiety exacerbate this.

Children with psychological disorders creating organic problems
Anxiety, depression, or adverse emotional reactions to the difficult family relationships may cause children to stop eating. Woolston (1983) has described three types of non-organic failure to thrive:

Type 1, when the parent under-nourishes and under-stimulates the child to the extent that the child suffers nutritional, emotional, social and intellectual neglect. The parent may be depressed and isolated and show little pleasure in interacting with the child. The child is often apathetic, withdrawn and showing significant delay in all areas of development (Crockenburg 1981). Onset is usually under 8 months of age (Chatoor *et al.* 1985).

Type 2, when the parent is not providing sufficient nutrition for the child. This may be because of misinformation, lack of understanding of the child's communication, or insufficient money to buy food. Parent–child stimulation may be adequate and the relationship will be normal. The child is likely to be co-operative and keen to eat when presented with food.

Type 3, when the child refuses to eat and uses meal-times as a battle ground with the parent. These children are often asserting their own independence and willpower in an effort to achieve control over the mother (Chatoor and Egan 1983). The relationship with the parents is usually angry and negative in quality (Egan *et al.* 1980) and onset is during the second half of the first year of life. The child shows developmentally inappropriate feeding behaviour and food preferences.

Most professionals view failure to thrive as resulting from maternal emotional deprivation (Green *et al.* 1984) but recent views indicate that the process is more complex. The individual characteristics of the child are important risk indicators (Kotelchuck 1980). The parent–child feeding interaction is a bidirectional process with each person affecting the behaviour of the other (Thompson *et al.* 1977). Some of these children were irritable, non-cuddly babies (Evans *et al.* 1972) while others were apathetic, withdrawn, and showed delay (Glaser *et al.* 1968). The effect of this type of baby on an overstressed and poorly supported mother can culminate in a situation of neglect or emotional abuse. Insufficient food may be provided because of maternal disorganization and the mother may be unaware of how much the child is eating. Chronic under-nutrition will lead to the child's demanding less and becoming withdrawn so that the mother fails to provide any more. The cycle can continue until professional intervention takes place (Skuse 1985).

Assessment of feeding problems

Assessment of feeding difficulties should take several stages.

Keep a food diary

Details of daily nutritional intake are required. A food diary can be given to the mother to fill in each day. Some mothers will be too disorganized to do this: either they may demonstrate a lack of concern about the problem or the stresses at home may be too great for it to be filled in reliably. If the problem is severe then the child and mother may need to be admitted to hospital for observation of nutritional intake.

Observation of a meal

This is best done at home so that the physical arrangements can be assessed. Some homes do not have a table; food may be provided while the child is playing or walking around. Other families may not have meal-times but eat at erratic times of the day. A family with more than one child may be so chaotic at meal-times that the mother is too pre-occupied with feeding the youngest that she fails to see what is happening with the others. Meal-times may be a signal for disruption to occur with children running around and not coming to the table to eat. The parents may become very angry and frustrated, shouting and hitting the children, and adding to the general level of tension and disturbance.

A detailed observation of the mother feeding the child can give a guide to the emotional nature of the relationship. The mother's uninterest and lack of enthusiasm will be apparent. Poor timing of spoonfuls can lead to the child's feeling frustrated and angry. The child may not have enough time to finish one before the next is shovelled in and so gag. This causes anger in the mother who interprets it as acting up and being naughty. Alternatively the mother may not offer the food quickly enough and so eventually the child loses concentration and interest. Overloading the spoon, awkward presentation, irritated or cold emotional effect will all influence the feeding interaction.

An over-intrusive mother can equally affect the child's feeding. Not allowing the child independence for self-feeding or getting dirty can interfere with normal developmental learning. The mother's anxiety will be communicated to the child and cause the child to feel upset and so refuse to eat. Removal of the food decreases anxiety in both the mother and child initially and so is reinforcing, but later when the mother realizes that there is a problem the anxiety never resolves and the child is fussed over in order to encourage eating. Meal-times become progressively more tense and the child starts to show more difficult behaviour.

The following checklist of observations during a meal can be a useful aid to identifying areas of concern and treatment:

Child's behaviour

Level of interest in food: looks at it, touches it, pays attention.

Level of activity at the table: restless or calm, demands to get down or sits quietly, happy or not happy.

Manner of feeding: finger-feeds self, accepts spoonfuls from mother, spoon-feeds self, drinks by self.

Eating style: opens mouth in anticipation, chews well and fast, swallows food.

Mother's behaviour

Emotional state: tense/relaxed, calm/angry, confident/tentative, intrusive/uninterested.

Presentation of food to child: speed, amount on spoon, angle offered, variety offered.

Observation of general mother–child interaction

The problems with eating are often reflected in a general relationship difficulty. The temperament of the child may clash with the mother and so the eating problems occur in the context of a wide range of other management problems. The child may be very obstinate and self-willed and the parents may not have learned how to manage the child's general behaviour. Depression will also affect the mother's ability to respond to her child's needs.

In some families the child with the eating problem may be the one with long-standing difficulties since birth. There may have been complications or separation at birth and the mother may have never really felt completely bonded to the child. The emotional distance felt by the mother will affect all of her interactions with the child. Favouritism may develop towards another child in the family and the child with the eating difficulties may be progressively left out.

Assessment of the environmental and emotional stresses on the parent

Marital difficulties, single parenthood, and interfering relatives all contribute to disrupting the parent's confidence in managing the child. Poor housing, poverty, and overcrowding all contribute to difficulties in parenting (Linscheid and Rasnake 1985). The level of responsivity a mother shows towards her infant can be influenced by temperament, care-giver attitudes, and availability of a social support system (Crockenburg 1981; Drotar *et al.* 1985). In severe cases of failure to thrive admission to hospital provides an environment where close observation of feeding patterns and mother–child interaction can occur (Goldbloom 1982).

Management of feeding problems

Advice to parents is based on a mixture of behaviour management skills, nutritional help, reassurance, and building up the parents' confidence in coping with the child and at times long-term support with careful monitoring of the child's weight and the parent–child relationship (Douglas and Richman 1984). Prevention of feeding problems is an important area to consider. Health visitors and family doctors can help parents anticipate areas of difficulty by providing literature about different stages and issues in feeding young children as well as discussing the parents' individual concerns and worries (Finney 1986). The more entrenched feeding problems can be very difficult to treat and take a long time to show improvement. In other instances medical intervention via naso-gastric feeding may be necessary to aid the child gain weight sufficiently to be out of immediate danger (Goldbloom 1984).

Aiding weaning

The mother has to be completely sure that she wants to wean her child from the breast or bottle: her motivation is essential for this to succeed. If she is ambivalent, she can be reassured that some mothers breastfeed into the child's third year of life with no adverse consequences. Making up her mind is the first stage as this gives her a clear aim and plan. The sequence of action can be negotiated by helping her see the importance of achieving small steps in the weaning process.

A gradual but firm approach to weaning is the most successful. Establishing some limits on the number of feeds in a day and moving to a schedule of roughly four-hour feeds for a 6-month-old baby is perfectly reasonable instead of demand feeding continuously. Discussing how to do this and preparing plans for alternative comforting will help her gain confidence and anticipation of the problems. Starting to offer drinks in teacher beakers or on a spoon, encouraging thumb or finger sucking, cuddling a doll or teddy or a piece of clothing are all good alternatives. Once a routine of breastfeeds is established the mother can then choose to eliminate them in gradual succession. The choice is up to her; some mothers opt to drop night feeds at first, others prefer to eliminate the lunchtime feed as they are confident that their child is having plenty to eat instead. It is often helpful for mothers to start offering the breast only after a solid feed so that the child is already quite full.

It is essential once a feed has been dropped that it should not be reinstated in a moment of weakness. The baby may well protest loudly but the mother has to keep in mind her ultimate goal. Any ambivalence or uncertainty will only make the child's demands more intense. Once the mother has made up her mind her firmness of resolve is often communicated to the child.

Bedtime or early morning feeds are often the last to go and the mother may decide just to maintain this one feed until the child loses interest.

Introducing solids

A gradual thickening of baby food is often a preferable way to introduce more solid food. Second-stage baby foods may be rejected but the child may accept some puréed foods cooked by the mother. Moving progressively towards a thick mashed potato consistency is well on the way to a normal diet. Many young children stay at the mince and mash stage for many months and are often still reluctant to chew meat when they start school. This need not be of concern as easily chewed food like fish fingers, beefburgers, and rissoles are commonly provided as children's foods.

Children manage better if they are left to touch and play with their food experimenting at their own rates. A variety of finger food can be introduced for them to suck and usually they start to chew on ones that they prefer during the second half of the first year.

Combating faddiness

Offering a varied diet that includes fresh fruit and vegetables can be difficult when a child is faddy. It is expensive to buy food that children do not eat and it is very easy for the mother to fall into the trap of offering the child only what she thinks the child still likes. It is important for parents not to supplement the diet with high sugar and salt content snacks in an effort to get their child to eat. Faddiness is a manipulation and once it starts to work the problem becomes progressively worse.

All children have fads at different times which resolve as quickly as they arrive and so it can be difficult for parents to determine where they should start to draw the line. A confrontation with the child can work when food is offered at regular meal-times and if it is refused it is thrown away but nothing else is offered in its place. The child will eat when hunger strikes and the problem is resolved. Planning and deciding to use this approach requires parental confidence.

A more gradual approach is encouraging the child to try out one new food each day in the context of the preferred diet. Reward charts can be utilized to back-up this attempt at increasing variety.

Increasing quantity eaten

This requires a lot of persistence by the parent particularly when the child is not interested in food. Children with poor appetites are often put off when faced by a large mound of food on their plates. Initially the quantity expected to be eaten should be very small and gradually the amount increased up to a normal portion for the age of the child. If the child normally manages only half a fish finger and a teaspoon of potato for lunch then this is all that should be placed on the plate so that the child can be encouraged to clear the plate. Very small increases in quantity can then be introduced over successive days as long as the child is continuing to clear the plate. Progress is often slow and the child should not feel forced or confronted to eat large quantities. As soon as children start to feel upset about food their appetite disappears and the process of eating becomes much more difficult. Rewards linked to clearing the plate can also help so that the child learns to accept the rule of eating what is on the plate. Parents may need help and training in reacting positively when their child is eating. Initially parents need to learn to smile and look or touch their child when food is being placed in the child's mouth and also for chewing and swallowing (McGuinn Koepke and Thyer 1985).

Some children with a small appetite can be helped by having smaller meals more frequently. Nutritious snacks will supplement the normal meals and avoid the child feeling overfull at any one point but then smaller quantities will be eaten at meal-times. Dietary supplements may also be important to ensure adequate vitamins and minerals are being absorbed.

Parents may also need some advice and discussion about the types of high-calorie food that are important for weight gain and growth. Sandwiches can have thicker layers of butter or more filling; milky drinks and snacks can be offered which are not low fat.

Improving the quality of parenting

Parents and children may require help in developing more effective and pleasurable relationships. Parenting skills often need to be taught so that parents accurately recognize and understand their child's behaviour and reactions (Lieberman and Birch 1985). The child and parents may need to be exposed to intensive care and contact with each other (Iwaniec and Herbert 1982). Many children who fail to thrive will have suffered neglect and deprivation both of food and emotional warmth. They need a gentle introduction to physical contact with an adult in order to learn to trust (Euler 1982). In the most severe cases these children are taken into care and professional care-givers or foster-parents will start to build up a relationship with the child.

In-patient care can be one way of helping the parent and child learn to relate more appropriately. These parents require extensive support, guidance, and help in learning what to do. The child will need the opportunity to develop a sense of competence and control in the relationship and learn how to gain pleasure from interaction with their parents. Special nutritional treatment may be required. Gradually the parent is helped to learn how to play with, talk to, and enjoy their child. Concurrent stimulation and therapy from professional staff – play therapists, speech therapists, nursery teachers – can encourage development within the child so that his or her behaviour changes and becomes more rewarding to the parent (Linscheid and Rasnake 1985).

Social network support for the parents may be essential. Financial and housing help from social services, support for other children in the family, use of nurseries and home helps can all enable the parent to begin to feel competent and organized.

Darren (3½ years) was admitted to hospital for severe failure to thrive. His mother had been concerned about his weight for nearly three years and a previous admission for investigation of the cause had found nothing organically wrong. He had been discharged but a year later there had been little change in his weight. A bout of sickness and diarrhoea exacerbated the problem intensely to the point of Darren refusing to eat at all and becoming extremely weak and debilitated. When admitted he weighed 9.4 kilos (well below the third centile for weight) and was 89.5 cms tall (between the third and tenth centile). Another medical check could find no organic reason for his failure to thrive and so psychological help was requested.

During the admission he had shown very disturbed behaviour on the ward, attacking nurses, screaming and shouting at them, and threatening to kill them. He began attendance with his mother and younger brother at a Day Centre where detailed observation of his behaviour, general interaction, and feeding was possible. He showed marked rivalry towards his younger brother and despite achieving normal results on a developmental test his social and emotional behaviour was very immature. His language consisted of babble plus muttering and echolalic phrases.

His mother had a flat affect, showed little emotion, and appeared to give up with most of his difficult behaviour. She was mostly absorbed in looking after the younger brother. At meal-times she fed the younger child but left Darren to eat his own food which he did not touch. Occasionally she would ineffectually encourage him to eat. If he did eat any food he would either chew very slowly or just hold it in his mouth. He took small sips of drink but refused milk.

His early history indicated problems since birth. He was underweight for age at birth and had been placed in an incubator for ten days after a difficult delivery. His mother had returned home without him and stated that she had never felt he was really her baby. Maternal grandmother had started to take control once the baby came home and undermined mother's confidence in her own abilities to care for the baby. Darren had been a poor feeder even in the early days and mother remembered spending hours with him trying to get him to take the bottle. When the second baby was born she had felt completely different. She had been determined that this baby would be hers. She found him very rewarding; he fed well and was thriving.

The treatment plan was

1 to help mother persevere with feeding Darren, increase his calorie intake, and take responsibility for his weight gain

2 to help mother stand up to maternal grandmother and take over control of Darren

3 to help mother express more appropriate feelings towards Darren, to show anger as well as affection

4 to help mother balance the needs of the two children more equally

5 to teach mother how to play with Darren and gain enjoyment from interacting with him.

Intensive help over the course of one year started to show some therapeutic effects. Darren had become much more attached to his mother and she was showing much more affection towards him. They played well together but she was still having difficulty balancing the needs of two children since the younger one could walk and demand a lot of attention.

Darren had made some slight weight gain – 1.2 kg over the course of this time – and mother was persevering with feeding. Most meal-times took an hour or more but she had realized how important it was for him to eat. His general behaviour had improved and his language was now appropriate for his age.

Further work with this family is required as Darren's weight gain is not yet sufficient for him to thrive in the long term, but it demonstrates the intensity and the long-term nature of the help required.

This type of case requires a long-term treatment plan using multi-disciplinary resources and requires careful monitoring over the course of many months or perhaps years if the child is to stay with the family. The infant may gain weight and make progress developmentally while in hospital but the changes in personality and behaviour may be slower. Although the initial concern of weight gain may be eliminated in some cases, the parent–child relationship may need much more help (Harris 1982).

Increasing calorie/protein intake

Observation of the parent–child feeding style and parental attitude should elucidate the particular nutritional problem that the child is showing. Such a child will rapidly thrive once an appropriate nutritional diet is provided. The family may need help with financial support and with clear dietary guidelines. Parental food fads and particular diets (e.g. Zen macrobiotic diets) have put many children at risk for malnutrition. Corrective dietary advice and supplements can avoid this problem (Howard 1984).

Managing meal-time behaviour problems

Management of these problems focuses closely on the meal-time interaction. The child is controlling the situation and the parent by difficult and unco-operative behaviour (Iwata *et al.* 1982). Consequences of this behaviour can be

1 prolonged adult attention

2 being offered a wide range of attractive foods that replace what is being offered

3 removal from the restraints of the feeding situation, that is being able to run around and play

Linscheid and Rasnake (1985) have found that the length of the meal-time is a good indicator of a behaviourally based feeding problem. Meals that last longer than twenty minutes indicate that the child is gaining more from the parent interaction than from the food.

The parents may be trying different techniques, coaxing and offering a wide variety of foods. They may have tried force-feeding, threatening, offers of rewards, punishing, modelling, or ignoring the problem. Another indicator of this type of problem is the existence of strong food preferences and a gradual reduction in the number of foods the child will accept.

A variety of management techniques are suitable for different problems. These are usually based on removal of attention for inappropriate behaviour like not eating (extinction) and on setting the scene for appropriate behaviour by eating only at the table (discriminative learning). Rewards (reinforcement) can be offered for finishing a meal, eating quietly at the table without getting up, or trying a new food. A graded step approach to teaching the child to eat everything on the plate is carried out by presenting the child with very small helpings initially.

The child who eats only puréed foods These children need a gradual introduction to a variety of textures. Palmer *et al.* (1975) describe in detail the treatment of such a child. Purée can be gradually thickened by adding flour, oatmeal, potato, rice, or any staple that the family uses until it reaches the consistency of mashed potato. Finger foods can be introduced as a way of showing the child that solid food can have an interesting taste. Encouraging the licking of spreads and jams off pieces of bread, toast, crackers, or biscuits may be the first step. Letting the child play with food for a while without the expectation of eating it will reduce the tension around meal-times. Different textures and colours to handle and lick off fingers will increase the child's interest. The parents can join in the play and reduce the level of attention given to not eating, but look at and smile when their children are putting food near or in their mouth.

Maria, aged 18 months, would drink milk only with a rusk mashed up in her bottle. She refused all solid foods at home and seemed fastidious about getting her fingers sticky or dirty. Her mother had tried to force feed her in the past as her doctor had said that Maria had to gain some weight but Maria had only cried and refused to swallow the solid food.

Treatment was aimed to reduce Maria's dependence on the bottle by providing it only at bedtime and in the morning. During the day she was offered milk in a cup in small quantities with a small portion of food at meal-times only. Her meals had a variety of dry finger foods like bread and butter, fish fingers or chips and some mushy foods like apple purée. She was encouraged to touch the foods but her mother otherwise ignored her during the meal-time.

Over the course of several months, Maria began to show

more interest in food. She would often pick up finger foods and eat them, but only in small quantities, and developed a preference for lumps of butter which she would eat in her fingers. Her mother had by now recognized her favourite foods and deliberately offered her one new food every day in order to increase the range of foods she would try.

Some children have little idea of how to chew and so parents demonstrating biting and chewing and talking about it shows the child how to do it. Good rotary chewing does not develop until around 2½ years of age. Many young children chew meat into small balls and then spit it out (Howard 1984). Some children get worried or feel uncomfortable because they fail to chew and then try to swallow large lumps of food which cause them to gag and vomit. Careful observation of how the child manages pieces of solid food can be very informative. They may suck on it until it dissolves sufficiently to swallow rather than chew it and so meal-times take a very long time.

An immaturity in the oral musculature which affects the child's co-ordination in chewing, moving food around the mouth, and swallowing can cause a delay in the acceptance of solids. This is often associated with a delay in language development and co-ordination of the musculature used for clear articulation of speech (Lewis 1982). Games at times other than meal-times that involve the child using their tongue can help develop co-ordination. Licking honey from around their lips, blowing bubbles, blowing through a straw into water are all games that children enjoy and help this area of development.

The child who refuses food Observation of meal-time will demonstrate the parents' over-concerned reactions. They usually need help in becoming disengaged from the eating process and let the child show independence.

The parent needs to learn to present food to the child and then not pay attention to what happens. If the child plays with it and makes a mess, the parent should not be concerned but just clear up the mess afterwards. Giving the mother a small job to do in the same room as the child during the meal will help distract her. Preparing potatoes at the sink with her back turned to the child can be a helpful way of encouraging her to ignore the child during eating. When the child takes the occasional mouthful she can smile and praise but otherwise no attention should be given to the food refusal. No additional food should be offered during the day apart from meal-times so that the child has the opportunity to develop an appetite in time for the next meal. The child also needs to learn that food is only offered at the table or in the high-chair. If food is not eaten it is then thrown away until the next meal is presented.

Ben, aged 3 years, started to refuse food gradually over a period of months. He had begun to drink a lot during the day as he had learned to go to the fridge and help himself to prepared squash. His mother had begun to feel very angry about his refusal to eat as he had started to lose weight, which worried her.

A plan to reduce the quantity of drink Ben had during the day and to offer drinks only after meals was implemented. The mother also agreed to place a small plate of Ben's favourite food (chunks of cheese and pieces of apple) in front of him at meal-times but then not to watch him eat by getting on with a job in the kitchen. She found that if she turned her back he was more likely to put food in his mouth. A drink was then offered after he had finished his small plate of food.

Over the course of two months, Ben had started to eat at meal-times and his mother had been able to introduce more variety into his diet and increase the quantity offered.

With young children it is often not appropriate to offer food as a reward for eating the main course. Many parents find that if they put a pudding or sweets in front of the child as an incentive the child is likely to refuse to eat and just demand the reward. If it is kept out of sight and offered at the end of the meal as a special treat, the child will start to learn appropriate eating patterns. Parents who are very concerned about weight loss are often tempted to give the pudding even if the child has not finished the main course because they are getting some calories into the child. Often this process is detrimental as the child starts to eat less and less savoury food. Pudding can be given once the child has complied with the parents' wishes and eaten the small portion of main course first.

The child who refuses to sit at the table or in a high chair These children may be showing specific food-related problems or the difficulty may be part of a much wider behavioural and emotional problem. If the child is also refusing food, the problem could have developed with the parent's trying to distract the child during feeding. Allowing the child to play is one way parents will have used of spooning food into the child's mouth. This rapidly progresses into following the child around the room with a spoon. In such cases it is important for food only to be given when the child is seated at the table or in the high-chair. If the child resists this to the extent of crying and screaming, the parent can desensitize the child by occasionally placing him or her in the high-chair during the day to play with a favourite toy.

Hyperactive and overactive young children often cannot concentrate long enough to sit at the table and so teaching this is a very important part of learning to control them generally. Children can learn that food is available only at the table so they may manage a few minutes sitting down to eat and then get up and run around. They can be encouraged to sit for gradually longer and longer periods of time until they can finish their meal in one sitting.

Simple reward charts can be used to reinforce either sitting at the table or finishing a meal for the 3-year-old and older. A kitchen timer that rings to indicate to the child when they have managed to sit for a specific length of time can be linked to the reward chart.

Obesity

Obesity is defined as weight above the ninety-seventh centile compared to normal height or more than 20 per cent above the mean weight for the child's age. Other measurements include triceps skin fold thickness (Garn and Clark 1976) or an obesity index that combines weight gain, suprailiac skin fold, and waist-size (Crawford et al. 1974).

There has been a lot of confusion about the importance of obesity in infancy as a determinant of obesity later in life. Recent studies have shown that the risk of continued obesity is less than originally thought (Shapiro et al. 1984; Poskitt 1980). The relative risk of an overweight baby becoming an overweight 5-year-old is about two and a half times more than for a normal weight baby.

Most overweight babies do not become overweight children.

The view that fat cell proliferation is triggered in infancy is now being questioned as it would appear that there seems to be a critical phase in infancy for this to occur. During the first year of life weight gain is due to increase in size of fat cells, but from 12 to 18 months increase in weight is due primarily to an increase in fat cell number (Knittle *et al*. 1979). It is now thought that the severity and length of time obesity has continued is the major determinant of the total number of fat cells in adult life (Kirtland and Gurr 1979).

Prevalence of obesity

Obesity appears to be related to cultural practice as it varies according to class. It occurs more frequently in children of single parents, of older parents, and in only children. One study has shown that there is a prevalence rate of 5–10 per cent of pre-school children (Maloney and Klykylo 1983). Some years ago in Britain (1960–75) there was a period of a much higher level of obesity in babies when the general view was that 'you cannot overfeed a baby'. Mothers were encouraged to give solids at a very early age and bottle feeding was predominant, with mothers incorrectly making up the feeds. This created an imbalance in the baby's salts, leading to thirst and the provision of more milk which created obesity. The habit of sweetening feeds also added to the problem. But in the very early 1970s the dangers of infantile obesity and dehydration were well publicized and the rate of tiny babies in Sheffield being fed unmodified milk powder dropped from 90 per cent to 0 per cent. Consequently the rate of babies above the fiftieth centile in weight dropped from 79 per cent to 43 per cent (Taitz 1971; 1977).

The present view that a breastfed baby cannot be overfed also has to be treated with caution. There is no firm evidence that this is so (Dietz 1984). The difficulty is with the advent of demand feeding. Some breastfed babies may have eight feeds in twenty-four hours while others may have thirty feeds in the same time. Many mothers have difficulty in interpreting the demands of their baby and tend to feed rather than play or comfort in other ways.

A strong correlation exists between the fatness of parents and their children (Dietz 1981). By 17 years of age the children of obese parents are three times more likely to be obese than children of thin parents. If one sibling is fat there is a 40 per cent chance that the second sibling will also be fat (Garn and Clark 1976). This is not a genetic link as these researchers have shown that if one spouse is fat there is a 30 per cent chance that the other spouse will also be fat. Similarly an association has been found between obesity in pet dogs and their owners (Mason 1976). The relative risk of a child being overweight is five times that of a child with normal weight parents (Poskitt 1980). Studies that have examined parental influences on children's eating patterns have shown that parents have a significant influence. Parental prompts and encouragement to eat are highly correlated to the relative weight of the child and increasing probability that the child will eat. Presenting food to the child is not correlated with weight while prompts are highly correlated; the higher the intensity of the prompt the higher the correlation (Klesges *et al.* 1983; Waxman and Stunkard 1980).

Types of obesity

Woolston (1987) has proposed a simple classification of obesity in childhood which takes into account the variety of different etiologies. The primary distinction is between organic-based obesity (endogenous), which includes metabolic disorders, and inorganic obesity (exogenous). Multiple factors contribute to this latter form and he has identified four groups.

1 Simple excessive calorie intake where the parent is overfeeding the child due to misinformation or cultural practice.

2 Familial obesity where there is possibly a familial vulnerability to being overweight. The obesity is gradual and progressive, often starting by age 4 or 5 years.

3 Psychogenic obesity where there is strong evidence of psychopathology in the child or parent or both. In these families there is no evidence of a family tendency to be overweight. It may have sudden onset and progress rapidly. Possibly a traumatic separation may trigger the condition (Kahn 1973).

4 Mixed etiology when more than one of the above factors occur in a family.

Treatment methods

The implication of such a classification is important for the development of treatment strategies. Attempts to get parents to reduce calorific intake, if the cause of the obesity is psychogenic, are doomed to failure; possibly this is why these families are often so difficult to treat.

Behavioural management Keeping a diary of what the child eats in a day and when it is eaten can help the parent become aware of the eating pattern. Parents may then need help in establishing the setting cues associated with eating. Simple guidelines about only eating at the table at meal-times and not snacking may be required. Parents can be motivated by keeping a weight chart for the child so that they see progress or failure and the aim of treatment is kept in mind. Placing it on the fridge door may encourage mothers not to indulge their child. But this alone is unlikely to be effective in many cases where underlying psychogenic factors are the root cause of the problem.

Dietary habits Some researchers have emphasized the importance of dietary habits. Long-term eating patterns need to be taught and avoidance of inappropriate dieting for children. A Traffic Light Diet has been developed (Epstein *et al.* 1981) where foods are grouped into three colour-coded categories, green ('go' foods), yellow ('approach with caution' foods), and red ('stop' foods). Parents are trained to develop menus and eating habits based on this system so that a balanced and healthy diet is provided.

At a simpler level parents can be reminded not to keep biscuits and sweets in the house as it is easier to say 'no' to a whining child if the foods are not easily accessible.

General child management Parents may need help in general child management methods. This can enhance the effectiveness of treatment (Epstein *et al.* 1985; Israel *et al.* 1985; Senediak and Spence 1985). Although these studies apply to older children the principle should hold for younger children where management problems are frequently linked with obesity. Over-pampered children often have few limits set for their general behaviour or their eating habits. Parents often need help in anticipating how to cope with demands outside sweet shops or in supermarkets. It has been easier in the past to give in to the child's demands, so learning to set limits across all aspects of the child's behaviour can be critical for coping with the battles about food.

Exercise Increasing expenditure of surplus calories through exercise and increasing metabolic rate has not been widely used in treatment strategies, although Cohen *et al.* (1980) found that children who maintained their improved weight one to three years after treatment had higher levels of exercise than peers who failed to do so. The incorporation of higher levels of exercise into children's life-style seems to be an important preventive factor for the future (Spence 1986).

Family therapy Involving the whole family in treatment is important, particularly if there is a family trait of obesity. All members of the family may need help in adjusting attitudes to food and mealtimes. The importance of food to the family can be as a social process or a centre around which all family communication and interaction takes place. The mother may feel that her role in the family is cook and food-giver: she may identify herself as a good mother and wife if she continually feeds her family. She and the family may need considerable help to change this viewpoint. Just to deny her that role or restrict what she can offer the family to eat can be strongly resisted by her as she can lose her identity. Her central role in the family can be continued by helping her provide emotional support and care to other family members. Relabelling her importance as being in control of her family's health by providing a healthy diet, encouraging and participating in physical activities is one method of cognitive restructuring that can help.

Food can be a pacifier to disturbed feelings. Adults often eat to comfort themselves, and will repeat this process with their children. The child learns this during the pre-school years and will also start to eat for comfort. The fact that unhappy feelings are pushed away with food is an avoidance style of coping with stress. Parents and children need to learn how to communicate unhappy feelings to each other and how to comfort each other without food. 'Talk rather than eat' should be the family motto.

Some parents feed their children to keep them quiet, not realizing that they can provide emotional support in other ways.

Suzy, an obese 3-year-old girl, was failing to lose weight even though her mother had been given a strict diet. Eventually mother was able to reveal that she gave Suzy a packet of biscuits every time she had an argument with her husband. The marital relationship was very tense and often violent so mother wanted Suzy well out of the way when her husband was angry. The parents needed not only extensive marital therapy but also to realize that Suzy needed sympathy and understanding about the distress she felt when her parents argued. She had already started to retreat into eating when she felt upset.

A clear analysis of the way food is used in the family is important in determining the treatment mode. The aim of treatment is not for a young child to lose weight as it would be in an adult, but to maintain their weight or make below normal weight gain (Dietz 1984). As the child grows, a more appropriate match between height and weight will then develop.

Cultural and social factors are more pervasive when parents like to see a fat child. Fatness may indicate avoiding the deprivation they experienced in their own childhood. Societal expectations are changing in Britain and the fat toddler is no longer looked on with affection, but some cultural minority groups still feel that the young child should be fed and pampered.

Pica

Pica is when a child regularly and excessively eats inappropriate objects, such as dirt, coal, stones, fluffy materials.

Maria, a 5-year-old girl, ate large quantities of material. She would chew her clothes, her bedclothes, her teddy, furniture materials, and the foam stuffing. If left sitting on a chair she would pick at the cloth cover until she made a little hole and then would pull out the threads and small pieces of the inside padding to eat. This habit had caused severe bowel difficulties which had culminated in repeated manual extractions of a large bolus of clogged material in her rectum.

She was an only child of a single, unsupported mother who was trying to maintain them both by working full-time and also having an evening job three nights a week. Maria attended a play centre at school in the evening and was then looked after by a neighbour. She was often bored and spent long hours watching television. She played in an immature manner and was very under-stimulated. The mother was unaware of how much time and attention a young child required as she herself had a very deprived childhood in the West Indies where her role was as a maid to help her mother bring up her brothers and sisters. She never remembered her parents playing with her.

The pica stopped once Maria's mother agreed to stop her evening job and provide more care and attention to Maria. This was a difficult decision as it meant a drop in their poor standard of living. They needed to learn how to play together and enjoy each other's company. Mother's own experience as a child had taught her to be self-sufficient and she needed a lot of support and practice at learning how to meet Maria's emotional and social needs.

Children often mouthe, bite, and chew on non-edible items. The pleasure of oral stimulation is clear but most children do not eat these items deliberately. Regular eating of these objects should be treated with special attention as it is a deviant behaviour and often indicates a high level of social deprivation. It is more common among severely mentally handicapped children where again the best treatment is keeping the child well occupied and busy.

Summary

This chapter covers a range of feeding problems found in young children, from not eating to excessively over-eating or eating non-edible items. These problems can vary in intensity from parents concerned about how to wean, to parents' neglecting and under-feeding their children. Assessment methods are described and management of these problems is discussed using a variety of techniques including reinforcement, extinction, discrimination learning, and graded steps to learning.

Some families require extensive help over a prolonged period to overcome long-standing emotional problems in the family which have culminated in a child who is failing to thrive or is obese.

Chapter six

Toilet training

Toilet training covers three main areas of management

1 daytime bladder control
2 night-time bladder control
3 bowel control.

There is a strong maturational component in the learning of these skills as well as cultural and societal differences in expectations.

Potty training

There has been a trend over recent years for professionals to advise mothers not to toilet train their children early. Many mothers do not even try to toilet train their children until the age of 2 years or later while others deliberately train their child during the first year of life (Douglas and Richman 1984).

One study of Scottish babies showed that 90 per cent of mothers started to train their babies during the first year with half of the middle class and a quarter of the working class starting before 6 months of age (Drillien 1964). The Newsons (1965) in Nottingham in the late 1950s similarly found 83 per cent of mothers potting their babies before 1 year, with 63 per cent starting before 8 months, and 20 per cent in the first days after birth. They found that the social class V mothers placed less emphasis on early training and appeared to have very casual attitudes. This contradicts the view that home appliances eased the pressure on the mother to toilet train early because these families were less likely to have washing machines. The casual attitude may be related to the observation that the children were rarely changed and were often left in wet nappies. Bowel training showed less social class difference possibly because there are clearer anticipating signs of passing a motion. At that time there was a widespread practice of holding the child over a newspaper for passing a motion. This practice was divorced from using a potty and may also indicate the reason for the difference in attitude.

The question about the early training approach is whether it is the mother or the child who is trained. Children do not recognize the physical cues of when they want to empty their bladder until they reach the ages of 12 to 18 months (Leach 1975; Lask 1985) and so it is unlikely that children trained before this age are reliable or in control. A developmental progression of toilet training emerges during the first four years of life. From birth the child is dry for increasingly longer periods. Reflex training can occur when the mother places the baby on the potty after feeds. The baby passes urine into the potty and the mother thinks that the baby is trained. The mother has become attuned to anticipating the possibility of the baby's need to pass water. Babies cannot therefore really be considered to be trained as they do not realize when they want to go, do not indicate that they want to, and do not go to the potty by themselves. Mothers may vehemently oppose this view and say that their child is clean at age 1 year but usually they mean that their child has regular bowel habits. The mother learns that if the child is placed on a pot at these particular times she is likely to avoid having dirty nappies. Many mothers can and do achieve this and are highly motivated to avoid cleaning up soiled nappies.

Between the ages of 18 months and 2½ years children will start to report that they have a dirty nappy and will use different words for urine and faeces. Given the opportunity not to be continually wrapped in a nappy a 1-year-old child will show a lot of interest in urination and indicate what has happened. Between 18 months and 2½ years many parents start to introduce the potty. Children may learn to pass urine and faeces in it but accidents will still happen when they are preoccupied in play or are in a place where they do not know where the lavatory is. By the age of 3 years most children can voluntarily initiate emptying a full bladder and later a partly full bladder.

The age at which a mother starts to toilet train her child is unlikely to have much effect on the age at which the child will be fully trained. Drillien (1964) found that children at 2 years of age who were potted early were neither wetter nor dryer, cleaner nor dirtier than children trained later. Similarly the Newsons (1965) could find no relationship between early or late training and reliability or unreliability at 4 years of age. This indicates that the maturational factor is very important in the majority of children and that this will determine when they are reliably dry and clean.

Richman *et al.* (1982) found that a quarter of normal 3-year-olds are still wetting in the day at least once a week but that this rapidly reduces to 8 per cent at 4 years and 2 per cent at 8 years. This progress occurs regardless of whether a child shows emotional and behavioural disturbance. In the behaviour problem group that was studied one-third of 3-year-olds showed daytime wetting while 17 per cent of 4-year-olds and no 8-year-olds did.

Management of potty training

Some parents are very unsure about how to start toilet training their child and need guidance in the early stages. Usually evidence of about two hours of a dry nappy indicates that the child has the capacity to retain urine in the bladder. The child needs to learn how and why to use a potty and parents may need to be encouraged to take their child to the lavatory with them so that the child can imitate what happens, have a potty around, tell the child what it is for, and encourage him or her to get used to it by sitting on it. Catching the first 'wee' in the potty is an important milestone and usually this is more by luck than judgement. The child can be encouraged to sit on the potty after a meal or a drink; providing books to look at and toys to play with may help the child stay seated. If the child shows no interest the parent need not feel concerned but try again another day. If there is no luck after a few days or the child is showing antagonism to the potty then the parent should leave the training for a few more weeks. If parents are beginning to feel anxious or upset about it then they should abandon the whole attempt until all the worry has died down.

Summertime is a good time to start training as the child wears fewer clothes and can go around outside without a nappy. If there are 'accidents' in the garden it is not so important as on the lounge carpet. Often children need to realize where their urine comes from. Being well encased in a nappy for most of their lives they are often surprised when they first see the urine coming out. Learning to pass urine in the correct place is the next stage of awareness and learning. Once a child is maturationally ready to toilet train the process usually only takes one or two weeks, but the teaching still has to come from the mother and she may be very uncertain about when to do it.

A recent study has shown that with very careful training over the course of five months, babies between 8½ and 10½ months of age can be taught to indicate their need to defecate or pass urine (Sweets *et al.* 1985). This intensive programming involves careful observation of the baby's cues on urination and defecation and linking these to the presence of a potty. The baby's attention is drawn to the potty before being placed on it: the aim was to teach the babies to reach out for the potty to indicate they wanted to use it. At the end of training this was achieved. The babies had fifteen consecutive days with no 'accidents' and were reaching for the potty followed by elimination 80 per cent of the time. All of the babies were successfully trained before they could walk although there were sporadic accidents if the potty was completely out of sight. The researchers question the maturation view and state that careful training at an early age can occur if the parental motivation and perseverance is great enough. But they admit that these babies had not achieved complete and independent toileting as they could only hold on to their eliminations for a few minutes and needed help to undress and get on the potty. Parental responsiveness to the child's early cues is an important factor. Cross-cultural studies have demonstrated that Bantu mothers establish night and day dryness by 5 to 6 months of age by being aware of their child's signs (de Vries and de Vries 1977).

Occasionally toilet training becomes part of the fight for supremacy between parent and child with the child refusing to do what is asked because of the overall management problem. It is important for the parent to realize that the child's resistance is not a separate problem from the general behaviour difficulty. A more general look at discipline and management in the family may then be appropriate.

Other children are too active to sit on the pot for any reasonable length of time and mothers may despair at ever being able to get them to sit still. Boys like this can be encouraged to pass urine standing up with mother holding the potty up to them.

Diurnal enuresis

It is rare to find diurnal enuresis (daytime wetting) without nocturnal enuresis as well (bed wetting). Girls more often have this difficulty: 40 per cent are more likely to wet by day than boys (Butler and Golding 1986). Sometimes this is giggle micturition when the girl loses bladder control when laughing (Berg 1979; Cooper 1973).

There is a required level of maturation of the mechanisms for the control of micturition. These include

1 reduction of activity of the micturition reflex

2 development of consciousness of bladder distension

3 development of conscious ability to postpone or initiate micturition.

Incontinence can be precipitated by a number of factors that influence this progression. Conditions that increase sensory input like severe cystitis and urinary tract infections will encourage frequent micturition, emotionally stressful events can reduce inhibition, and bladder sensation can be reduced by deep sleep or events that preoccupy the child like play or worry (Schmitt 1982b; Yeates 1973).

Most children who suffer from day wetting have primary enuresis, that is they have never been dry by day. An association with 'urgency' has been found when the child passes urine frequently and with great urgency, often not reaching the lavatory in time (Berg *et al.* 1977). In some children this may be due to small functional bladder capacity, or to incomplete voiding when they do go to the lavatory (Berg 1979; de Jonge 1973). Girls are more frequently affected than boys (10:1 or 20:1 ratio). The age of onset is often between 3 and 5 years. The urgency is unpredictable and comes on suddenly, These girls will often control the sensation by pressure on the perineum either by holding themselves, crossing their legs, or by sitting on their foot. Sometimes a urinary tract infection is associated with this condition so treatment with antibiotics can help. Parents need to be helped to understand the problem and not punish the child for not getting to the lavatory in time (Schmitt 1982a).

There is also a connection between day wetting and urinary infections. A survey of nearly a thousand girls starting primary school found that 2 per cent of them had bacteriuria and of these children two-thirds had day and night wetting (Savage *et al.* 1969), so a check for urinary infection is indicated when there is evidence of daytime wetting after the age of 4 years.

Management of diurnal enuresis

Reminding Management of diurnal enuresis has been attempted with initially asking the parent to remind the child regularly when to go to the lavatory and gradually pass that responsibility on to the child. Helping them recognize the feeling of when they want to go can be an important component for the older pre-school child.

Retention control Retention control training involves the child's learning to wait longer and longer once the sensation of wanting to pass urine occurs. This approach attempts to reduce the frequency of passing urine and increase bladder capacity. Starfield and Mellits (1968) were successful in teaching 5-year-olds to hold on to their urine for as long as possible once a day for six months and enabled one-third of the children to become dry.

Pants alarm Recent research has shown that a pants alarm can help children attain daytime bladder control after the age of 5 years (Halliday *et al.* 1987). This alarm is similar to the type used at night but is a sensor attached inside the pants with a small portable buzzer alarm attached to the child's clothes. This study found that intermittent buzzing reminded the child to go to the lavatory and so avoided wetting in 68 per cent, but in the group when the buzzer was related to actual wetting there was a bigger improvement rate of 80 per cent. The mean age of these children was 8½ years and most were girls. Improvement was maintained over a follow-up period of six months.

Such an approach appears to have better effects than medication. A previous study showed no significant difference between giving imipramine and a placebo with only one-fifth of the children becoming reliably dry (Meadow and Berg 1982).

Some parents feel that the problem centres on the child's not getting to the lavatory in time (Berg *et al.* 1977) and so a non-contingent alarm to remind them to go can be effective. The child needs to be motivated and so receiving rewards for going to the lavatory when reminded or for staying dry can be an incentive for the younger child. A simple timer could be used for this instead of buying the special pants alarm.

Family therapy Secondary onset day wetting (excluding urinary tract infections) is often due to emotional causes. The child may deliberately wet in various places in the house. An extensive psychiatric investigation of the family and their relationships is then indicated.

Darren, aged 5 years, had been found deliberately passing urine in the corner of his bedroom carpet. His parents had detected a smell in the room over the past few weeks and had noticed a damp patch. His mother had caught him doing it one day and had been extremely angry with him.

Darren's mother had recently been diagnosed as diabetic and had a period of several weeks in hospital. She had been very ill and suddenly taken to hospital without Darren's knowing why. His father had been too upset to talk to Darren about it and he had been sent to stay with an aunt that he did not know very well. Darren had always been a good and well-behaved boy but once he had returned home he had been waking repeatedly in the night and been difficult to manage in the day. He was very angry at having been sent away and was very confused about what had happened to his mother.

The family needed help to discuss these unhappy times with Darren and understand the immense distress and confusion he must have felt. He was able to express his own upset at his mother's absence and said that he thought she had gone away because he had been naughty. Once his parents were able to reassure him that his mummy had been very ill for a while but now she was better but had to take medicine he became a much easier boy to handle and stopped urinating on the carpet.

Nocturnal enuresis

The causes and assessment of bedwetting

There are several causes of bedwetting which can occur in combination and provide indication for the most effective form of treatment. Some of these causes fall into an 'organic' category, such as delayed maturation, heredity, or age of the child, while others can be considered to be emotional in origin, for example parents' management method, stress and disturbance in the family. Detailed assessment of the problem should include

1 the child's history of toilet training both during the day and at night to determine whether it is primary or secondary in origin and its continuity

2 the family history of enuresis to determine any hereditary factors

3 the parents' approach to toilet training and methods of managing the enuresis to determine whether the child has had appropriate opportunity to learn to be dry or whether undue stress and anxiety has been generated

4 the emotional environment at home to determine whether the child's behaviour is a reflection of the tension and distress in the family.

Delayed maturation Some researchers have indicated that persistence of bedwetting after the age of 5 years is due to delayed maturation of the necessary mechanisms (Bakwin and Bakwin 1972). This has been postulated as failure to develop cortical control over subcortical reflex mechanisms (Lovibond and Coote 1971). This can be seen as physiological immaturity or a deficiency in learning where the child has not learned the series of conditioned reflexes necessary for achieving bladder control. But many children of this age show intermittent bedwetting so the mechanisms of bladder control must already be present (MacKeith *et al.* 1973).

Heredity The strongest predictor of bedwetting is the family history. Children who have two or more first-order relatives with a history of enuresis are likely to be later in attaining nocturnal bladder control (Fergusson *et al*. 1986). The frequency in other family members is directly related to the closeness of the genetic relationship. Monozygotic (identical) twins that both show enuresis are twice as frequent as dizygotic (non-identical) twins (Bakwin 1973). The mechanism for this is not clear and leads some researchers to accept the physiological view that delayed maturation or physical differences (such as reduced functional bladder capacity) may be the cause of the problem (Zaleski *et al*. 1973). The importance of genetic factors in determining the occurrence of enuresis is generally higher for primary than secondary enuresis, which is what would be anticipated. But the ambivalence that some studies have shown must call into question the relative importance of the history of family attitudes to bedwetting as perhaps being equally or more important than any postulated physical reasons.

Age Clearly the age of the child is highly associated with the occurrence of bedwetting. Richman *et al*. (1982) found that one-third of normal 3-year-olds still wet the bed three or more times a week. This reduces to 19 per cent of 4-year-olds and 5 per cent of 8-year-olds. Weir (1982) found higher rates of bedwetting in 3-year-olds. Nearly a half of all 3-year-old boys were bedwetting more than twice a week while 30 per cent of girls were.

Another recent study in New Zealand (Fergusson *et al*. 1986) found that by 8 years of age only 3.3 per cent of children had never been dry at night but another 4 per cent had relapsed after achieving control (secondary enuresis). From the age of 5 years between a half and one-third of cases of bedwetting were primary enuresis while the rest were secondary onset.

Reports on prevalence rates in different countries vary but there appears to be a 'sensitive period' between the ages of 18 months and 4 years (especially the third year) for learning to stay dry at night. In the third year of life 40 per cent of children who are still wet achieve dryness at night. This time is followed by a period in which the chances of becoming dry are low (MacKeith *et al*. 1973).

Depth of sleep Many parents say that they think their child wets the bed because of being in such deep sleep. Research findings have been ambivalent in this area and no firm results have been shown. Children appear to wet in any phase of sleep except during REM (rapid eye movement) sleep (Graham 1973).

Emotional problems Emotional disturbance and stress in the family has been found to be linked with bedwetting under the age of 5 years (Miller *et al.* 1960); Richman *et al.* (1982) found that the proportions of bedwetting children were higher when the child showed other behavioural disturbance. Half of 3-year-olds, 31 per cent of 4-year-olds, and 12 per cent of 8-year-olds still bedwet. This group of disturbed children also had a greater persistence of bedwetting.

Pre-school children are less likely to be dry by 3 years if they are anxious or depressed. Physical and mental stress between the ages of 2 and 3 years cause a significant increase in persistence of bedwetting after the age of 4 years (Stein and Susser 1967). J.W.B. Douglas (1973) found that children who have no stressful event reported in the first four years of life (especially the third and fourth) are much less likely to wet their beds than children who have experienced these events. In his sample, one-third of bedwetting was associated with anxiety-provoking events:

1 break-up of family through death, divorce, separation (especially when the child was not cared for by the mother)

2 temporary separation from mother for one month or more (greatly exacerbated if the child stayed in unfamiliar surroundings or with unfamiliar care-takers)

3 birth of a younger sibling

4 moves of house

5 repeated admissions to hospital

6 accidents

7 operations.

Treatment of bedwetting

Part of the difficulty with young children is deciding when bedwetting should be treated. It depends on the frequency of the wetting, the age of the child, and the sex of the child. The DSM III (American Psychiatric Association 1980) definition of nocturnal enuresis is bedwetting twice a month for children between the ages of 5 and 6 years. But there has been some argument that the criteria should be increased for boys to the age of 8 years (Verhulst *et al.* 1985).

In general, children over the age of 5 or 6 years are mostly treated by enuresis clinics. Before this age parents can be given ideas about encouraging children to go to the lavatory before going to bed, and waking them at the parents' bedtime so providing another chance to empty their bladder. Making sure that the parents praise the child for dry beds and not punish the child for wet beds is also important, as the anxiety generated by punishment and anger from the parents may exacerbate the problem. Some parents find restricting drinks during the night or at bedtime can help.

Reward charts This is a very commonly used technique for young children aged over 3 years. A special chart can be drawn by the parents showing the days of the week and every night the child has a dry bed a special sticker is awarded the next morning for the child to stick on the chart. The incentive plus praise and pleasure shown by the parents encourages the child to try to stay dry at night. As in the use of any chart of this type, parents must not remove stickers once they have been earned and no black marks should be given for wet beds. The parents' enthusiasm is critical for this work. Unfortunately many clinicians use this approach in an incorrect manner and do not follow up at regular intervals. Children and parents can be left with these charts for months. Their effect will be rapid if they are to have any effect at all. The motivation of both the child and the parents is highest in the first two or three weeks. If it is not working in that time then the chart should be discontinued. Parents should also be carefully questioned about how they are using it and should describe in detail what they do. The therapist should listen to the parents rather than just tell them what to do.

In some cases it is appropriate to choose other rewards that are more motivating to children, like a surprise bag with little gifts in it into which children can place their hands and find a surprise. Awareness of the opportunity to earn the rewards must be made clear to the children so that their interest and motivation is increased.

Enuresis alarms The 'bell and pad' is another commonly used method of treating bedwetting that can be very successful (Taylor and Turner 1975). There are a variety of different types available (Mountjoy *et al*. 1984; Schmitt 1982b) but the one most often used in Britain consists of two pads of wire mesh that are placed on the child's bed with a sheet separating them and another sheet on top for the child to lie on. They are attached to an alarm and when the child wets during the night the circuit is connected which activates the alarm. The child should get up, go to the lavatory to finish urinating, and then with the help of the parents change the bed and reset the alarm. The rationale for the use of this technique is a conditioning process in which the child associates relaxing of the bladder sphincter with being woken up.

The family needs to be motivated to make this work. Some parents just switch off the alarm after the initial wetting, fail to change the bed, and leave the child so that there is no real opportunity for the child to learn. They then complain that the alarm does not work. Again careful questioning about how the bell and pad is used will indicate any misuse. Occasionally the technology can go wrong. The alarm may go off at the wrong times and this can be very irritating but the fault can be capitalized on and the child encouraged to get up and go to the lavatory anyway. Erratic alarms will occur if the separating sheet has been allowed to dry without being washed or if there are holes in the separating sheet. Also the battery needs to be checked regularly especially if the child is wetting frequently.

Inadequate parental co-operation is the major difficulty with this form of treatment. Inappropriate expectations about the speed of change may reduce motivation or the social conditions may present real difficulties (Turner 1973). The relapse rate is a result of the inefficiencies in treatment rather than features associated with the child or background variable (Young and Morgan 1973).

In general it is a safe, economic, and effective treatment for nocturnal enuresis (Houts *et al*. 1983). There is about an 80 per cent improvement rate after a relatively short course of treatment (eight to ten weeks). One-quarter of children treated in this way become dry in two to six weeks, a half dry in one to three months, and 90 per cent dry in four to six months (Dische 1973). But some children do relapse into bedwetting once the alarm has been withdrawn and so re-treatment may be necessary in about one-third of children (Turner 1973). Young and Martin (1973) have evaluated 'over-learning' in the approach to help prevent relapse. After fourteen dry nights the child has to drink two pints of fluid during the hour before bed in order to stress their bladders and test the children's ability to wake up during the night. A higher proportion of children did not relapse after this procedure.

Usually parents are permitted to stop using the alarm if the child has had fourteen to twenty-one dry nights, but need to be warned that the child may relapse for a short time. During the period of improvement the parents will notice a reduction in the number of times the child wets at night and also in the size of the wet patch.

Dische (1973) has outlined the criteria for suitability with this approach:

1 when organic disease has been excluded

2 when there has been no satisfactory response to simple supportive measures

3 when the child is wetting at least three times a week

4 when the child understands the purpose of the routine and can carry it out

5 when the parents are prepared to co-operate in treatment, persist with it, and attend for regular supervision.

If the social conditions do not seem favourable for consistent use of the alarm then social support services may need to be alerted to help the family with the stress and problems that they are encountering. Social workers can help with benefits, housing, provisions of laundry services, and plastic covers for mattresses.

Dry bed procedure This is an intensive one-night training process that uses a bell and pad plus frequent drinks and hourly waking (Azrin *et al.* 1974; Foxx and Azrin 1973). It requires an adult to participate and stay up for the night. The child is given drinks throughout the night to increase the probability of urinating and providing a lot of opportunities to practise. The child is woken every hour and taken to the lavatory. For children older than 6 years they are asked if they can inhibit urination for an hour to teach bladder retention. On the next waking they are then encouraged again to inhibit urination if they can. The child is praised for having a dry bed and another drink is given before they go back to sleep. If the child does wet the bed the alarm goes off, the child is taken to the lavatory, and is then asked to help change the bed sheets. They then practise several times lying down, counting to fifty, getting up, going to the toilet, and trying to urinate.

This has been shown to be an effective and rapid method of training but it does require intensive supervision from an adult. Parents are mostly unwilling to carry it out unless they are very desperate and nothing else has worked. When the programme was originally devised in the USA the families had a therapy aide who slept in the house and carried out the programme with the child.

Medication Imipramine (a tricyclic antidepressant, Tofranil) is the only drug that has been shown to be significantly more effective than a placebo in reducing wetting frequency. The effect is generally noted in the first week when a gradual reduction in the frequency of wetting is noted. Total remission is seen in under half of the children but more often only 10–20 per cent completely stop bedwetting. Relapses are common immediately after the drug is withdrawn (Blackwell and Currah 1973). Negative side effects of the drug can occur and increases in the child's drowsiness, irritability, restlessness are noted as well as loss of appetite and headaches (Doleys 1978).

Night waking Some professionals suggest that parents should wake their children at certain times during the night to get them to go to the lavatory. Erratic and staggered waking is more effective than a fixed waking schedule but both show only moderate effects and are not as effective as the bell and pad. Part of the problem is that the children become dependent on the parents to wake them and take no responsibility themselves. The children can also become antagonistic towards the parents and refuse to get out of bed or to go to the lavatory. This problem is not so common with the bell and pad as it is the alarm doing the waking of the child and the child is already wet. Another concern is that it can also promote compulsive night-time wetting as the child learns to urinate at night rather than inhibit urination (Doleys 1978).

Encopresis

Prevalence

Most parents expect their children to be clean by the age of 2½ years, but 16 per cent of 3-year-olds still show signs of faecal incontinence once a week or more. By the age of 4 years this has reduced to 3 per cent (Richman et al. 1982). By 7 years only 1.5 per cent of children are still soiling and by 10 to 11 years this is down to 0.8 per cent (Bellman 1966). Boys are three or four times more likely to show this problem than girls.

Types of encopresis

There are several different types of faecal incontinence so the clear assessment of the problem is crucial in choosing the most appropriate method of treatment (Doleys 1983).

Primary encopresis These children have never achieved bowel control possibly due to faulty or inconsistent training. Families may have to share lavatories with other families or it may be inconveniently placed and so parents find that it is too much bother to take children to the lavatory and continue to let them soil. Developmental considerations should be taken into account as the intellectual maturity and the age of the child will affect continence. Voluntary defecation is a total neuromuscular response and involves maturational factors interacting with social learning (Hersov 1985). The stools are normal in consistency and appearance but are deposited randomly.

Secondary encopresis Children's bowel control may have relapsed in response to a stressful event like the birth of a baby, a traumatic separation or loss, and this can be seen as a regression to an earlier level of emotional development. Usually this lasts for only a short period if the problem is acknowledged. In other children the soiling indicates a marked level of emotional disturbance. The child may start to hide faeces in inappropriate places or smear faeces on the walls or bedclothes. This inappropriate behaviour can indicate the level of distress or anger that the child is feeling and extensive investigations into family functioning are indicated. Smearing occurs more frequently in severely learning disabled children and is often part of exploring sensation or deliberate behaviour to evoke reactions from care-takers.

Overflow soiling and constipation Constipation has been recognized as a common cause of encopresis (Levine 1975; 1982). As the rectum and colon become impacted with a hardened mass of faeces there is usually leakage of watery stools around the mass. The child is not capable of controlling this flow and will show staining of his or her pants. Parents may interpret this as very loose stools. Children often have distended abdomens and may suffer severe cramping pains as they try to retain their faeces. A vicious cycle becomes established with the child being constipated, having overflow but retaining the faeces because it is painful to pass.

The cause of constipation may be:

1 An aversive conditioned response of feeling pain on passing a motion because of a small anal fissure. The child becomes frightened and holds back the faeces making the constipation worse (Levine and Bakow 1976).

2 Toilet phobia developing when the child has had an unpleasant experience in the toilet and has become frightened to use it (Ashkenazi 1975).

3 Over-restrictive and punitive toilet training methods. Children become frightened of soiling themselves and learn to hold in their faeces so that they become constipated.

4 Refusing to use the lavatory in a battle of wills with the parent and a fight for power and control.

5 Bad diet.

6 Parental concern and attention gained from the condition.

Psychological and emotional factors are very important in the etiology of this problem (Balson 1973). Some parents have very high expectations of cleanliness and expect complete conformity from their child. Fraught family relationships and a negative mother–child interaction can maintain the problem.

Treatment of encopresis

The evidence indicates that soiling has a multi-factorial etiology and that physiological predisposition and emotional influences around the toilet training process both play a part. No single treatment exists for the range of soiling that is presented but a programme that uses a number of different approaches can be effective (Hersov 1985).

Primary encopresis A full assessment of the reasons why the child has never achieved continence is required. Laxness or inconsistency by the parents in toilet training needs to be understood and discussed with them. They need to be motivated to teach the child and this may come with the prospect of starting nursery where the child has to be clean.

When toilet training, a systematic approach of putting the child on the potty or the lavatory after each meal and before going to bed can start to establish a routine and pattern (Levine and Bakow 1976). Children can be given toys and books to look at and encouraged to sit for at least five minutes. Parents may need to sit with their children during this learning phase to encourage them to stay seated and to talk to them and distract them with stories and play. Once the child starts to relax while seated on the potty the parent can gradually reduce the amount of attention and start to leave the room for short periods. Some families find that seating the child on the potty in the living-room or kitchen helps as the child stays part of the family and does not feel left out. Later the child is encouraged to pass motions while in the bathroom or lavatory. If the lavatory is inaccessible, down a corridor, or dark and cold, the child may be reluctant to use it but if the parent accompanies the child and waits, he or she can gradually learn confidence.

Several studies have described this gradual procedure of teaching the child to sit on the lavatory. Refusal to sit is often associated with constipation and soiling and may have to be taught before bowel movements can be encouraged. Doleys and Arnold

(1975) treated an 8-year-old mentally handicapped boy by encouraging him to copy another child and by reinforcing attempts to sit on the lavatory for longer periods. He learned to sit after one day of clinic treatment. Similarly Ashkenazi (1975) reports parents being successful at teaching five young children to sit on the lavatory within five days at home by offering toys and sweets as rewards.

With the 3-year-old and older a sticker chart is a useful incentive to using the lavatory correctly. A sticker is earned for initially sitting on the lavatory for the required length of time. Once this is well established the sticker is only awarded for passing a motion into the lavatory. Some clinicians make the mistake of giving stickers for staying clean but this can easily cause additional problems of the child's becoming constipated to stay clean rather than passing motions in the correct place. Gaining parental attention and praise is a vital part of the programme as often the parents' lack of interest is the reason for the problem having continued. Parents need to learn patience and show their child that they are pleased with the progress.

If a sticker chart is used it is helpful to encourage the family to bring this to the next session at the clinic so that the child can demonstrate his or her achievements and gain additional praise. In conjunction with this the therapist will need to know how much soiling is accompanying the learning of appropriate toilet habits. Parents may be asked to keep a simple diary and check the child's pants four times a day to see if there is any soiling. If soiling has occurred the child should be informed immediately, the parents indicate their displeasure at this, and the child should have his or her pants changed. A code in the diary of 1 for a stain, 2 for a small piece of faeces, and 3 for a large amount will help the therapist understand what is happening. Some parents become confused when staining is due to children not wiping themselves properly and so they may need to teach their children more precisely how to wipe their bottom.

In general, the development of a systematic approach to toileting plus rewards for appropriate behaviour can be successful in teaching these children (Berg *et al.* 1983). Some studies have used money, toys, or sweets as rewards. Bach and Moylan (1975) offered a 6-year-old boy 25 cents for each appropriate bowel movement, while Blechman (1979) used money and toys to eliminate primary encopresis and constipation in a 6-year-old girl and a 7-year-old boy.

Susan, aged 3½ years, had never been out of nappies for passing a motion. She was dry by day and night but insisted that her mother put on her nappy for her to pass a motion. Her mother felt that Susan had an aversion to the sight and smell of her motions. She would go and stand behind the sofa to pass her motion and when finished would demand that her mother remove the nappy immediately. Previous attempts at encouraging her to sit on the lavatory or the potty for this had ended in tantrums and tears so mother had given up trying.

Mother needed to be reassured that it would be all right to stop putting a nappy on Susan and to talk to her about doing her 'poo' in the lavatory. She talked to Susan about it being flushed away and that Susan could flush the lavatory when she had finished. She bought a toilet seat to fit inside the big one and planned two visits each day to the toilet after meals or when Susan indicated that she wanted to pass a motion. Mother took books and crayons and accompanied Susan while she was seated on the lavatory, encouraging and talking to her about doing her 'poo' in it. Susan was initially upset about not being allowed to have a nappy but mother's persistence and confidence was quickly communicated to Susan and within three days she was happily using the lavatory to pass a motion.

Secondary encopresis The reason for the onset of soiling needs to be clarified initially. Changes in the emotional atmosphere at home, marital problems, trauma, and illness can all affect the child and parents may need help in understanding the link between the emotional state and the physical state (Rappaport and Levine 1986). It is likely that the child has received criticism, ridicule, and anger about the soiling which will exacerbate their distressed emotional state. Talking about the problem and aiding open family communication is often crucial in helping the problem (Young and Goldsmith 1972). Some simple toileting guidelines and reward charts as described above will also help break the vicious cycle and make parents feel able to act positively.

Overflow and constipation Once it is detected that the child is showing severe constipation it is necessary for the impacted mass of faeces to be removed before the normal elimination training can take place. This can be done with washouts but these are distressing for the child and the parent. Enemas and suppositories may be of use but habitual use of these can create an unhappy and strained parent–child relationship. These artificial methods of emptying the bowel just produce a temporary emptying but do not deal with the basic problem of retention (Jolly 1976; Berg and Jones 1964). O'Brien *et al.* (1986) have described a successful treatment programme using initial enemas, regular toilet sitting for five minutes morning and afternoon, plus a suppository if there was no bowel movement.

A regular bowel training programme has to be implemented so that the child learns to pass a normal soft stool. Repeated experiences of it not hurting will help overcome the fear of the child who has experienced pain. The use of a laxative (Senokot) and a stool softener (Dioctyl-Medo) or lactulose (Duphalac) can help ensure that the stools are soft (Graham 1986). The standard use of Senokot together with behaviour management is not necessarily indicated in all cases. Berg and his associates (1983) found that the use of Senokot did not affect the improvement rate over behavioural methods. Increasing the amount of roughage and fibre in the child's diet will also help to soften the stools. Parents can be encouraged to use bran in breakfast cereals, soups, and stews as well as giving the child fresh fruit and vegetables. It may take a little while for the bowel motions to become settled into a regular pattern. Impacted faeces stretches the colon and the muscles become loose. It needs time to regain its normal elasticity and reduce in size so a period of loose stools is often desirable.

The child who shows stool retention and consequent constipation due to emotional disturbance will need this 'physical' approach to treatment plus additional therapy in the family. The cause of the retention needs to be determined and therapy aimed at alleviating the stress and tension that are contributing to it. The problem often arises in response to marital disharmony (Douglas 1981).

Luke, a 4-year-old boy, would sit on his heels in order not to pass a motion. He refused to pass motions in the toilet and had phases of extreme stomach-ache and lethargy due to his extreme constipation. He could hold in his motions for two weeks and then would pass an enormous quantity under great strain and pain. His mother felt angry and incompetent about not being able to manage this problem. She directed her anger at her husband as well as Luke and was frustrated by her husband's passivity and lack of activity in helping her with the problem as well as more generally in their relationship. She would verbally attack her husband but the more she shouted the more he withdrew from confrontation.

Therapy was aimed at helping the parents establish a more balanced and satisfactory relationship, learning to negotiate rather than lapse into their habitual pattern of attack and withdraw at the same time as providing a reward programme for Luke just to sit on the lavatory. As mother began to feel more relaxed and understood by her husband she became more positive in her attitude towards Luke. She was able to carry out the simple reward programme which worked very well and then progressed to rewarding Luke for passing a motion in the lavatory. The success of the programme built up her self-esteem and improved her general relationship with Luke.

Wakefield *et al*. (1984) describe a treatment programme that combines several treatment approaches to managing faecal incontinence. The programme has five main aims:

1 to reduce the anxiety caused by the problem
2 to restore the child's confidence
3 to provide some hope for the future
4 to empty the bowel of retained faecal matter
5 to restore or create a regular toileting regime.

A relaxed regime of visiting the lavatory after each main meal and at bedtime is established with the parents keeping a record. Parents are encouraged to ensure that the child is seated safely and comfortably. Advice on diet is offered and the child receives abdominal massage, anti-constipation exercises, and hydrotherapy from a physiotherapist. Play therapy is also used as a method of relieving anxiety.

It is possible to use a wide range of techniques to treat encopresis. The most effective procedures appear to be those that use reinforcement for appropriate elimination and a punitive consequence for soiling, such as washing out dirty pants (Doleys 1978). But it is necessary to link the treatment to the different types of problems. Non-compliance is the principal factor in therapeutic failure and studies report over one-third of treatment failure is due to this (Taitz *et al.* 1986; Davis *et al.* 1977; Berg *et al.* 1983).

Prevention

New parents may need some information in understanding the developmental progress of bowel function. Concern about a baby's bowel movements can set the scene for concern and anxiety. Knowledge about diet and good nutrition can offset any tendency to constipation and avoid the constipation-pain-retention cycle building up.

The child also needs time to go to the lavatory; a hurried and pressurizing parent or an overactive child who cannot sit still can start a pattern of difficult bowel habits. Encouraging a relaxed atmosphere, provision of toys, and letting the child sit on the potty in the middle of family activities can help establish positive attitudes to toileting. Young children often show a great interest and delight in their faeces and expect others to do the same. Understanding this developmental stage is important for parents (Rappaport and Levine 1986).

Summary

This chapter includes an introduction to the process of basic toilet training a young child and then examines the problems in continence that young children show. Physical maturation is a critical factor in the attainment of continence although emotional factors are of importance particularly in secondary enuresis. The causes and management of daytime and night-time wetting are discussed and described in detail.

Encopresis and the problems of constipation with overflow soiling often cause great concern to parents and the management of these difficulties are also described. Practical advice for parents is outlined but there is a high treatment failure rate: the therapeutic relationship may be very important in gaining full co-operation from the parents and a family approach to treatment is often indicated.

Chapter seven

Bedtime and sleep problems

Parents of young children often face extensive night-time disturbance. The stress caused by this problem can be very great and some parents have chronically disturbed sleep for five or more years, especially if they have more than one child. Although adults can adjust to reduced amounts of sleep their reserves of emotional energy become depleted and they are likely to be more irritable, prone to mood changes, and less patient. This can affect both the marital relationship and the parent–child relationship.

Prevalence

Frequent night waking occurs in about 20 per cent of 1–2-year-olds, 14 per cent of 3-year-olds and 8 per cent of 4-year-olds (Jenkins *et al.* 1980; Richman *et al.* 1975). Richman (1981a and b) carried out a survey of 771 children with sleep disruption and found the following rates of disturbance in the 1–2-year-age range:

56 per cent woke up to one night a week
24 per cent woke between two and four nights a week
20 per cent woke between five and seven nights a week.

Of these children, 10 per cent were considered to have a severe waking problem. This was defined as having existed for more than three months, waking five or more nights a week as well as either waking three or more times a night, being awake for more than twenty minutes in the night, or going into the parents' bed.

There are also differences in the level of disturbance that

parents can tolerate. Some parents become very distressed at being woken regularly once a night, while other parents may feel that this is to be expected with young children and are not concerned about it. Some parents enjoy having their child in bed with them while others find it irritating and disturbing and one partner usually goes off to sleep on the sofa or swops beds with the child in an effort to get some sleep.

There are no sex differences in the rates of sleep disturbance in young children and no social class difference (Richman *et al.* 1982). But there is a persistence of the problem: 46 per cent of children with sleeping problems as a baby still have sleep problems at age 5 years (Butler and Golding 1986). The more severe the sleeping difficulties the greater the likelihood of persistence of the problem. More of the wakers have no siblings (Richman 1981a; Butler and Golding 1986). About one-third of children with sleep disturbance also show other behavioural difficulties; this may be partly due to lack of sleep.

Causes of sleep problems

Perinatal problems

Researchers have attempted to identify the characteristics of the child that are associated with sleep disturbance and some evidence is available that perinatal adversity is linked (Blurton-Jones *et al.* 1978). Obstetric factors during pregnancy, labour, and delivery plus descriptions of behaviour in early infancy were found to be the best indicators of later night waking. The length of labour was longer, the time for first cry was longer, and the babies had lower Apgar scores (Bernal 1973). Babies who were reported to wake regularly during the night at 14–15 months of age were more fussy and wakeful in the neonatal period, slept for shorter periods in the first year, had lower sensory thresholds, and had mothers who responded more quickly to their crying.

Children who have suffered brain damage as a result of prematurity or complicated deliveries often show a pattern of irritable behaviour that is linked with sleeping difficulties. These children may be more difficult to feed and fit into established routines.

117

Physical illness

Children who have eczema, asthma, or other uncomfortable illnesses are likely to show chronically disturbed sleep patterns. Sometimes the concern of the parent is so great that a continual checking to see the child is all right occurs. Creaming the eczematous child at night can escalate into a complex and lengthy process with the child gaining a lot of additional attention and care.

Any child who feels ill through a blocked nose, ear ache, or sore throat may have disturbed sleep for short periods but usually the child settles again once the illness has passed.

Behaviour problems

Sleep difficulties may be part of a wider behavioural problem. Toddlers can be out of control of their parents either through general obstinacy, strong will, and refusal to co-operate, or through being over-indulged. The interaction between the child and parent may need help on a more general level apart from sleep management advice. A parent who is unable to set limits on behaviour during the day is unlikely to be able to do so at night.

Although children are temperamentally different and this does affect the way the child reacts to environmental events it is not possible to ignore the effects of the parents' responses to the child. Just because children had neonatal difficulties does not imply that they are necessarily going to be poor sleepers. Similarly children with a good birth history may be terrible sleepers despite having no other organic difficulties. The interaction between child and parent is the critical issue. Parents should not give up on trying to sort out the problem just because other identifiable factors may be present. A child who has an illness may require additional time and attention in the middle of the night but this can occur without a larger behavioural problem evolving, as long as the parents do not reinforce any behaviour that encourages wakefulness.

Some parents find that their three other children were all good sleepers but the fourth presents great difficulties. The approach that they used with the other three may not work for the fourth. So although predisposing factors may exist it is also the parental response to the problem that can increase or decrease the problem.

Types of sleep problems

Night waking

Sleep patterns and problems vary widely. Some children may wake many times during the night but settle quickly once they have been comforted by their parents. The numbers of waking will vary widely but many parents report being disturbed five or six times a night and feel that they have been awake most of the night. Other children wake only once or twice but are difficult to settle and will stay up for an hour or more in the night either wanting to play or crying and being unhappy. Other children will sleep only in their parents' bed but can be restless and repeatedly disturb their parents.

Parents vary in their tolerance of disturbed nights. Anger and frustration can build up to unpleasant scenes in the middle of the night with marital rows as well as shouting and aggression expressed towards the child. Very often they will feel unable to cope with the crying and so do anything to avoid it. A cyclical interaction can then build up of parents unwittingly maintaining the child's wakefulness with extra cuddles, feeds, play, and food. Short-term solutions are sought to deal with the long-term problem.

A pattern often exists of a baby who was initially difficult to manage who undermines the parents' attempts at pacifying. The parents lose confidence and use a wide variety of settling techniques which vary and alter regularly. The child never has the opportunity to learn what is expected or what are the limits. In other instances the parents may be overconcerned with the child due to fears about illness or cot death. Any number of events can contribute to the unfortunate spiral of developing sleep disturbance. The common feature in these families is the parents' lack of confidence and direction in how to manage the sleep problem. Once the parents become uncertain or slightly anxious the child senses the ambivalence and immediately escalates demands for attention.

Problems settling to sleep

Children often have difficulty in settling to sleep and demand that

119

their parents stay with them for up to a couple of hours at bedtime until they fall asleep. Others may refuse to go to bed at all and fall asleep in the living-room or on someone's lap. In the sample surveyed by Richman (1981a) 62 per cent of the waking group were reluctant to go to bed and the same number took a long time to settle once they were in bed.

Nightmares

Young children do have nightmares although it is not until the child can speak that we clearly know that this is what has wakened them in the night. The child may wake up screaming and require comfort to go back to sleep or remember bits of the nightmare and may be frightened to go back to sleep in case it recurs.

Nightmares can be triggered by something frightening that the child has heard during the day on television, in a story, or that they have experienced themselves. They may start to be frightened of the dark or of shadows. If a general anxiety state is present then it may be that factors in the family may be causing concern.

These dreams occur in the light stage of sleep called REM (rapid eye movement). They usually resolve by themselves and the child just requires reassurance and comfort.

Night terrors

These are in contrast to nightmares as the child is not aware of them. The child may scream and look terrified in the night but not be fully awake. In the morning the child cannot remember what happened. The terror will resolve in a few minutes and the child can be tucked up to go back to a restful sleep. It is difficult to wake the child so it is usually recommended not to try this but just let the child calm down.

Terrors occur in deep sleep (stages 3 and 4) and often in the first few hours. They tend to run in families and occur more commonly in boys and in older children between 5 and 12 years (Anders and Weinstein 1972). They are a rare sleep disorder and no treatment is required. Waking the child during the initial hours of sleep may disrupt the sleep cycle and prevent the night terror in the early part of the night.

Sleep walking and talking

This state is similar to night terrors in that it occurs in deep sleep and the child has no memory of it in the morning. The child is best taken quietly back to bed and the house made safe against nocturnal wanderings. A child can fall downstairs or climb out of a window when sleep walking. It occurs regularly in about 15 per cent of children, more often in boys and also runs in families. It is also more common in the older age range of 5 to 12 years.

Headbanging and rocking

Rhythmical movement is a soothing process used to induce sleep in babies. Children will use this process themselves as a comforter and to help themselves fall asleep (Sallustro and Atwell 1978). They will not hurt themselves if this is the only purpose of the headbanging. Problems can arise when parents become concerned and give in to the child's demands for extra time or attention. Violent headbanging of this nature may be part of a wider behavioural problem as the child uses it to gain a response from the parents and gain control. Bruising and bumps on the head will result as the child escalates the movements. It is no longer a comforting process but an expression of anger, frustration, or a method to get their own way.

> Clive, aged 18 months, was a severe headbanger at night. He disliked going to bed and would headbang as soon as he was put in his cot in the evening in order to make his parent take him out again. The parents had a lot of difficulties with Clive's aggressive behaviour during the day and were inconsistent in how they managed him. At night they were very erratic in their response to him. They would try to leave him to fall asleep but usually gave in after he had headbanged for half an hour or had started to increase the strength of the banging. Over the course of six months Clive had become a master at using headbanging as a way of avoiding going to bed. His forehead was a mass of lumps and bruises.

Rocking in bed can be a nuisance because of the noise it can create. Children can move cots across rooms or bump them against walls during the night. In some children this may reflect a high level of tension that may be present during the day as well. Usually it is not associated with gaining parental attention but is just a rhythmical comforting habit that helps the child settle to sleep.

Assessment of sleep problems

A detailed assessment of the child's sleep pattern and the parents' style of management is essential for an effective treatment plan to be devised.

History of the problem

The history should identify when the problem started and how long it has been continuing. Often sleep problems have existed since the birth of the child and may be a continuation of waking for feeds. In other cases the child may have been through a well-settled phase but been disrupted by a separation, a move of house, an emotional upset, or an illness. Parents should have the opportunity to express their worries and concerns about the problem and only then is it possible to move on to planning intervention. It is most helpful to have both parents involved at this stage of assessment as it will avoid misunderstanding or one partner undermining the other's attempts to change later in the programme. They both should come to some agreement on what is the problem and how they would like the situation to change. Joint action by parents can be most beneficial in some cases. They need to decide when they are going to start, who is going to carry out the programme, and will they share the responsibility? Many fathers are pleased to be involved as they may have felt excluded by their wives. Disagreements and tensions about managing the child can be expressed openly and an offer to share the responsibility may be gratefully received.

Fathers can be very important when the waking problem is combined with a difficulty in weaning. Mothers can find themselves trapped in a pattern of continually breastfeeding at night, feeling that it is the only way the child will settle to sleep. Fathers can be crucial in developing alternative methods of settling the child to sleep particularly when mothers keep responding to the 'let down' reflex of milk flow when the child cries.

Sleep diaries

To understand exactly what is happening in the middle of the night the therapist requires some detailed information. Asking parents to keep a sleep diary can provide a picture of the child's sleep pattern and is vital in planning an effective intervention.

Some children will not have developed a clear diurnal rhythm and still be having multiple daytime naps which interfere with a prolonged sleep at night, so the pattern over twenty-four hours is helpful. The chart records the total time that the child is awake during the night including the frequency of waking and the duration of time awake. The parents' reactions to the waking are also recorded so that they can check what they are doing.

	Monday	Tuesday	Wednesday	Thursday
Time woke in a.m.				
Time of day naps				
Time went to bed				
Time went to sleep				
Times woke in night				
Parents' action				
Time went to sleep again				

The diary has several functions:

1 It gives a clear record of what is happening at night and avoids distorted memories.

2 It checks the level of motivation of the parents. Parents who do not keep the diary are unlikely to carry out any agreed plan of action.

3 It records the effectiveness of the change in parents' management and so provides feedback to the parents and therapist.

4 It checks that the parents are carrying out the programme.

Methods of treatment

Two main methods of treatment exist for the management of sleep disturbance: medication and behavioural management.

Medication

Medication has been the most widely used treatment for sleep problems. One report indicates that 25 per cent of a group of first-born children had been prescribed sedatives by the age of 18 months (Ounsted and Hendrick 1977).

A controlled trial of Vallogan forte (trimeprazine tartrate) against a placebo with children aged between 1 and 2 years indicated that parents reported a difference in the child's ability to fall asleep and an improvement in night wakings when taking the medication. But when the total number of disturbed nights was examined there was no difference between the drug and placebo groups. The overall number of wakings was the same but they were sometimes of shorter duration. There was no permanent effect on sleep patterns and at six-months follow-up severe difficulties still persisted (Richman 1985a).

There is no evidence in this study that medication affects sleep patterns in the long term and that it is of limited use for most wakeful children. Drugs seem to have their best effect being used for a brief period of two to three weeks at maximum. The effects should be carefully monitored (Richman *et al.* 1985). Some parents keep their child on medication for long periods worried that if they stop the drugs the night waking will become even worse. These families need help in gradually reducing the dependence on medication and then thinking about alternative methods of coping with the problem.

Behavioural management

A management approach aims at altering the parents' style of coping with the problem. There are many views and attitudes about how to do this. Some professionals advocate taking children into the parents' bed as babies and letting them decide when they want to leave the family bed, often at about the age of 2 years (Jolly 1877). Others advocate a firm line of leaving the child to cry. Part of the difficulty in giving appropriate advice is the range of different sleeping difficulties that children show and the emotional responses of the parents and child (Douglas and Richman 1984). It is not possible to give one piece of advice to cover all eventualities and so both of the above suggestions may be appropriate in different families with different problems.

Management advice should cater for all problems and be individually tailored to the needs of the family and the child. Parents need to be very motivated to change their style of management before this approach can work. Sleep problems are often a topic of complaint but the underlying feelings may be that the child will eventually grow out of the problem and so the parents are not really concerned.

Management techniques in treating settling and waking problems have been found to be successful in 90 per cent of children between 1 and 5 years old and the improvements maintained over a four-month follow-up period (Richman *et al.* 1985). Another study based on the same format and carried out by health visitors found a 68 per cent improvement rate (Farnes and Wallace 1987). Health visitors have found the techniques transferable to their community clinics (Thornton *et al.* 1984) using a manual of behavioural techniques (Douglas and Richman 1985).

There are several basic behavioural techniques that can be applied to the management of sleep disturbance. It is through open discussion with the parents that the most appropriate method is chosen. The pace of change and the type of technique can be tailored to the family and the parents have to be encouraged to express their views fully about what they think they can or cannot manage. Direct advice is often not utilized by parents; they need to come to a decision themselves with some guidance.

There are four basic methods of behaviour change: graded stages, setting the scene and teaching cues, rewards and incentives, and ignoring and extinction.

Graded stages This is the most commonly used method when parents feel anxious about their child, cannot stand to hear crying, or have difficulty in setting limits and boundaries to their child's behaviour at night. It requires planning a sequence of small changes that combine to achieve the overall aim. A classic example is the child who needs to be rocked or patted to sleep at bedtime as well as at every waking during the night. Once the parents have agreed that the overall aim will be to teach the child to fall asleep unaided, an outline of the different stages of settling can be discussed. The stages of change can be slow (fifteen small steps) or fast (four steps) depending on the parents' feelings of how they can cope. The therapist needs to help parents clarify what they can realistically hope to achieve so that they don't set themselves too high a goal and then fail.

The following example of settling-to-sleep stages demonstrates the gradual progression that can occur. Each stage can be achieved in a couple of nights but the parent needs to feel sure that the child has accepted one stage before the next one is introduced. The aim is for the child not to show marked protest and for the parents to feel confident in the small limits that are being set. The starting-point will vary according to the pattern that each family has already established about encouraging their child to settle to sleep.

1 Stand still and hold the child while he or she falls asleep.
2 Sit down and hold the child.
3 Place child on cushion on lap, still holding.
4 Place child in cot, bend over side and hold.
5 Loosen hold while leaning over cot side.
6 Sit by cot and hold hands through bars.
7 Sit by cot and don't touch child.
8 Sit away from cot and don't look at child.
9 Sit out of sight in bedroom.
10 Stand by bedroom door.
11 Stand outside door.

The process of gradual separation involves the parent's being less responsive, having less physical contact, and becoming more boring. Not making eye contact can help to prevent parents engaging in chatting, playing, or smiling at their child.

Setting the scene and teaching cues Children who refuse to go to bed or who wake early are often responding to inappropriate cues about how they are expected to behave. Getting ready for bed may have become dissociated from actually going to bed and falling asleep. There can be a gap of four hours of play between getting changed and falling asleep. The cues for falling asleep may be linked to the parents' going to bed. The child needs to learn a set routine which is relatively brief (up to half an hour) of getting ready for bed and falling asleep. A regular and finite sequence of wash, change, drink, story, song, and cuddle enables the child to calm down and learn the next stage in the pattern. The parents need to be organized and consistent in their approach to bedtime.

Similarly getting up in the morning can be delayed by the child being taught not to expect to get out of the cot immediately on waking. The child can often be encouraged to play quietly or even doze if given an early morning drink. Older pre-school children can learn not to go into their parents' room until the parents indicate that they are allowed in. Waiting for an alarm clock to go off or a light on a timer switch to come on can give the cue that it is now time to wake up everyone.

Rewards and incentives Children can benefit from incentives to speed up learning. Children who repeatedly go into the parents' bed at night can be encouraged to stay in their own bed with a promise of a reward the next morning. A sticker chart on the bedroom wall or a surprise bag in the morning can act as an incentive to comply with the parents' wishes.

This approach can be used to encourage a child to stay in bed in the evening instead of repeatedly coming downstairs. The expectations and the contract about how to earn the reward need to be explained very clearly to the child. Children should also be able to earn the first rewards relatively easily so that they realize how the system works. The standards can be raised once the child has shown the potential to be able to succeed.

Ignoring and extinction Most parents realize that if they ignore difficult behaviour, it will start to decrease and they may well have been told by relatives or other professionals to leave their child to cry at night. This confrontational method often works rapidly but it is difficult to apply and requires parents to have very strong willpower and a sense of desperation. Children learn that previous patterns of behaving no longer achieve the same effect.

To apply this technique to children who go into the parents' bed at night involves the parents' being committed to returning the children to their own bed every time they enter the parents' room. To have the best effect the parents need to prevent the child from even putting one leg in their bed. The parents have to be firm and committed to returning the child to bed as well as being consistent in carrying it out. Sometimes taking turns at the chore can help. The first night this is attempted is the worst as children will try very persistently to get their own way. But once the child has realized that the parents' attitude has changed the attempts will reduce in frequency.

The history will often reveal previous failed attempts to use this approach. Parents will have tried for a time and then given up. Unfortunately the child learns to persevere even more when this happens and so the problem is exacerbated. In effect the parents will have taught their child to carry on trying.

The child who cries at night and cannot be pacified by any other means or children who demand their parents' presence to help them settle to sleep can also be managed by this method. Parents have to learn to ignore the crying until the child falls asleep. Sometimes children can cry for a couple of hours if this approach has failed previously and so parents need to be warned how difficult it may be. If parents are distressed by the crying they can go in every five minutes and quickly check the child is safe. But they should not comfort or touch the child but just tell them firmly to go to sleep.

It is a difficult method to use for some parents as the child can become very upset. Children may vomit with crying and so parents need to be prepared to go in to clean up the child and change the bedclothes quickly and, with the minimum of fuss, put the child back to bed, and walk out. It is very important if parents opt to use this method that they be warned how the problem can be made much worse if they do give in. If they doubt their strength of resolve on any night then they should give in to the child's demands immediately and so the child learns to cry only for a very short time, or go into the parents' room only once. Results are rapid. Most night crying children will stop within four nights. If the problem is lasting longer then it is important to check what parents are doing very carefully as they may be unwittingly undermining their own attempts to leave the child.

Multiple techniques Sleep problems often require the creative application of several behaviour change techniques. For example the child who goes to bed very late needs to learn a bedtime routine (setting cues) and also an earlier bedtime (extinction or graded stages). Once the child has learned the bedtime routine at the later bedtime the whole process can be gradually edged earlier on successive nights until a more appropriate bedtime is achieved. Young children do not realize that bedtime is becoming earlier as they respond to the routine.

Children who visit the parents' room at night can be helped to stay in their own beds by being repeatedly taken back (extinction) and by receiving a sticker on a chart for staying in their own bed all night (reward). The same two approaches can be used for children who come down during the evening and won't settle to sleep.

Twins and waking siblings

Children do not usually wake each other up with crying at night. A family with twins or more than one young child who wakes at night will find that the children wake at different times. This can effectively keep the parents up all night.

In families with two parents it can be possible for each parent to take on responsibility for dealing with one child. This allows some slight peace but is important for mutual support and encouragement. When families with multiple wakers start treatment the parents can become competitive in the speed of settling and reducing the number of night wakings. This motivation and enthusiasm will aid the treatment programme and speed up success.

Occasionally a pattern can develop where one child wakes regularly and the other child who is in fact a good sleeper starts to realize that exciting events are occurring in the middle of the night which are being missed. But once parents start to reduce the amount of attention the children receive in the middle of the night the new problem will rapidly disappear.

Sibling rivalry can be a component particularly when a new baby arrives in the family and the older toddler starts to wake in response to the change in family patterns. Visits to the parents' room while the new baby is feeding are common just to check out what is happening and not to be left out. Considerate handling of this is important and the toddler returned to bed when the baby is settled. Reassurance and understanding is all that is required and this phase will rapidly pass.

Single parents

Single parents may require a great deal of support during the treatment programme as they have only themselves to depend on to carry out the changes. They need to be single minded and confident in their approach and have a lot of feedback from the therapist about their progress and success. Managing night waking alone can be very distressing. Single parents may feel that it can be easier just to give up and let their child sleep with them. Conversely anger and desperation can easily erupt, so careful judgement is required about the speed of change possible and the level of stress that the parents can tolerate.

Housing

Families in bedsits or cramped accommodation experience severe environmental stress as well as the demands of the child. Night-waking children can tip the balance as there may be no way to avoid the noise or to get out of the room. Children often stay up late because the parents are watching television in the room and it can be very difficult for parents to establish a clear bedtime routine when other members of the family are having their supper or talking. A strong psychological boundary needs to be established so that the child knows what is expected. The lack of physical boundaries makes the need for psychological boundaries that much greater.

The principles of management are the same but may be harder to apply in families that live in these conditions or do not have the reserves or the commitment to carry through the plans of change.

Children in a cot in a bedsit need to understand that a separate stage of the day has been reached at night-time so that they learn to settle to sleep. Unfortunately many of these children may spend long periods of the day in their cots playing because there is nowhere else safe for them to be. Day melds into night and the child never really establishes a clear diurnal rhythm. These families can be helped by the child's attending nursery provisions as this clarifies the discrimination between day and night.

Night feeding

The majority of children give up night feeds by the end of the first year of life. But some night-waking children develop a pattern of falling asleep only while sucking on the bottle or breast. Parents may despair of ever achieving another way of settling the child to sleep. Weaning can be an issue in such cases and the mother needs to be completely sure that this is what she wants to do. She can be reassured that she can try in six months' time if she has not yet made up her mind.

As in managing other types of sleep problems, weaning can be achieved by different methods. Some parents will just throw out the bottle, tell the child that it has gone in the dustbin, and put up with the upset for a couple of nights until the child finds an alternative method of falling asleep. Others cannot do this and choose a gentler approach of reducing the quantity in the bottle or reducing the number of bottles per night or changing gradually to a non-preferred drink in the bottle, for example diluting milk with water. The parents may need reassurance that the child can have a drink of water if thirsty but that this drink should not be warm milk or juice which can be reinforcing. There is usually a crisis point in this type of approach when children realize that there is not enough drink in the bottle or that it is not the drink they expected, so parents should be prepared to face the anger and know how they want to manage it. Some choose to line up a series of drinks and encourage children to help themselves without disturbing their parents.

It is often helpful for parents to practise the new method at the child's bedtime as this is the easiest settling period to manage. They may decide initially to try without the bottle at bedtime but have it in reserve for the night. The older child of 2½ to 3 years can also be told clearly what is expected and a simple reward approach can be used as an additional incentive to settle without the bottle.

Parents may need time to adjust their expectations about drinks and feeds at night. Mothers who are reluctant to give up breastfeeding but want to reduce the frequency of feeds can be helped to teach the child the cues associated with breastfeeds.

Mary was keen to carry on feeding her 2-year-old son but found the number of times that he latched on to her breast during the night was severely disrupting her sleep. She enjoyed having him sleeping in her bed but wanted help with how to reduce the number of night feeds.

A plan of teaching Tom cues about when to feed was agreed. Mary bought a nightie that buttoned up to the neck so that Tom could not continue to help himself to the breast during the night. She decided on four feeds per night initially which was a marked reduction from the eleven or twelve short bursts of sucking that had been established. When it was a feed-time she sat up in bed, switched on the side light, unbuttoned herself and allowed Tom to feed in a correct feeding position.

Within a week this pattern was well established and Mary then felt able to reduce the number of night feeds to one at bedtime and one in the early morning.

Prevention

During the first six months of life some babies will have erratic sleep patterns and may not easily adopt a diurnal rhythm, but parents can help the baby settle by creating the right conditions and regularity in daily pattern. Flexibility to cope with the baby's varying needs is important so that the baby feels that its communications are being understood. But a confident approach to handling the baby, enabling and allowing the baby to have regular rest periods interspersed with play, is necessary. Some mothers overstimulate their babies, expecting them to indicate when they want to sleep; others feel undermined by the baby's erratic demands and lack confidence in understanding the baby's needs. Breastfeeding is often used as a palliative for all events so that every time the baby cries the breast is offered. Feeding becomes confused with comforting and sleeping.

Prevention of sleep problems is possible through helping new parents become aware of the pitfalls of parenthood. Being aware that patterns do become established in the first year that affect the later years is important. By 6 months of age mothers should understand that continuing to settle baby to sleep with feeding could lead to a continuation of this habit. Babies of this age can learn to settle themselves to sleep without sucking, so mothers may need consciously to wake their baby after a feed by changing the nappy and then putting the baby down to rest while awake.

Establishing simple routines about going to bed often start between 6 and 12 months. Closing curtains, reducing light level, bedtime routine, and their own cot all become associated with falling asleep. Some parents resist this idea and want freedom with their new baby, taking baby with them everywhere and not curtailing social activities. That is fine as long as they do not complain that the baby does not go to sleep when they want some peace during a quiet evening at home.

Once babies reach the age of about 10 months they can wilfully keep themselves awake. Mothers report children of this age fighting to stay awake after a feed, screaming if put to bed, and smiling as soon as the parent goes to see what is the matter.

Parents may need help in realizing how the patterns in the first year of life can continue unless they are prepared to change how they manage the situation. Being aware of how their attitudes to the baby affect the baby's behaviour will enable them to make the choices suitable to their life-style and needs. Discussion about sleep patterns often arises in post-natal support groups. Health visitors who have attempted these discussions in ante-natal groups find that mothers are often not aware of the problems that can arise because the pregnancy has not yet materialized into a real baby and the discussion feels too distant.

Summary

Night-time disturbance is a very common problem faced by parents of young children. There are a range of techniques that can be used to manage the behaviour but the choice of method should reflect the parents' ability and motivation to change their reactions. Parental confidence is a key aspect of success in managing sleep problems and so joint decision-making between the therapist and the parents is critical for advice to be successful. There is no one technique that solves all sleeping problems but each family can be helped to choose a method of change that suits their needs. In most cases change occurs once parents can establish limits for the child's behaviour.

Chapter eight

Emotional problems

Anxiety and fears are common in young children and can stem from widely differing experiences. Some children are fearful and withdrawn as a feature of their personality. They are shy socially, rarely speak out, and hide behind their mothers. Some have great difficulties with separation and cling to their mothers in a developmentally inappropriate manner. Other children will have experienced a traumatic event in their lives that caused their problem. Parents' divorcing or the experience of a bereavement are significant triggers. Children will also develop fears and phobias, like adults, in response to unpleasant experiences.

Fears

There is a developmental pattern to children's fears. Most children demonstrate fear of separation and strange adults after the age of 8 months. These decline in the second year of life but are often replaced by fears of animals or of the dark (Marks 1987a). Despite widely differing patterns of child-rearing, fears of separation, and of strangers are common in children all over the world (Marks 1987b). The development of separation fears or fears about animals are very difficult to suppress completely. Marks (1987a) feels that there are certain prepotent cues which cause a child to learn these fears more quickly. This may be related to survival and is part of a species self-protective mechanism.

Shyness appears between 3 and 9 months of age. Mothers have reported observing distress, anger, interest, joy, and surprise on their baby's face from the age of 1 to 3 months, and 59 per cent also reported fear, but shyness was reported in only 9 per cent

(Johnson *et al*. 1982). Children will actively search for emotional information from their parents from this age when in an uncertain situation. This has been called social referencing and entails the children looking for reassurance from familiar adults.

In one study where 2-year-olds were placed in a strange room with lots of toys and their mothers not facing them, 50 per cent of the children abandoned the toys and moved to where they could see mother's face (Klinnert *et al*. 1983). In another study of 1–4-month-old babies, if mothers were asked to sit still-faced and not respond to their child for three minutes the babies became distressed and then withdrew and the mothers felt very uncomfortable.

Social referencing takes time to mature. Between 2 and 5 months of age the baby will look at a face but may not use the information meaningfully. After 5 months the baby starts to react appropriately to the emotional expressions of others and by 10 to 12 months can understand the mother's pointing and her direction of gaze.

Uncertainty can increase the child's search for emotional guidance. 'Visual cliff' experiments where babies have been placed on the other side of an apparent drop from their mothers raise a mild level of uncertainty and fear in the baby. The baby is completely safe because a glass screen covers the drop and the baby can crawl across it safely to reach the mother but the baby does not realize this and feels unsure about crossing over the edge of the apparent drop. Children aged 1 year using a 'visual cliff' demonstrated that if mothers on the other side of the pretend drop showed fear the children retreated from the edge in distress, if the mothers show joy or interest 74 per cent of the children crossed the cliff, if the mothers showed sadness 33 per cent crossed and if mothers showed anger 11 per cent crossed.

Mother's expression can also affect the child's emotional state. When mothers showed fear when looking at a new toy their 12–18-month-old children moved close to the mother, but if she showed interest and joy they moved towards the toy; if she was neutral they stayed between (Klinnert *et al*. 1983). So it is important to assess the parents' emotional state when examining the fearful and anxious reactions of young children.

Fear and emotion can be reduced by learning that one's actions can influence events. A feeling of power and competence replaces the fear. Babies who were given a clockwork toy showed less fear when they had learned how to switch it on and off. Parents often automatically do this with children, demonstrating how to cope with fearful objects by handling and experiencing the object.

Children between the ages of 5 and 8 years commonly develop rituals which are self-made rules to stave off imagined terrors and give the child self-confidence. These can be as simple as not stepping on the cracks in the pavement or asking parents to come and check them in five minutes once they have settled to sleep. Repetitive counting, singing rhyming songs, or putting objects in certain positions repeatedly can help the child feel protected and safe.

Girls are consistently reported as being more fearful than boys but it is not clear whether boys are less reluctant to express their fears than girls or whether parents are less willing to perceive their boys as fearful (Harris and Ferrari 1983).

Some fears develop after an unpleasant experience while others have no apparent trigger. Fear is often triggered in dangerous situations and is increased by social deprivation, novel settings, changes in familiar settings, and rejecting or punishing mothers (Marks 1987a).

Management of fear

Separation As we have just discussed, parents can transmit fear and anxiety to their children and affect their ability to learn and cope with their feelings.

Maturation in the development and decline of fears is affected by environmental interaction. It is possible by early exposure of the child to fearful objects or situations to prevent fear emerging later (Marks 1987a). For example, giving the child repeated safe and brief opportunities for separation can offset a later more extreme reaction. This has been called stress immunization (Stacey *et al*. 1970). Children need to have graduated experiences in learning independence and self-reliance so that they learn how to cope with anxiety without relying on their parents. Most mothers will encourage their child to have brief separations during the second year of life. Going to stay with a grandparent or play at a friend's house for a short period is a common first step. This prepares the child for transition to playgroup or nursery. The nursery attendance similarly prepares the child for attendance at school.

Some mothers find separation from their young child very stressful. The child provides company during the day or the mother may feel very protective and unable to let the child demonstrate any independence. The anxiety generated in the mother by the separation can be transmitted to the child. As the child starts to protest the mother may immediately respond to her child's distress, either complying with the child's demands not to leave or abandoning the playgroup with the feeling that it is not suitable. Some mothers will try several playgroups in an attempt to separate but repeat the same experience in each one. The child learns that by protesting the mother will not leave and the mother feels unable to leave while the child is distressed.

Mothers caught in this situation will need help from playgroup staff about how to structure the separation. If she indicates firmly to the child that she is leaving for a short time but will come back at juice time the child is helped to understand the limits of the separation. She then needs to leave the playgroup while the staff distract the child and engage in play activities. When the mother returns she should tell her child that she has come back as she said she would. Once the children have learned the new pattern of being left at playgroup they settle down very quickly. Repeated experiences like this teach the child that the mother is trustworthy and will return. The pattern of saying goodbye is important as a cue for the child to anticipate the course of events.

If mothers start to creep out quietly without warning then the child can easily become clingy and unsure. Anxiety is increased by not knowing what is going to happen. Some mothers find the stress at hearing their child cry on separation too great and so opt for this avoidance tactic but usually it creates more problems than it solves.

Many nursery teachers say that they have mothers hanging around outside the classroom door unable to leave the school on the first day, while the child may have made the transition in the class very easily. It can be helpful for these mothers to have prepared a series of activities to do during the day to fill the time while their child is away. Gradually the pain at separation time starts to diminish as the mother adapts to the new routine.

Everyday fears Young children can show fearful reactions to a wide number of objects and events, for example animals, loud noises, insects.

> Terry, aged 3 years, refused to go out and play in the garden as he had become frightened of bees. His fear had started one day when he had been playing with his grandmother in the garden and a bee had started to buzz around him. His grandmother's fear that he might be stung was so extreme that he had run into the house and the bee had followed him up the garden and indoors. He had started to cry in terror and the whole family had rushed in trying to get rid of the bee.
>
> During treatment of this fear his parents were encouraged to take him twice a day into the garden for a period of fifteen minutes to play in the sand pit. They were to reassure him once about the bees but then to ignore any further talk about them. Initially he had cried and struggled against being taken outside but once in the sand pit would start to play after the first five minutes. The following week the parents planned more active play in the garden, pushing him around on his bike and standing further away from him and encouraging him to ride around by himself. Within two weeks the problem had resolved and Terry was able to play outside by himself although he still felt quite anxious if he heard a buzzing insect.

To overcome fears and phobias children need the opportunity to face up to the feared object in a safe and contained manner. Being held by parents, who reassure and calm them while they gradually approach a feared object, is the most common way of managing fears. Parents need to feel confident while doing this. The steps of introduction to the feared object can be very small so that no anxiety is aroused.

> Susan, aged 2 years, showed great fear of the bath. As a young baby her mother had accidentally dropped her under the water and she had become very distressed. Since that time she had resisted going in the bath and her mother had always washed her from the basin with a flannel.
>
> A simple programme of reducing her fear (desensitization) was started. Her mother was encouraged to put Susan in the bath every day fully dressed, with no water in it, to play with

her dolls for a short period. A bathmat was also placed in the bath so that Susan would not slip over. A period of water play in the kitchen was arranged each day for Susan to wash her dolls and play with her tea set. Although Susan was initially very fearful of being put in the bath, when she realized that there was no water in it she stopped being frightened.

After two weeks mother took off Susan's clothes to go in the bath and set up the water play time in the bath. A doll's bath was put in the big bath with Susan and she was encouraged to splash and get wet if she wanted to. Once Susan was relaxed and enjoying it the bath plug was put in so that extra water collected at the bottom of the bath and she was standing in it. Gradually more and more water was added and Susan was encouraged to use the bath taps for additional water for the doll's bath.

Over the course of three weeks Susan had become accustomed to playing in the bath with her dolls and tolerated a couple of inches of water to sit in.

Habits

Young children show a wide range of habits. 17 per cent of 3-year-olds and 14 per cent of 4-year-olds have three or more habits (Passman and Halonen 1979).

Comfort habits

Some parents feel that comfort habits like thumb and finger sucking, holding cuddly toys or rags and blankets indicates that a child is anxious. The 'transitional' object is seen as a way of reducing this anxiety and helping the child cope with the world. Research has indicated that children who show these habits are no different in their levels of anxiety from children who do not have the habits (Davidson et al. 1967; Tryon 1968; Ozturk and Ozturk 1977). Another study even found a positive finding that 16.4 per cent of children with a favourite cuddly cloth tended to show less disturbed behaviour (Boniface and Graham 1979).

A much longer follow-up study that examined children who had insisted on a cuddly toy at 4 years of age could detect no differences at 16 years of age in an index of emotional adjustment or in terms of how difficult the children were to control and influence. Also fewer of them had become regular smokers at age 16. The conclusion was that the dependence on a comfort habit in the pre-school years does not indicate persistent insecurity, nor does it indicate potential psychological problems later in life (Newson *et al.* 1982).

The comfort blanket Sometimes a child's comfort habit can start to interfere with everyday life. The 3-year-old who insists on taking a blanket out to the shops to hold and cuddle can become so absorbed with keeping hold of the great bundle that normal experiences during shopping are ignored. Most parents will start to teach the child that there are appropriate places and times when the cuddly can be held. Keeping it in the child's cot or bed is one way of containing the spread of the habit. Alternatively they may allow the child just to use it in the house when feeling tired or unhappy.

Another approach is to reduce the size of the cuddly progressively. Many mothers cut a comfort blanket in half so that there is one in the wash and the child does not feel bereft of comfort on wash day. Cutting it into smaller pieces can gradually reduce the dependence. Some young children starting nursery have been seen clutching a few strands of blanket on their first morning. Once the final piece has been lost or thrown away the child then forgets about it.

Thumb and finger sucking Thumb and finger sucking are generally more difficult to stop. The major concern comes when second teeth emerge and there is the possibility of pushing them out of alignment. Dentists, in general, are not concerned about this until the child is over the age of 6 years; 10 per cent of children between the ages of 6 and 12 years suck their fingers or thumbs (Christensen and Sanders 1987).

A wide range of strategies to encourage children to stop this sucking has been tried although mostly with older children. Avoidance methods have included putting on finger or thumb splints (Lewis *et al.* 1981), making the child wear woollen gloves (Lassen and Fluet 1978), or putting a bitter-tasting substance on the finger (Haryett *et al.* 1970). Many dentists introduce an oral device like a palatal crib that interferes with the normal stimulation received from thumb sucking (Haryett *et al.* 1970).

Other behavioural management techniques have concentrated more on the responses of parents to the thumbsucking. Many parents find that just reminding their child not to suck is not effective, and the child's habit may be reinforced by the additional attention. Becoming angry with the child can set up unpleasant interactions which can increase the child's level of anxiety and consequently increase rather than decrease thumb sucking. Parents who have been trained to reinforce the child for not sucking have been more effective (Clowes-Hollins and King 1982; Knight and McKenzie 1974).

There are often certain times in the day when thumb sucking occurs more frequently. These are at bedtime, while watching television, listening to a story, or when tired. Parents can tell the child that they want to stop the thumb sucking at these times and indicate that the child can earn rewards for not thumb sucking for a certain period of time. The reward can be stickers on a chart, something to eat, or any other small gift. Parents can include interrupting the pleasurable event if the child does put in the thumb. The television can be switched off immediately for five minutes, or the story stopped for a couple of minutes.

Christensen and Sanders (1987) compared two types of parental management of thumb sucking in a group of thirty children aged between 4 and 9 years. They taught the parents to use

1 Habit reversal method where the children were taught to clench their fists around their thumbs and slowly count to twenty (Azrin *et al.* 1980) when they felt like sucking their thumbs. Whenever the children did thumb suck they were instructed to clench their fists and count to twenty three times.

2 Reinforcement of other behaviour which was a straightforward reward approach of receiving a token for a period of no thumb sucking. A thirty-minute training time was set and the child could initially receive a token every three minutes for no thumbsucking. Gradually the time intervals were increased until the child received tokens for every half an hour of not thumb sucking during the day.

Both these approaches proved successful in significantly reducing the amount of thumb sucking although it was totally eliminated in only a small number of children, while the control group had not changed. The improvements were maintained at three months follow-up.

A difficulty in assessing the effectiveness of treatment of self-stimulating behaviour is that the treatment effect may not generalize across different situations. When parents are out of sight children could easily suck their thumb. Also some studies have reported a slight increase in difficult behaviour once the comfort habit is stopped and some parents may prefer to have a child thumb sucking rather than being difficult.

Tension habits

Tics and twitches These are habits that are clearly related to the child's level of anxiety, stress, and tension. Involuntary movements like eye twitches, hair flicking, sniffing, and tics of facial muscles all increase with tension. They rarely occur in very young children but are frequent in the 5 to 7 age range. They vary in their occurrence and may disappear as suddenly as they appear. A child will often have a series of different tics one after another.

Tension in the young child is most often related to the emotional environment at home. Marital tension or an anxious and irritable parent influence the child's emotional state. Usually when parents calm down the child calms down as well. So management of the habits is best approached by helping the family recognize and cope with the existing tensions in the relationships.

Changes in the child's daily life-style such as starting nursery or infant school can also create stress. This stress may be short lived as the child learns to adjust to the new surroundings and starts to make friends. Parental confidence and support during this phase is important. Reassuring children that they will soon get used to the nursery, perhaps asking a specific child home so that they can make special friends and support each other at nursery, can speed up the process of adjustment.

When involuntary movements seem to be continuing over a longer period than expected the child may be helped to gain control of them by practising them. Setting aside a time each day when the child has to try deliberately to do the movement repeatedly perhaps twenty or thirty times brings them under voluntary control.

Stammering Stuttering and stammering can be related to tension particularly when children are learning to speak between the ages of 2 and 3 years and are in a rush to get out what they want to say. A second group of children develops stammers and stutters at the ages of 6 and 7 years when they start school, after having had a period of talking fluently. The speech interruption can make children feel very self-conscious and they may be teased by friends. Some parents get angry with the speech difficulty and force the child to repeat what has been said.

The normal dysfluency of the young child often spontaneously disappears as the child gets older. But a small proportion of children will continue to have fluency difficulties and show true stammering behaviour (Rustin 1987). There is a predisposition to stammering that is inherited and so a family history of the condition is often an indication that the child's stammering is not just normal dysfluency and referral to a speech therapist will be required. The children most at risk for this are sons of women who are stammerers themselves (Rustin *et al*. 1987).

The parent's rate and speed of talking can be linked to children's stuttering and so instructions to slow down and speak more clearly to the child will help language development to progress normally. Taking a special quiet time each day to play and talk with the child will aid this.

Although true stammering behaviour is related to physical aspects of the child's development – that is the child often has a slower voice onset time, has more difficulties in processing information, and in co-ordinating the movements of tongue and lips – it is also affected by the child's psychological state. The child needs time in which to speak and not to feel agitated by listeners who are either embarrassed or irritated. Parents who feel anxious about their child's speech pattern can transfer their feelings of anxiety to the child. These children may need some special help from a speech therapist to learn how to slow down their rate of speech.

For normal dysfluency problems the parent's reaction can similarly make the situation worse. Most young children are not upset by their stammering but their parents are and start to label it as a problem. The child can then start to feel frustrated and annoyed because people around are reflecting those feelings.

Bereavement

The child's concept of death

The concept of death is not fully acquired until around 8 years of age. The full understanding of death entails awareness of a number of components. Lansdown and Benjamin (1985) have identified these as:

1 separation
2 universality
3 causality
4 irrevocability
5 appearance
6 insensitivity
7 cessation of body function.

They found that about 60 per cent of 5-year-olds, 70 per cent of 6-year-olds and 66 per cent of 7-year-olds had complete or almost complete concepts of death. They concluded that many children younger than 7 or 8 have a good understanding of the meaning of death and that discussions about death with 4- and 5-year-olds should not be underestimated.

Other research has indicated that most children under the age of 5 years are unlikely to understand the finality of death (Kastenbaum and Aisenberg 1972) although all 3-year-olds know that death occurs (Kane 1979). But by the age of 6 years many children understand that death is inevitable and irreversible (Smilansky 1981); 73 per cent of 6-year-olds indicate that they believe that they will die some day (Reilly *et al.* 1983).

Very young children will have an awareness and curiosity about the fact of death which can distress parents and relatives. The young child can understand the reasons for burial or cremation. Previous experience of having a pet die or seeing animals being prepared in a butcher's shop gives them an awareness of dead bodies. In fact they may seem rather ghoulish and cold-blooded in their curiosity at times. Visits to graveyards can incite many questions about where the bodies are or whether they can get one out to look at it. The child's questioning about what happens to the body when it is in the ground, or questions that indicate a lack of understanding of the finality of death like 'Will mummy come and see me again?' are often hard for the bereaved parent to manage. The child's need for acknowledgement and explanation about the meaning of death is difficult when adults are feeling vulnerable themselves. So it is understandable when parents do not want to discuss this very emotional topic with young children for fear of feeling hurt themselves.

Loss of a parent

Behaviour problems and anxiety symptoms are common among children who have suffered bereavement of a parent. Caplan and Douglas (1969) found a higher incidence of depressed mood, phobic disorders, and school refusal among children bereaved of one parent than among other clinic attenders. Raphael (1982) rated thirty-five children aged between 2 and 8 years within a few weeks of a bereavement and found that 92 per cent showed behaviour disturbance. This included high levels of anxiety, exaggerated separation difficulties, clinging, excessive crying, marked aggressive behaviour, sleep disturbance, and disorders of eating and toileting.

Toddlers can show a number of regressive behaviours when under the stress of a bereavement. Return to immature speech, incontinence, and clinging behaviour are all common. They may show withdrawn behaviour and suffer nightmares or even run away to look for the lost parent. Children as young as 18 months can show an emotional reaction to loss but they are unable to grieve if they do not understand what death means (Black 1987).

Some children continue to show behavioural problems long after the bereavement. Studies have shown that after nearly four years 39 per cent of children who had lost a father in a war still had symptoms that required professional help (Kauffman and Elizur 1979; Elizur and Kauffman 1983). Another study showed that, over a year after bereavement, children still had withdrawn behaviour, minor depressive symptoms, and a decrease in school performance (Van Eerdewegh *et al.* 1982; 1985).

Loss of a sibling

Loss of a sibling involves a variety of mixed feelings that parents should acknowledge. Surviving children may have feelings of having 'won' the parents. They can now have the parents all to themselves and so may feel an element of pleasure. But they have also lost a playmate, they feel lonely, and they may feel guilty about having 'caused' the death through bad thoughts about the sibling. They may also fear catching the same disease or having the same disorder that caused the death.

Many of the behavioural problems associated with losing a sibling are due to the parents' reactions after the loss. They may become preoccupied with the lost child, mourning the loss for an excessively long period, and consequently depriving the surviving child of adequate attention, care, and love. They may consciously or unconsciously blame the surviving child for still being alive or idealize the dead child to the detriment of the surviving one. They may alternatively become so overprotective and concerned with the surviving child that the child becomes smothered and unable to express appropriate levels of independence.

Jonathan, aged 6 years, was referred because he seemed very unhappy and miserable and was soiling. The history revealed that eighteen months previously his 3-year-old sister had drowned in a family boating holiday. While the boat was moored on the banks of the Thames the little girl had been playing a game of hide and seek and had fallen into the water while walking around with a coat over her head. She had never surfaced and the family had been distraught. Since that time Jonathan had become a changed personality. From a lively and happy boy he had become solemn, frequently cried, was solitary at school, and was soiling himself during the day.

Therapy was aimed at the family reliving the terrible scene together and each explaining how they felt and how terrible it had been. All of the family cried freely in front of each other and were able to comfort each other. The parents had been reluctant to discuss the incident with their son for fear of making him feel worse and so had hidden their grief from him. He said that he thought his parents did not talk about his sister because they were angry with him for having caused her death. The opportunity to discuss the event openly and the painful feelings allowed the family to comfort each other constructively. Jonathan was reassured that he held no blame for the accident and that his parents had been trying to protect him from feeling unhappy but unwittingly had made him feel worse.

Management of bereavement

Mourning A cause of long-term distress in children is the failure of adults to help them understand what has happened. The surviving parent or relatives need to allow the child to express their grief and share in the mourning. Protecting the child from seeing adults crying or unhappy may make the child feel that there is something wrong about expressing feelings openly. Children appear to cope with their feelings about the death better when they have had the opportunity to cry and talk about the dead parent in the month after bereavement (Black and Urbanowitz 1987).

Explanation Understanding the cause of death can help a child cope better with the loss of a parent. Giving information sensitively helps break through the secrecy and denial about what has happened (Rosenheim and Reicher 1985). Complex medical details are not necessary but a simple explanation about a part of the body not working properly and that the doctors could not make it better is often sufficient. Children who do not hear about the cause of death may assume personal responsibility for the death. The child's developmental stage of egocentric thinking can induce these thoughts: the child may feel guilty about having been naughty or being angry with the parent before death and link this with causing the death.

Preparing a child for death of a parent is sometimes an issue if a parent is chronically ill. The illness needs a simple explanation, plus awareness that the parent is not going to get better. Death can be discussed and the child reassured that death does not hurt. Preparation for the fact that the parent will be missed is important. But despite full discussion and preparation the aim is not to prevent the child showing upset at the death. The aim is more to help the child understand the process to avoid long-term difficulties like guilt.

Visiting the sick parent in hospital is a very helpful way for the child to realize how ill the parent is. They may need careful preparation for the changed appearance of the parent but seeing the parent helps them adjust to the death when it happens. Saying goodbye can be important. The young child after the age of 18 months can benefit from this opportunity to understand what is happening (Black 1987).

Religion The inclusion of religious concepts is very much the family's decision. Some relatives find it easier to say that 'Mummy has gone to live in Heaven' but they need to be aware of the confusion and misconceptions that a child can develop. Young children have very concrete concepts about God and Heaven and may wonder why they cannot go to visit mummy there. It is important for parents not to retreat into using abstract religious concepts if they do not believe in them (Black 1987).

Continuing care The continuity and security of care after a parent's death is another major influence on the young child. The mental health of the surviving parent is critical for the child's future emotional development. Having a depressed widowed mother has been associated with high scores of behaviour disturbance in children (Van Eerdewegh *et al.* 1985).

The loss of a husband often severely affects the family's standard of living. Loss of income, status, having to move home and lose friends will all exacerbate the problems of loss. Prolonged depression in the surviving parent affects the parent–child relationship and extends its influence into the daily management of the child (Black and Urbanowicz 1985).

Loss of a mother may mean that care-taking of the young child is transferred out of the family to another relative or to a substitute parent. The child needs the opportunity to develop a consistent relationship with the new care-taker and not be moved around different people. The child's emotional needs and security should be the major consideration of the father at this point rather than his own feelings of wanting to hold on to the child.

Divorce and parental separation

There is a trend at present in the USA for more couples with pre-school children to separate and also have disputes over custody (Wallerstein 1985). In Britain there is an increasing rate of divorce: in 1982 27 per cent of children under 16 years of age had experienced family break-up (Donovan 1984). The issue of the break-up of families with young children is now becoming very important.

The child's understanding of divorce

Young children have a simple understanding of what constitutes a family and what constitutes family membership. Living in the same house is a necessary condition for family membership to the young child, while at older ages of 11 and 12 years the ideas of blood ties and legal relations emerge as important; 60 per cent of 4-year-olds from intact homes thought that the defining attribute of parenthood was physical location and less than 10 per cent thought that parenthood continued once the parent permanently moved out of the house, while 30 per cent had no understanding of divorce at all and thought that parents would always be there. Experience of divorce can modify these views and young children can learn that emotional bonds can be maintained over distance (Gilby and Pederson 1982).

The young child may feel that a parent is no longer theirs after a divorce because they do not live in the same house. This can seem like a bereavement unless the child is helped to understand that the other parent will still come to visit. It is therefore possible to understand why many young children show fear and anxiety about being abandoned by the departing parent or by both parents during a divorce (Wallerstein and Kelly 1980; Richards 1982).

The child's view of the cause of the divorce is also strongly age related. Children under 8 years old tend to blame themselves for the break-up and feel guilty and anxious (Kalter and Plunkett 1984; Wallerstein and Kelly 1980).

The effects of divorce on young children

The age of the child at the time of divorce or separation is important in determining the reaction and the process of adjustment (McGurk and Glachan 1987). Pre-school children can show considerable behavioural regression, clinging, increased bedwetting, while older children show increased anger and aggression to both parents.

A six-year follow-up of 144 pre-school children and families found that divorce has more long-term effects on boys, but remarriage of the mother is associated with increased behaviour problems in girls and a reduction in boys (Hetherington *et al.* 1979).

In general, children in divorcing families are more likely to develop emotional disorders (Zill 1984). Some of these are long-term effects and 15–25 per cent may require psychiatric treatment (Waters and Dimock 1983). Many parents marry again within five years of divorce but 20 per cent of those will separate again and so the children may be exposed to several marriage breakdowns (Wallerstein 1985). The adjustment to step-parents, step-siblings, and new extended families can be stressful and children can face continued readjustment difficulties throughout their early years (Kalter *et al.* 1984).

The changes in the emotional climate in the family will affect the child's behaviour. Mood changes in the parents, irritability, and depression will all influence the interaction between parent and child. Children may feel confused at the unpredictability of their parents' reactions. Lack of consistency in management can be reflected in sudden indulgence of the child when the parent feels guilty, or excessive provision of material possessions to gain allegiance with the child against the other parent. One parent may try to gain an inappropriate alliance with the child, complaining about the other parent openly in an effort to gain support (Hildebrand 1988).

The experience of divorce can vary markedly from child to child. The emotional environment in the family during the period preceding the divorce or separation can have a great effect on the child's behavioural and emotional state (Rutter 1984). Some parents' break-up is vitriolic and painful, others manage it amicably and without severe distress.

Divorce should be recognized as a process rather than a single event. Wallerstein (1985) has described three stages in the divorcing process:

1 the acute phase lasting two years during which time the

partners gradually disengage from each other and re-establish their separate lives

2 a transitional phase during which the parents experience failure, success, and ambivalence about the separation

3 the post-divorce phase when the single-parent unit becomes stable and clearly established or the parent remarries.

The parents not only are learning to cope with their own emotional adjustment and needs during this time but also may have to fight extensive legal battles about custody and access, the division of financial resources, and the split of the family home and possessions. Children can suddenly become a focus for the aggression and antagonism between the partners. One parent may try to deprive the other from seeing the children more from their own anger and disappointment than from understanding the needs of the children. The children can then become pawns in the battle and drawn in to take sides. They can feel split loyalty when they still love each parent equally and desperately want the whole family to stay together and live happily under one roof.

Management of children's reactions to divorce

Not all children show emotional or behavioural problems related to their parents' divorce. In a study of fifty-one families with joint custody of the child 27 per cent of the families were doing well after three years (Steinman *et al.* 1985). These parents showed mutual respect, had high self-esteem, were flexible and open to help. They viewed the other parent as a co-parent and co-operated in management and care of the children.

Wallerstein and Kelly (1980) have stressed the importance of the parent–child relationship before the break-up. An open and caring relationship where the parent is aware of the child's emotional needs will enable the parent to continue to meet these needs even in times of stress. The extent of extended family support and other network support is also valuable. A caring grandmother can help offset some of the confusion and disruption that is happening at home.

There are two simple guidelines for parents to help cope with children during marital breakdown:

1 The child should be informed as soon as possible about the imminent break-up. Trying to keep a secret in a fraught atmosphere just creates more tension and the child may feel frightened and confused. Children hear what is being said in arguments in the house and if the position is not made clear they may carry a burden of guilt that they are causing all the problems.

2 Explanations should include information that affects the child directly. Children do not want complex descriptions of why the break-up is occurring but reassurance that it is not their fault and the explanation that mummy and daddy are feeling very cross with each other. The effects on the child should be explained very clearly, for example one parent may not be living in the house any more, or daily details about who collects them from school or who takes them swimming.

Many parents will need professional help during this time in dealing with their own feelings as well as those of the children (Fine 1987). They need to understand that children need good continuity of care both physically and emotionally and that children suffer immensely when drawn into the fight between the parents as they have no reason to dislike either parent. Their allegiance to their parents may be equal and the stress that there is going to be a separation is enough for them to cope with.

Summary

Emotional problems in young children cover a wide variety of symptoms and causes. Fear is aroused by a number of events and experiences. All children have a phase of fear of separation which they gradually grow through and learn to manage, although some have a heightened reaction to separation experiences and become very distressed and upset. The behaviour can concern parents who often capitulate to the child's demands and exacerbate or maintain the problem. A desensitization approach to managing fear is the most useful technique of coping.

Bereavement can cause a number of long-term emotional reactions in children if there has not been adequate explanation about events or the child has not been helped to understand and discuss the loss. Experiences of parents' separating or divorcing can have a similar impact. Children readily interpret events as having been caused by them and carry a sense of guilt. Separated parents who can co-operate in child-rearing and remain on good terms can enable children to cope with family break-up.

Habits are common in young children. These may be self-comforting like thumb sucking or holding a soft cloth, while others are indicative of tension like twitches and involuntary movements.

Parents can be helped to be aware of their child's emotional state. Often this reflects the parents' emotional disturbance and so help may need to be directed at how the parents are coping in their own lives.

Chapter nine

The overactive and hyperactive child

Parents and nursery staff often use the term 'hyperactive' to describe children who are very lively or restless. It is a term that has been used rather loosely to describe a number of behaviours that include restlessness, inattentiveness, excitability, overactivity, impulsiveness, fidgetiness, distractibility, and disruptiveness (Taylor 1985a). There has been a lot of confusion over the terminology used about overactivity and hyperactivity and so it is helpful to distinguish between the different terms used (Taylor 1986a). There is a vast literature about this topic and the problems of attempting to define discrete categories of behaviour. Clear diagnosis is important in determining the best form of treatment for the condition. Taylor (1985b) has presented the following definitions:

1 Overactivity refers to an excess of physical movements. The child moves about more than the average child, may have fidgety movements, or may have difficulty in sitting down for any significant period of time. Despite being lively, these children will often have good concentration when they do pay attention. In general, they are vigorous and energetic children but sometimes the high level of activity is generated by agitation and anxiety. Occasionally they are described as non-compliant children as they will refuse to sit down when told to stay in one place. The behaviour is often not a problem to the child but is irritating and exhausting for the adults.

2 Hyperactivity or attention deficit disorder describes a child who has a high level of physical activity because of a short attention span and is disorganized and chaotic. These children

show a combination of restless and inattentive behaviour that is inappropriate to their chronological age. They are impulsive in their actions which can lead them to appear fearless and foolhardy. The children have no apparent sense of danger because they react immediately to the situation without thinking or anticipating events; consequently they can appear clumsy and have many accidents. The children can be disruptive and difficult to handle both at home and in nursery school. The distinction between the hyperactive child and the conduct-disordered child can be difficult to make, particularly as the hyperactive behaviour is sometimes situation specific.

3 Hyperkinesis refers to a psychiatric syndrome of children with hyperactive and inattentive behaviour. It implies that the condition is not just a feature of the child's reactions to situations but is severe and pervasive. The behaviour occurs in all situations regardless of who is present. The behaviour is handicapping to the child both socially and academically. These children also frequently show delays in intellectual development with clumsiness and speech delay (Taylor 1985a).

Research studies on hyperactive behaviour in children have been beset by difficulties because of the varying definitions of the behaviour under study. A twenty-fold difference in the diagnosis rate of hyperactivity has been found between the USA and Britain. In Britain and Europe the diagnosis of hyperkinetic syndrome is reserved for children who show the pervasive hyperactivity across all situations and so occurs in about 1 per cent of the population. In the USA this diagnosis is applied to children who would be called conduct-disordered in Europe (Schachar *et al.* 1981).

The confusion in terminology has extended outside professional circles to the public. Hyperactive children are often seen as naughty and wilfully disobedient and may be considered to be conduct-disordered but the defiant behaviour is often a result of the child's problems with attention and poor ability to modulate their activity level. Although hyperactivity is a risk factor for later development of conduct disorder it is not always associated with the adverse family and social problems that are characteristic of conduct problems in children. Aggressive and defiant behaviour in children is closely related to the family and social environment of the child, while hyperactivity does not have this same close association.

Hyperactive behaviour that starts early in the child's development is strongly related to later anti-social behaviour. Parents' and teachers' reactions to the child can contribute to the development of conduct disorder. A child who is continually active, cannot concentrate, is chaotic and disorganized can tax a parent's abilities to the utmost. These children receive a lot of negative feedback and readily elicit anger and exasperation from adults. The child and parent may develop an aversive system of interaction where all communication is either controlling or negative. Hyperactivity is just one of several routes that lead to anti-social behaviour.

Causes of hyperactivity

Brain damage

There is no evidence that superficial brain damage to the cortex is related to hyperactive behaviour (Rutter 1983). Nor is there any evidence of localized lesions to the brain that cause hyperactivity although the possibility of deeper-level brain damage still exists and has not been disproved. No common neurological cause has been found (Rapoport and Ferguson 1981).

But in contrast children who show hyperkinetic behaviour have a higher frequency of seizures, speech problems, hemiplegia, or diplegia. As a higher proportion of developmentally delayed children show hyperkinetic behaviour, and as structural brain damage is more common among this group of children than in the normal population, it is likely that links with brain damage do exist. But there is no identifiable brain lesion and not all children with brain damage have hyperactive behaviour (Taylor 1986a).

Prenatal and perinatal adversity

There is a consistent and small association between behaviour problems in general and stresses in pregnancy and the neonatal period but only a very severe trauma is significant. Complications in pregnancy and delivery contribute only a little to the prediction of hyperactivity when other factors like maternal smoking during pregnancy and low foetal heart rate during second-stage labour are accounted for (Nichols and Chen 1981).

Lead in the environment

Exposure to lead has been shown to have a slight effect on cognitive development in children (Lansdown and Yule 1986; Harvey 1984; Yule *et al*. 1981) but this is not associated specifically with hyperactivity. High lead levels in children are associated with poor concentration (Taylor 1986c) but high levels of activity have only a low association. So although lead in the environment does affect children it is neither a necessary nor sufficient cause for hyperactive behaviour to develop.

Diet

The effects of a child's diet has been linked to hyperactive behaviour although the mechanism by which this occurs is not yet clear. There have been two main areas of research about the effect of diet on behaviour:

1 Some children may be particularly susceptible to toxic effects of additives in the diet (Feingold 1973; 1975).

2 Some children may be allergic to one or more different foods in their diet (Egger *et al*. 1985).

These two areas of research have both come up with positive results for some but not all hyperactive children (Taylor 1984).

First, Feingold's research in the early 1970s indicated that eating food that contained food colouring (especially red and yellow dyes), a preservative (BHT or butolated hydroxytolulene), and natural salicylates (e.g. in apricots, prunes, raspberries, tomatoes, and cucumbers) could cause behaviour disturbance in children. He reported that when he placed hyperactive children on a salicylate-free diet 30 per cent showed a dramatic improvement (Feingold 1973; 1975). This research provoked a wide reaction and many studies were carried out to try and replicate his findings. Some detailed studies were unable to demonstrate similar findings

(Harley *et al*. 1978a; 1978b; Conners 1970; Mattes and Gittelman 1981). But when the results of these studies are examined more closely positive results were found (Weiss 1982). Children do not all respond to one particular additive or even a similar combination of additives and so grouping together findings over a large number of children can negate any positive findings in individuals. The general view now appears to be that an additive-free diet can occasionally be a helpful form of treatment for some children. There is a good response in a minority of children but the effect is normally a placebo effect.

Second, research on allergic reactions to foods has shown that dietary manipulations do have a significant effect on children's hyperactive behaviour (Egger *et al*. 1985). Seventy-six hyperactive children were given an oligoantigenic diet for four weeks. This diet was based on providing very few varieties of food in the initial stages and gradually reintroducing new foods in a controlled and carefully monitored manner over the course of several weeks. The basic diet consisted of two meats (lamb and chicken), two carbo-hydrates (potatoes and rice), two fruits (banana and apple), vegetables (any brassicas), water, calcium, and vitamins. Every week a new food was introduced in the diet and if no reaction was noted it was included in the diet. The child's behaviour was recorded every day by the parents.

The children who appeared to react to a particular food were then asked to participate in a further test of their response by reverting to the original diet and taking capsules that might or might not have contained the identified food. This phase of the research was included to avoid the possibility of a placebo effect. If neither the parents, the child, nor the researcher knew the contents of the capsules until the end of the trial, there was no possibility of expectation affecting the results. Twenty-eight families completed this second phase and all identified the placebo period as being the time when the child showed better behaviour (that is the child was not receiving any of the identified foods). So it was possible to discriminate by observing the child whether the capsule contained the identified food or not.

The foods that caused the most frequent behavioural reactions were benzoic acid and tartrazine, which were usually involved together. No child reacted to them alone. Forty-six other provocative foods were identified. The top ten were

Foods	Reaction
colourants, preservatives	79%
soya	73%
cow's milk	64%
chocolate	59%
grapes	50%
wheat	49%
oranges	45%
cow's cheese	40%
hen's eggs	39%
peanuts	32%

The indication from this study is that combinations of any foods can affect behaviour and that is likely to be an allergic reaction rather than an idiosyncratic response to one particular type of food. Removal of the identified foods from the diet is very effective treatment for some children.

Assessment of hyperactive behaviour

Due to the variation in view and confusion about the existence and the etiology of hyperactivity in young children a number of treatment approaches have been advocated. The essential characteristic for successful treatment is accurate assessment of the problem so that the most appropriate style of management of the problem can be applied.

Behaviour of the child

Parental reports about the child's behaviour at home are usually the starting-point for assessment. Generalizations by parents about how the child behaves need to be identified and made more specific. What does the parent mean by restless or hyperactive? Examples of precise instances of how the child behaves need to be discussed. Questioning about the child's behaviour should cover the following areas.

Level of activity How long can the child sit down for? What type of fidgeting is shown? Does the child appear agitated or anxious? When is the child overactive? Does the child show evidence of being able to relax and have quiet times? Is the level of activity described appropriate for the child's age and developmental status, for example is it normal inquisitiveness and exploration? Is the child's level of activity the same in all situations or is it situation specific?

Attention span Does the child maintain attention on tasks that are interesting? How long will the child play with any one activity? Does the child's attention vary according to who is present? What distracts the child from an activity? Can the child resist distraction?

Aggression and anti-social behaviour Does the child show aggressive behaviour? If so, what instigates the problem and what does the child do? Is the child destructive? Does the child tell lies? How does the child get on with peers or siblings? Are there any difficulties with learning to share and co-operate?

Developmental status Is the child showing any delays in development, particularly language development? Is there any evidence of adverse perinatal or post-natal history? Is there any neurological abnormality?

Evidence of allergy Does the child or any close relative show any allergies such as skin rashes, migraine, asthma?

Evidence for food responsiveness Has the parent noted any relation between the child's behaviour and anything that the child has eaten? Is the child a fussy eater? Does the child eat any food excessively? Does the child drink excessively?

These areas of questioning will start to reveal the severity of the problem and whether the child's behaviour is situation specific or more pervasive. The relationship of the behaviour to the developmental and intellectual level of the child indicates whether the parents have excessively high expectations of their child's behaviour or whether the child is behaving inappropriately for his or her age. Identification of general behaviour problems or disobedient and aggressive behaviour can reveal a problem of management rather than hyperactivity; evidence of allergy or food responsiveness will give indications that a dietary approach may be effective.

Behaviour of the parents

Family and social factors also influence how a child behaves and these need to be assessed to determine how much an influence the parents are having on their child's behaviour problems.

Parent–child relationship How do the parents discipline the child? How effective are they at controlling the child's general behaviour? Does the child appear to be generally out of control or is the overactive behaviour of primary concern?

Emotional environment at home Is the mother showing any psychiatric or emotional difficulties such as depression or anxiety? Are the parental expectations appropriate for the child's age and developmental level? Is there a marital problem? Are there any other family emotional stresses apart from the child's level of activity?

A detailed interview should be supported by observation of the child either in a play setting or during an assessment period. A parent's view of overactivity may be an over-reaction to normal behaviour and it can be helpful to point out how the child is able to maintain attention and inhibit movement when really interested and motivated in doing a task. Many children who show a tendency to be overactive will be disruptive and wild when they are in an unstructured setting or have nothing to do, but once occupied they settle down well. Similarly some children have difficulties in choosing appropriate activities to do and are unable to occupy themselves without adult help. Consequently they appear to be making continual demands for attention and interrupt the parents' activities.

Observation of parent–child interaction is also valuable to reinforce the information already obtained. The problem may be more of a general management and discipline problem than one of hyperactivity. The child may be non-compliant because the parents are unable to carry through their demands and be consistent rather than because the child does not pay attention to what the parent says. Aggressive and anti-social behaviour are also much more related to the parental management style and the emotional environment at home than to hyperactivity. Conflicts between the parent and child and an ongoing family stress can exacerbate a tendency that the child has to be overactive.

Management of hyperactive behaviour

The choice of treatment approach may not be entirely clear after the assessment and sometimes a combination of approaches is needed to manage the problem successfully.

Diet

Indications for trying a dietary approach include:

1 The child is showing a significant level of pervasive overactivity that has been continuing for a period of time plus a short attention span.

2 The home environment should be relatively stable with parents who have appropriate expectations of the child's behaviour and who manage the child adequately.

3 The child is showing evidence of a behavioural reaction to certain foods that are eaten.

4 The child or a very close relative has some form of allergy, for example skin rashes, eczema, asthma.

5 The parents and child are motivated and committed to trying a dietary approach.

Keeping a detailed record of the child's behaviour is a very useful starting-point when a dietary approach is being used. The parent needs to keep a sense of objectivity rather than being carried away with over-enthusiasm. The problem behaviour can be recorded on a chart, devised by the therapist and parent, which breaks the day into segments. The parent can rate the child's level of activity, concentration, and co-operation on specific activities or generally over the time period. More formal rating charts can also be used (Conners 1973; Goyette *et al.* 1978; Zukow *et al.* 1978). These provide a baseline against which any changes in behaviour can be recorded once the diet commences. Also during the diet when alterations are made the effect on behaviour can be noted.

Some health visitors have found that an early starting-point is for mother to write down exactly what the child eats in a day and match this with a rating of behaviour. This can reveal some simple associations that parents had not recognized previously and may prevent a long, detailed diet being undertaken.

Mark, 5 years old and the second child in the family, had shown extremely overactive and restless behaviour since a baby. He had cried incessantly as a young baby and had always been very difficult to settle. Life had been so stressful for his mother that she had needed her husband to stay at home with her to help manage him during the day and night. He was a very poor sleeper and was irritable all day. His routines had never been properly established despite great attempts by both parents.

The parents were very caring and showed great tolerance towards him but had become progressively more worried as his school had indicated that although he was bright he was not possible to teach in the normal classroom. At home his behaviour was disorganized and erratic. He was continually moving and then would suddenly collapse in exhaustion. He could be very aggressive but then extremely sorry and truly contrite a few minutes later. He had also started to masturbate excessively while lying on his front on the carpet which distressed his parents.

His father had an extensive history of allergic reaction to foods, pollen, and dust. The parents had also noticed that Mark came out in rashes on his face and body erratically. They had felt that he might be allergic but they had tried excluding foods from his diet to no effect.

Detailed observation of the child and his parents reinforced the view that they could not be helped in improving their management of him and so an oligoantigenic diet was started. Within the first week a marked improvement occurred in Mark's behaviour. He stopped masturbating completely, he was calmer and was more manageable at home. During successive weeks every time a new food was introduced he managed well for a day or two and then his behaviour began to deteriorate again. Once returned to the basic diet he improved again. His mother eventually found that he was able to tolerate turkey, rice, green vegetables and pears but any other foods began the cycle back to overactive behaviour.

Mark came to accept his diet extremely well. During the initial stage he had a few lapses but it was evident in his behaviour when he had eaten something that was not on his diet. One morning he had taken a small crust of his brother's toast and within half an hour a red rash developed on his face and he had begun to feel unwell. Despite being so young he was aware of how food affected his behaviour and so complied with his diet.

The difficulty with applying a special diet is that it can be expensive and requires commitment and close co-operation by the parents. Some families are too disorganized and chaotic for this approach ever to work. When an overactive child is at home the parents' abilities to cope may be so overstretched that an additional request which involves setting very precise limits on the child's eating pattern may be just too much to expect. The child needs very close supervision to ensure that excluded foods are not eaten. When children go to play at friends' homes or attend parties, parents need to have good co-operation from friends and neighbours. Children easily feel excluded from the family when they are on a diet as they see other family members eating the forbidden foods. Some parents will include the whole family in the diet so that this exclusion does not occur, but this is difficult. The problems about eating at parties or in cafés or restaurants are great and so the child may be restricted from going out.

Similarly if a child stays for meals at a nursery, a crèche or with a child-minder clear instructions need to be given to other adults supervising the child. With some children even a very slight piece or portion of a target food can disrupt their behaviour markedly and unless the parent is aware of this an inaccurate picture can develop about the child's reactions to the diet. An additional danger is created for some children when a particular dietary item has been excluded for a period of time because a heightened reaction can occur to the food when it is reintroduced. This is particularly noticeable in children who are allergic to dairy products. Some clinicians feel that it is necessary to have a child admitted to hospital during a challenge phase when dairy products are reintroduced as the reactions can be dangerous.

Dietary restrictions for the pre-school child can be such a disruptive process to normal family and social life that some clinicians feel that it is contra-indicated. The reason for the diet has to be presented very carefully to the child who may feel that they are being punished by not being allowed to eat favourite foods. They may feel that the parents are angry and may not understand the necessity for the length of the 'punishment' when they have been trying to be good. This can create difficulties in the parent–child relationship. Some children start to steal food and have tantrums to get what they want. When a young child starts to resist the diet it becomes difficult to provide a balanced diet with the choice of foods left. Parental anxiety increases markedly and some parents start to feel that it is not worth the effort. They end up preferring to have their child overactive rather than cope with the fights about food at every meal-time.

Some children fantasize about having devils inside them that cause them to be bad and their reasoning as to why they are not allowed certain foods becomes confused and distorted. When banned foods are reintroduced they may become very frightened about eating them again unless they are helped to understand in a practical and realistic way the reason for the diet.

So selection of this treatment is dependent on not only the type of presenting problem and a possible sensitivity or allergy to foods but also the ability of the family to apply the diet consistently. Assessment of parenting skills and commitment to using the approach are essential. All of the difficulties inherent in the treatment need to be discussed fully with the parents. Details of the practical application should be considered so that parents understand fully what is expected of them.

Parents are often tempted by reports in the press or books to try children's diets unsupervised. It is possible to devise an additive-free diet but this rarely works as parents are not usually aware of the extent of additives in the diet, do not try for a long enough period, or are not aware of the need for complete consistency in the diet.

Michael, aged 5½ years, had epilepsy which was not completely controlled by medication. He still continued to have occasional grand mal attacks early in the morning while in bed and would have drop attacks during the day. He was a very active child who became uncontrollable in unstructured settings. At home he would climb on the furniture and rush around the flat. He found difficulty in settling to play unless his mother gave him undivided attention. He was often aggressive and would refuse to co-operate with instructions at home and at school.

His mother reported that she had tried an additive-free diet with him at home to no effect. She carefully looked at the contents of food that she bought and tried to prepare fresh foods in meals. On careful questioning it was evident that she still gave Michael a packet of sweets on the way home from school every day and she had no knowledge about the lunches he ate at school.

The dangers of parents attempting to carry out an oligoantigenic trial unsupervised are quite considerable. Removal of significant sources of vitamins, minerals, and proteins from the diet results in children suffering from malnutrition or severe dietary deficiencies. This diet needs to be closely monitored by a doctor and a dietician so that supplements can be provided for the child without affecting the dietary trial. Consequently it is a time-consuming and expensive treatment approach in terms of professional involvement.

Medication

Drugs are considered most effective for children with hyperkinetic syndrome whose hyperactivity is pervasive and severe and whose attention skills are very poor but who show little evidence of emotional disturbance. These children are usually described as showing an attention deficit disorder using diagnostic criteria developed in the USA (American Psychiatric Association 1980).

Drug treatment of hyperactive children has produced extensive research results (Ottenbacher and Cooper 1983; Taylor 1986e). Stimulant drugs (amphetamines, e.g. Ritalin) have been used most effectively with hyperactive children in the USA. The evidence for their effectiveness is now well documented; however, the prescription rate in North America greatly exceeds that in Britain. In fact the majority of doctors will not prescribe these drugs in this country (Taylor 1979). The long-term effects are still not clear and as many children are on them for many years in the USA there is a reluctance to commence this form of treatment in this country. Use of the drug requires careful monitoring and should be used in conjunction with alternative treatment approaches such as behavioural management or remedial education.

Part of the problem of using medication as the major form of treatment is the psychological dependence it creates in the family. Parents become used to how the child behaves while on medication and become terrified of stopping it in case the child reverts to the previous behaviour pattern. In fact little adaptation is made to the fact that their child has a significant behaviour problem and they carry on as if it does not exist. These families need to accept that medication may not be possible over the long term because of the lack of knowledge about its effects and efforts to learn and anticipate how to manage the child need to occur in conjunction with medication.

Use of medication has had a beneficial effect on some children's performance in school. This is not because it helps learning in a specific way but it reduces their level of inattention and so the child's productivity at school increases (Douglas *et al*. 1986). The drug-induced changes in junior-aged children have been shown across a wide range of academic, learning, cognitive, and behavioural measures. The beneficial effects extend beyond improving attitude to work and increasing on task behaviour to an improvement in self-regulating behaviour. This involves better organization and sustained effort, accurate and efficient information-processing and self-correction of errors. It does not just slow down the child's rate of response but enables them to make more effective use of the time spent on task.

It is still not clear how stimulants achieve their effect. Findings on adults taking amphetamines indicate that improvements in attention to tasks occur under conditions of boredom, fatigue, or low motivation. Also the finding that normal children show similar beneficial results in school work when taking these drugs indicates that hyperactive children are not unusual in their response. Douglas *et al*. (1986) has speculated that the effect may be mediated through a self-regulating mechanism so that children and adults all work at a higher level of capability. Hyperactive children may be different from normal children in that the discrepancy between their output and their capability is greater and so the improvements seem more marked. The children who improve most on medication are those who score worst on tests of concentration (Taylor 1985a).

When considering the treatment of the pre-school child the picture is not so clear. Many doctors and parents are even more reluctant to use medication with this age group. Two early studies found that stimulant medication gave some symptomatic improvement but that the effects were less dramatic and consistent than found with older children (Conners 1975; Schleifer *et al.* 1975). There is insufficient data to draw conclusions about drug effects with this age group.

Other evidence from use with school-age children indicates that stimulants can help the family cope better. Measures of family atmosphere demonstrate that parents show more warmth towards the child, and sibling relationships improve. This is one way of helping families reverse the angry and destructive interactions that have built up (Schacher *et al.* 1988). This helps to avoid the pre-school child being labelled as bad and the cause of all problems. Once parents recognize that the child's problem is not deliberate misbehaviour they are able to learn how to provide the best environment to help the child's development. A combination of therapeutic approaches is essential. Neither the child nor the parents should come to rely on the drug as the only way of coping. Alteration in attitude to the child, recognizing the scope of the behaviour problem, and learning how best to manage it are long-term goals. Short-term improvement on drugs provides time for an adjustment in feelings and expectations towards the child. It also provides space for planning how best to help the child's social functioning.

Behavioural management

Working with parents to devise ways of coping with a hyperactive child is the most frequently used mode of treatment. This approach is applicable to all forms of overactive, hyperactive, or conduct-disordered behaviour. In essence the style of management discussed in Chapters 3 and 4 is the basis of the approach. Observation of mother–child interaction has demonstrated that mothers of hyperactive boys give more commands and praise throughout the day than those of normal children (Befera and

Barkley 1985). This probably reflects the poor level of compliance these children show and so mothers feel they need to be more controlling. Studies using medication suggest that mother's behaviour is often a response to the child's non-compliance (Barkley and Cunningham 1979). When children were taking Ritalin and were consequently less active and showed improved concentration span, the mothers were less controlling and angry with them.

Parental management techniques have concentrated in three main areas: management skills, improving the child's attention span, and improving the child's social skills.

Management skills These include using positive control in order to prevent a spiral of aversive interaction building up, carrying through requests and commands, and ensuring that the child pays attention to what is being said (Barkley 1981). Parents may need to learn to crouch down to the child's level, direct the child's face towards them, and repeat the instruction clearly and simply until the child acknowledges that they have heard and understood. Very clear and deliberate instructions help the child become aware of what is expected. Continual prompting will help the child stay on the task or remember what has been asked. Once the child is distracted the job will be forgotten and although this appears to be wilful the child genuinely has a problem in concentrating on a task until it is completed.

Parents need to learn to set very clear limits for the child's behaviour. These need to be maintained rigorously and consistently so that the child learns what is expected and allowed. With most normal children it is possible to be inconsistent some of the time because they transfer learning across new situations and realize the special circumstances that apply when rules change. The hyperactive child finds this change very difficult to accept as their learning pattern is so erratic. The confusion and distress that change in routine brings is painful both to the child and the family. Parents who want to indulge their child on a special occasion, or because they are feeling sorry for the child, find that the child often becomes chaotic and much worse behaved because they are confused or overexcited.

Clear structure and precise limits work very well in conjunction with using rewards. The child learns the results of appropriate behaviour when feedback from the star chart or another reward is given. A tight structure and immediate feedback is very helpful to hyperactive children in aiding them to gain self-control and awareness of their actions. Many parents find that allowing a period of high activity, like rushing around the room or the garden, is an effective reward for the child after a period of self-control. The child needs to let off steam and use up some energy for a period before settling down to a task again. Reward approaches enable parents to be positive in their attitude and emphasize the good qualities of the child or the good events of the day. This aids a more positive relationship between parent and child.

Time out approaches to management where the child has to sit quietly on a chair or is removed to another room do not work well with hyperactive children. The child has to show so much self-restraint to sit on the chair that when they get off they are likely to rush around even more. Similarly if they are sent to another room they will rapidly forget that they have been naughty and start to amuse themselves or get into further trouble.

Improving the child's attention span The child will need aid in focusing attention on the correct cues. Learning to stop an activity in order to look at who is talking is a skill that needs to be taught. Simple cues can help this, for example always calling the child's name before requesting something, emphasizing what the child needs to notice by saying it louder, repeating it several times, using gestures, or physical prompts.

Routine and a structured day aids this process. Children learn where to put their shoes if there is a place organized for this. Similarly expectations about behaviour should remain constant so that the child learns by repeated experience what is, and what is not allowed. A sequence to the day helps the child feel settled and begin to anticipate events. Families of hyperactive children often find that a change in routine is often very disruptive. Holidays often cause problems and the readjustment of returning to home can also be difficult.

The process of learning is often longer for these children due to their fluctuating attention span. This is why frequent repetitions are necessary as the child often misses some of what is said the first time but picks up more the second and third times. This need for repetition is exhausting and emotionally wearing for parents who need to keep calm and patient. Seeing their children's problem as a learning disability helps parents take an educational rather than a purely disciplinary role. Conflicts arise when parents see that their children are bright and able but will not use their abilities to the full. It is easy to feel that the children are not trying and are not motivated to learn, or that they are deliberately disobedient or not listening. Once children start to be blamed for their characteristics, parents start to lose patience, and an aversive emotional environment begins to develop.

An increased attention span can be promoted by parents encouraging their child to attend to a task for progressively longer periods. The therapist needs to set up specific playtimes for the parent and child at prescribed points each day and the parent should rigorously record the amount of time the child stayed seated or maintained attention on the task. A quiet activity like looking at a book or playing a sedentary game can be used to encourage the child gradually to spend longer times on one activity. If initially the child stays still for only approximately thirty seconds, parents should consistently increase this length of time in small amounts across a number of activities. Increases of ten seconds may be all that can be expected initially but by persevering and helping the child maintain concentration this can be built up into minutes. A stop-watch is a useful tool for parents to tune their expectations finely to the child's ability. Daily routine such as sitting still for a meal, watching some television, helping around the house, or in the garden can all be used to increase attention span gradually.

More complex activities should be broken up into small steps so that the child has the opportunity to see the development of an activity. Each step requires only a brief amount of concentration but by coming back to the same task the child gradually builds up a sequence of activities in small steps. A task that another child would complete at one sitting may take several sittings with a hyperactive child and will need to be left out ready for the next time the child can settle to it. Small steps of concentration interspersed with time to let off steam helps the child learn and gain satisfaction from achievement.

One nursery teacher became expert at catching the attention of a hyperactive 4-year-old in her class. She estimated that he was able to concentrate for between thirty seconds and one minute at a time so she would encourage him to come to her desk where she would have a puzzle or a drawing that he was completing. She would work with him intensively for that brief period and then let him run off around the class for between five and ten minutes until she could call him again. She found that with a carefully structured approach like this she was able to get him to complete as much as the other children did but in the briefer and more concentrated time.

With older pre-school children parents can encourage them to pause and reflect on what they are doing. If the child is just about to misbehave or act on impulse a cue just to stop and think helps the child avoid a problem. Some children benefit from learning to talk out loud to themselves, repeating an instruction or talking their way through an activity. Strategies of problem-solving can be taught in this way. For example when doing a jigsaw or formboard the children need to remind themselves to try each piece in all directions or to say which colour piece they are looking for. At a later age this will progress into anticipating and considering alternative decisions which again require thinking and taking a little time instead of immediate action.

Improving the child's social skills Many hyperactive children need help in understanding the effect of their behaviour on other people. They feel upset when other children do not want to play with them or refuse to include them in games but do not understand why they are being excluded. Their level of activity easily isolates them from other children. They are often disruptive in games, inconsiderate of others' feelings, show poor self-control, and have problems with taking turns and sharing. Although all young children show these features at some time, hyperactive children will continue with these characteristics when other children have outgrown them and become more socially aware. The first place where children become aware of the rules of social behaviour is in the home. Opportunities in playgroups and toddler groups expand the experience. Mothers need the confidence not to feel embarrassed about managing their child in public. It is sometimes easier to stay at home but the child needs the safe opportunity to learn social skills while mother and other adults are around to help point out the problems and cope with the upsets.

The child may need to be held and contained while waiting for a turn on a slide and gradually the ability to wait will be incorporated by the child as the adult's grip loosens. Eventually the child will be able to wait, once reminded, and a verbal prompt may be all that is necessary. There can be a progression from taking turns with an adult in a game to including one other child and then helping the two children play the game together with an adult just supervising.

Learning to wait is probably one of the hardest skills to teach hyperactive children. Even with normal children the process is often fraught but frequently the hyperactive child does not stay around long enough to find out the result of waiting. Consequently the requisite social learning does not take place. To learn to wait the child has to be able to stay in one place. Being physically contained by an adult may be necessary for this to occur but these occasions should be very brief and not seen as a punishment by the child. Waiting needs to be taught in a progressive manner, increasing the time gap by perhaps only ten seconds at a time. The parent needs to be aware of the child's ability to wait and be responsive to the child's efforts. A final goal of a thirty-second delay may be a great achievement. This needs to be seen as a success rather than always comparing the hyperactive child to others.

John's mother would often feel upset that other children at nursery never invited John to their house to play. She had specifically asked several children to tea so that John could make friends with them. She recognized that he was isolated because of his hyperactive behaviour and tried desperately to help him. She spent long periods playing with him and teaching him to take turns in games and share his toys. When other children came round John would become so overexcited that he would rush around the house and the garden being unable to settle and play. His mother was becoming so desperate she found herself amusing the visiting child rather than the children playing together.

John's mother needed a lot of support and encouragement to continue in her attempts to help John mix socially. She had to learn to accept that John would not necessarily be invited back to play partly because the other mothers felt unsure about how to cope with him in their own houses. She was encouraged to keep asking children over but a plan was made to try choose one or two friends rather than lots of different children so that John would get used to them and not become so overexcited. John's mother needed to recognize that her time spent playing with the visiting child was an important time for John to get used to the new situation of a friend in his house. Once he started to feel he knew the friend he began to join in the activities and gradually his mother was able to leave them to play together.

One of the biggest problems for parents is the embarrassment they feel for their child. They need to recognize that other parents feel frightened and helpless and are not just being rude. They have to recognize that their child is different from others so the normal social rules do not apply. Being hyperactive can be a considerable social and academic handicap and so to help the child, parents need to keep their best interests in mind and become hardened to the reactions of others. Patience and perseverance are required in extraordinary quantities.

Summary

There is considerable confusion in the definition of hyperactive behaviour. There are differing levels of severity that affect the child's social and academic functioning. Detailed assessment of the child's behaviour in different settings is essential to understand the cause of the problem and indicate a useful treatment approach.

Dietary analysis and a number of behaviour management approaches are the main methods of treatment as medication is not often used in Britain, although it is common in the USA. Parents need a lot of support and encouragement in understanding their child's behaviour and in learning how to cope effectively with their child.

Chapter ten

Crying babies

A crying baby can cause parents great anxiety and stress. The tone of the cry, the length of time spent crying, and the ability to modify it all influence parents' feelings and reactions. Research studies have examined the acoustic features of babies' cries as an aid in diagnosis of organic disorder (Wasz-Höckert *et al.* 1985), adults' feelings and perceptions of babies' cries (Boukydis 1985; Murray 1985; Lounsbury and Bates 1982), and the effect of babies' cries on parents' behaviour (Donovan and Leavitt 1985; Frodi 1985).

Crying in young babies is described in varying ways by parents. In some babies it is time linked in the day, often in the evening, and has been called 'three-month colic'. This type of crying is often inconsolable and has the appearance that the child is in pain although no physical cause is found. Legs are drawn up or the baby's back arches, the baby may struggle, not snuggle down for comfort, and feeding is refused (Brazelton 1962; Rebelsky and Black 1972).

Other parents report that their baby cries nearly all day long. A pattern of general fussiness, irritability, crying, and whining is described with disturbed sleep and feeding patterns. Parents can become distraught with attempting to comfort such babies. Mothers may feel they have to carry the baby around all day and have no time to do any other household chores. The fact that there are different styles of crying and different levels of intensity and duration suggest that it is multifactorial in origin.

It can be helpful to see crying as a developmental process responding to physiological demands in the first few months of life but later developing into affective expression of the baby's emotional state. Crying can then be seen as a social communication, for example demand for more or less attention and stimulation, indication of frustration or anger (Lester 1985).

Prevalence

Results from an epidemiological study in the Isle of Wight has indicated that colic affected 16 per cent of babies and was present in most babies by the age of six weeks. Nearly half of the infants (47 per cent) who first had colic before the age of 6 weeks no longer had symptoms by the time they were 3 months old, a further 41 per cent stopped crying by 6 months while 12 per cent carried on with the symptoms of colic between 6 and 12 months of age (Hide and Guyer 1982). It rarely starts after the third month and in general seems to be a self-limiting problem.

Retrospective data from mothers of 5-year-old children indicated that they remembered 14 per cent of the children as having cried excessively as a baby (Butler and Golding 1986).

Estimates of the prevalence rate of colic in different studies vary from 13 per cent of babies (Carey 1968) to 35 per cent (Thomas 1981). A major difficulty is the lack of a uniform definition of colic and that most studies ask mothers about their babies' behaviour a considerable time after the event and so the data are retrospective. For precise information mothers need to keep clear diaries about the frequency, duration, and intensity of the babies' crying.

Bernal (1972) studied seventy-seven babies during their first ten days of life and found that there was a peak in crying between 6 pm and midnight and that first babies cried more than second babies.

Causes of crying

There has been a wide variety of hypotheses about the causes of crying in babies. One problem is the lack of clear understanding of the nature of 'colic' and whether this is different from other types of crying shown by young babies.

Birth complications and prematurity

Complications during pregnancy and birth can cause an irritable and crying baby (St James-Roberts and Wolke 1984) although there are no specific indications of how long this early phase of irritability lasts. Thomas (1981) followed up 130 babies and found that such events during labour as forceps delivery or prolonged labour were significantly related to the incidence of 'colic'. First babies were also more likely to have 'colic' crying particularly if the mother had an epidural block during the labour. He has made the suggestion that the increase in reports of colic in young babies in Australia could be linked to changes in obstetric practices and the greatly increased use of epidurals and anaesthesia during labour.

Children of low birthweight are reported to cry more than normal birthweight babies (Butler and Golding 1986) and a significant difference in the type of cry can differentiate premature babies from healthy full-term babies. Their cries are shorter and more high pitched (Wasz-Höckert *et al.* 1985). In a study where parents were shown videos of premature and full-term babies crying, they reported greater autonomic arousal and more negative emotions to the cry of the premature baby (Frodi *et al.* 1978). It could be that the more aversive a baby's cries are the less parents can tolerate it and start to feel increasingly stressed and upset. This could interact with the frequency and the actual amount of time the baby cries; some babies cry frequently though not for long periods but their cries are very arousing.

Feeding

There appears to be no difference in the incidence of crying between breastfed and bottle-fed babies although mothers who breastfed for less than two months remembered their babies as crying excessively (Butler and Golding 1986). This may be because mothers changed to bottle-feeding as they thought crying was due to insufficient nutrition. Hide and Guyer (1982) support this finding but report that the real difference in prevalence of colic is more related to social class than style of breastfeeding. The higher social classes babies are more likely to be breastfed.

In contrast to this finding Bernal (1972) reports that breastfed babies have a more marked twenty-four-hour pattern of crying with greater total time of crying and more crying after feeds than bottle-fed babies. She suggests that mothers often claim to give up breastfeeding because of the baby waking and crying so frequently. Similarly a study of babies in Norfolk found that there was a greater incidence of 'colic' crying in breastfed babies (Rubin and Prendergast 1984).

In fact many mothers are advised to give up breastfeeding crying babies because of possible concerns about allergy to substances in their milk or insufficient milk supply. A number of different substances transmitted through the mother's milk have been linked to crying, for example caffeine, brassicas, beans, and grapes, but no clear research findings support this anecdotal evidence. A hungry baby is often suggested and bottle-feeds are considered a more reliable method of the baby gaining sufficient nutrition. The fact that crying is more common in the evening has been linked to breast milk supply being low because the mother is tired and has been busy all day. It is not clear whether this advice is successful as mothers often give up breastfeeding around the three-month time when many babies will begin to reduce the amount of 'colic' crying.

Allergic reactions

There are quite contradictory research results about the effect of cows' milk protein in breast milk. A view exists that mothers' drinking and eating dairy products is linked to 'colic' in breastfed babies (Jacobssen and Lindberg 1978; 1983). A sample of eighteen mothers and babies who showed that a maternal diet free of cows' milk stopped colic also had a history of allergy in the family. This finding has not been supported by other studies where there has been a double-blind trial of milk products (Evans *et al.* 1981; Liebman 1981). In Evans's study there was no effect from a maternal history of allergy nor from evidence of cows' milk antigen in the maternal milk. The only effect noticed was that when mothers increased the range of their diet, particularly when they ate chocolate, there was an increase in the number of babies' colic attacks.

Allergic reactions to foods can cause a variety of symptoms, for example diarrhoea, vomiting, sleeplessness, skin rashes, eczema and rhinitis and 'colic' crying.

Maternal reactions

Anxiety and tension in the mother has been cited as a contributory factor to babies crying (Carey 1968). With the finding that first-born babies are more likely to cry excessively, it has been easy to blame a lack of confidence in handling by the mother. Bernal (1972) indicated that second-time mothers responded more quickly to crying and more often with feeding. Consideration should be paid to the fact that first-time mothers may take more account of what others say to them about how they should manage their child and so they may not be quite so flexible or may be more erratic than a second-time mother.

Carey (1968) emphasized the importance of the mother's level of anxiety when anxious mothers were found to be about nine times more likely to have colicky babies than non-anxious mothers. Part of the difficulty is separating out cause from effect. Naturally a mother whose baby cries a lot and is difficult to console will report higher anxiety in managing the child as she will feel less capable and undermined by her baby. This does not imply that the anxiety preceded the crying. The results of studies in this area can also be interpreted as anxious parents perceiving their babies to be crying more than they actually are.

Carey (1983) has proposed an interaction model for the development of colic when a physiologically predisposed baby is cared for by an anxious parent whose soothing methods are ineffective. Several studies have suggested that colicky babies are temperamentally more difficult (Barr et al. 1983; Carey 1972; Weissbluth et al. 1984).

The evening 'colic' pattern has also been linked to an increase in emotional tension in the mother and the house when father comes home from work (Brazelton 1985).

Illness

Acoustic cry analysis is starting to provide an important and new diagnostic tool to detect babies at risk for organic disorders. The *cri du chat* or very high-pitched cry of the hypothyroid baby has been known for many years (Wasz-Höckert et al. 1985). Sound spectrography of cries can reveal whether the baby has laryngeal or cerebral problems, particularly if the baby suffered from asphyxia. The changes in cry characteristics in asphyxiated newborns are so obvious that cry analysis could become a valuable tool in neurological examination. If the cries become more normal after a few days the baby is more likely to recover without any neurological sequelae than if the cry continues to remain abnormal (Michelsson 1971; Michelsson *et al.* 1977). Infants who were found to be neurologically damaged at later follow-up had more abnormal cries in the newborn period.

This aspect of research, although of great value, does not address the issue of prolonged crying in babyhood and its association with organic problems. A general medical check will identify whether the baby has any of the more obvious difficulties such as hernia, urinary tract infection, throat or ear infection. But mothers should be encouraged to describe all signs that concern them to the doctor, for example projectile vomiting, diarrhoea, rashes, or refusing feeds.

Parents often feel that their colicky baby has the appearance of the baby being in pain as the crying is usually inconsolable. Various theories have been offered: excessive gas or wind, immature intestinal tract (Asnes and Mones 1982). The view that colic is related to biological maturation is supported by the finding that the usual onset of colic in premature babies is within two weeks of the expected date of the birth regardless of when the baby was actually born (Meyer and Thaler 1971).

Assessment of crying babies

So many hypotheses exist as to why babies cry that parents become confused and need help to analyse what is happening. Helping parents to assess the problem in a systematic manner can sometimes expose connections that they did not realize. It also demonstrates the reality of what is happening at home. A mother may complain that her baby is crying all day, but when she records the crying incidents she can see that the baby does in fact sleep erratically during the day but always wakes up crying. Her difficulty is not being able to predict what will happen and so the crying episodes seem very frequent. Another mother may manage the problem by carrying the baby all day so that there is no crying. She avoids the problem but is bothered by the possibility of the baby's crying when put down. Another baby may winge and fuss all day without really screaming, while others will have full-bodied screaming attacks for short periods that cause panic in the parents.

A full assessment procedure has several components. Screening for medical problems with a full medical history and details of any worrying symptomatology such as vomiting, fits, diarrhoea, constipation, breathing problems, poor weight gain, and frequent colds is important. Checks for urinary tract infections and ENT problems are particularly relevant. Also a developmental check will determine whether the baby is showing normal behavioural progress.

A detailed history of the crying problem should include:

1 when the crying started

2 whether there have been any periods of improvement or deterioration

3 a description of the type of crying including its intensity, length of time spent crying, and the time of day it occurs

4 what the parents have tried and what helps stop the crying

5 the effect on the parents' emotional state and the level of stress that they are experiencing.

Further details of the baby's pattern during the day provide a full picture of events. Assessment of the feeding and sleeping pattern combined with the crying episodes reveals the routine or lack of routine that exists:

1 how the baby is fed and what is offered (breast or bottle, any solids)

2 quantity offered/length of feed

3 level of fussiness during feeding and quality of sucking

4 frequency of feeding (day and night)

5 pattern of sleeping during day and night

6 pattern of feeding and sleeping.

Parents can be given a diary to fill in to record the times and durations of feeding, sleeping, and crying periods (Pritchard 1986).

Management of crying babies

Parents usually go through a checklist in their own minds about the possible cause of crying and then try to link this with their management of the crying. If they think the baby is hungry they offer food; if the baby is too hot or too cold clothing and bedding is altered accordingly; if they think the baby is bored they play and distract; if tired the baby is encouraged to sleep; if in pain they check for teething, wind, or go to the doctor. A problem arises if the crying does not indicate to them what is the matter and so a guessing game develops that can undermine the parents' confidence.

Developing routines and patterns

Some parents are better than others at predicting what is the matter and often a routine at home will help this process. The mother will be able to anticipate certain behavioural conditions at certain times of the day and as the baby also starts to learn the routine the communication system between them becomes more effective. A small indication from the baby rather than prolonged screaming will indicate that the mother needs to help in a particular way. A mutual communication pattern develops that becomes more effective and avoids unnecessary crying.

Pritchard (1986) found that daily diaries filled in by parents about feeding, sleeping, and crying showed unstable routines indicating that the parents were having difficulty understanding the baby's needs. They lacked confidence in handling the baby and there was poorly synchronized interaction between mother and child which led to a build-up of frustration and more crying. These parents were given clear guidelines about feeding, that is quantity given, timing between feeds, as well as specific feeding techniques like correct positioning, winding, size of teat hole. Advice on developing a sleeping pattern for the baby was also provided. Settling routines and nap times were discussed and planned. After an initial period of change the baby's crying became more predictable and parents felt happier because they could correctly identify the message from their baby. The crying caused by temper, pain, or boredom then becomes easier to identify and manage. By the second week of intervention the parents' worries about the baby's crying had significantly reduced and within two months it was considered to be within normal limits.

Another study of thirty colicky babies matched with thirty controls demonstrated improvement when parents were given simple management advice and an outline of what to do when the baby started to cry (Taubman 1984). The colicky babies averaged more than twice the crying time of the normal control babies at the beginning of the study. The treatment group was divided into two with different strategies; in one decreased stimulation was used with parents instructed to let the babies cry for up to half an hour in the cot after having tried all methods of stopping the crying including feeding. They were then instructed to pick up the babies briefly and return them to their cots, repeating this until the babies fell asleep or until three hours have passed. After three hours the babies were to be fed again. The second treatment group had instructions on effective parental responses and were asked to try never to let the babies cry. If the babies did cry then to go through a checklist of whether they were hungry, wanted to suck but were not hungry, wanted to be held, were bored and wanted stimulation, or were tired and wanted to go to sleep. Parents were instructed to try each new response if the previous one had not worked in five minutes and not to be concerned about overfeeding or spoiling the baby.

In the first treatment group there were no significant changes in the babies' crying while the second treatment group showed a 70 per cent improvement. This was a significant difference compared to the first treatment group and to the control group.

This study stressed the importance of initial assessment diaries that recorded both the babies' crying and the parents' responses. The diaries indicated that many of the responses were illogical and ineffective. Some parents would let their babies cry for fifteen minutes or longer before responding, others would never consider that the baby was hungry if the crying occurred within one or two hours of feeding, while for others feeding was their only form of response. Many assumed that the crying was beyond their control and made no attempt to find an answer. The diaries demonstrated to the parents how effective or ineffective their strategies were being.

Rhythmical stimulation

It is an automatic reaction to try to soothe a crying baby with rhythmical movements like rocking, patting, and stroking. Parents will sing quiet lullabies in time with the rocking. Prams or cots are gently shaken or pushed by hand or foot, babies are taken for rides in the car, or carry-cots are placed on top of the tumble drier while it is working. Some of these efforts to calm crying babies have existed for centuries. Old wooden cradles were built with rockers just for this purpose so that they could be rocked by foot while the mother had her hands free to do the sewing or knitting; old rocking chairs also were designed for rhythmical rocking.

Research on the effect of rocking babies has found that distressed babies who were rocked all calmed more quickly than those who were just picked up and held on the shoulder. The direction and continuity of rocking are also important. Babies who are intermittently rocked in a vertical position are more likely to be calmed into a bright-alert state, while babies who are rocked continuously in a horizontal position will become drowsy (Byrne and Horowitz 1981; Korner and Thoman 1972).

The rate of rocking has also been investigated and the greater the speed the greater the effect. Rocking rates of over sixty rocks per minute seem most effective, and as this is close to maternal heart-beat rhythm a biological link is postulated (Ter Vrugt and Pederson 1973). It is interesting that the most comfortable rocking speed in an old wooden rocking chair is about this speed.

Soothing and rhythmical singing often accompanies rocking: this can be a meaningless combination and repetition of sounds. Continuous sound will decrease the arousal level of young babies (Brackbill 1973) and some mothers find the noise of the washing machine, hair drier or the tumble drier helpful in settling their baby. Many gadgets emitting 'white' noise exist on the market now and basically consist of a 'sshh' sound that blocks out a lot of other noise reaching the baby. Tapes and records of womb noises have a similar effect. One theory is that continuous stimulation suppresses the arousal system of very young babies.

Several soothing processes occurring together have the most effect on crying babies. Physical movement, sound, and sucking affect all of the baby's senses to reduce the level of arousal. Sucking is the primary method most mothers use when calming their babies, breastfeeding being the most frequent first choice. But many mothers choose to give their babies dummies or encourage thumb and finger sucking as a way of helping their babies regulate their own levels of upset. This non-nutritive sucking is a very powerful calming agent and many babies appear to need far more sucking time than is appropriate for feeding alone. The cue to providing non-nutritive sucking is when the baby starts to mouth or suck fingers and before the baby has become upset. In a study of fussy but healthy newborn babies, those who were given a dummy after feeding continued to suck for an average of one hour. This was followed by a long period when the babies were alert but quiet. The babies who did not have a dummy slept less, were less alert, and cried significantly more (Anderson 1983).

Some mothers feel concerned about babies' becoming addicted to dummies, but as long as the dummy is used at the time the baby wants it rather than when the mother wants the baby to have it there is no real concern. Difficulties arise when mothers continually push the dummy back into the mouth of their baby for every cry, effectively stopping all communication with the baby and not meeting the baby's needs in other ways.

Carrying the baby is another frequently used method of soothing fretful babies. It is not clear whether the movement and stimulation of being carried or the proximity of the mother is important. Hunziker and Barr (1986) found that asking mothers to carry around their 3-week-old babies for an additional minimum of three hours a day reduced the amount of crying at 6 weeks by 43 per cent during the whole day and by 51 per cent during the evening. The decreased crying and fussing was associated with increased contentment and feeding frequency but no change in length of feeding time or sleep. The additional carrying time was not a response to crying. The researchers suggest that normal crying probably represents a culture-specific pattern reflecting the interaction between biological factors and infant care giving practices typical of our society. A baby's cries are an adaptive behaviour that increases the proximity of the mother and provides the opportunity for social interaction (Murray 1979; Thoman *et al*. 1983). Increasing carrying promotes proximity and so reduces the need for crying. Carrying may have allowed the mothers to respond more rapidly to their baby's needs and facilitated a more synchronous mother–child interaction.

Medication

Use of drugs to help calm crying babies has been used until

relatively recently. Merbentyl syrup which contains an anti-spasmodic agent (dicyclomine hydrochloride) was often prescribed for babies with severe colic. The major action of it is thought to be a non-specific direct relaxant on smooth muscle. Research findings were favourable for the use of this medication (Weissbluth *et al*. 1984) but it has now been withdrawn from the British market because of concern about side effects. There has been concern about possible links with sudden infant death syndrome and the occurrence of apnea or respiratory difficulties (Dupuis 1985).

Many old remedies exist, gripe water still being freely available but of unknown effect. One double-blind study of the effect of various medication for colic in 110 babies revealed no improvement (O'Donovan and Bradstock 1979). The substances used were

1 homatropine/phenobarbitone/alcohol
2 phenobarbitone/alcohol
3 alcohol
4 placebo.

Increasing or reducing stimulation

Some babies over-react to stimulation around them, becoming frightened by loud noise, bright lights, and too much handling. This type of baby screams at nappy changes and hates having a bath or clothes changed, so sometimes it is necessary to check that the mother and baby are synchronized with each other. The mother may need help in modulating the way she handles her baby and learning to recognize the baby's cues about being overstressed rather than just carrying on regardless. Her reactions and attitudes to these situations should be examined or observed so that tips about gentler handling can be offered. Holding the baby so that it feels secure and contained, changing one-half of the baby at a time rather than a complete strip off, regulating the temperature carefully where the baby is changed are all useful hints. Also mothers may need to be reassured not to be too fussy about the baby's clothes, leaving on 'babygros' for sleeping as well as daytime and trying more 'top and tailing' rather than lots of baths.

Very young babies can often be calmed by wrapping them closely in a sheet or blanket to restrict gently the amount of movement. This traditional habit of swaddling was put to experimental test and it was found that the most physical restriction on the baby's movements seemed to be the most effective process (Lipton *et al.* 1965). Very young babies' own intermittent movements appear to be overstimulating and keep them awake. Similarly the position of the baby while in the cot can affect the baby's arousal level. When babies lie on their backs compared to being on their fronts they are more irritable (Brackbill *et al.* 1973).

In other instances babies may cry excessively due to being too tired and unable to regulate their arousal level and fall asleep. Parents may need to help in establishing routines or being aware of the limitations on the baby's wakefulness and the need for quiet times. Many babies moan and cry when put down for a rest; a well-meaning parent who then picks the baby up thinking it needs help to fall asleep unfortunately over-arouses the baby even more. Babies need time to learn their own skills at self-regulation.

Other babies show the complete opposite picture and appear to want a lot of stimulation much of the day. These babies may not sleep very much during the day or have brief cat-naps only to wake up full of energy. They are often alert and lively and want to be carried around so that they can see what is going on. They can be distracted from crying by showing them something. If amused they are happy but when left unattended they get miserable and frustrated. This can be very wearing on a mother who has many other jobs to do in the day apart from amusing her baby. These babies can be helped by strategic placing of baby bouncers, use of parachute swings, walks in the buggy, mobiles, lots of pictures and books, and frequent changes of position. If left on a rug on the floor they will enjoy squirming around and experimenting with their physical skills but may also become very frustrated. Having lots of friends and relatives around to share the load is often the best solution but unfortunately is not always possible.

Sharing the worry

Many mothers become worn out with the responsibility of looking after a crying baby. The emotional stress is immense and relief can be obtained through sharing experiences with other mothers who face or have faced the same problems. Self-support groups (CRYSIS, National Childbirth Trust, La Leche) play an essential role for the isolated mother at home with her baby all day. She needs to realize that she is not the only one suffering this problem, that there is nothing wrong with her or her baby, and that there are people around with whom to share the worry. Friends and relatives can be co-opted to take the baby out for a walk regularly to give the mother a break and half-an-hour to have a bath. Husbands may need help in realizing the stress and rather than expecting the house to be in perfect order and supper on the table when they come home from work, they may need to come in ready to take over the management of the baby for a period so that their wives can have a rest or time to do the jobs. A joint partnership in coping through this phase can ease the load (Gray 1987; Kirkland *et al.* 1983; Kirkland 1985).

Summary

Crying babies can cause severe stress within families and have been linked with child abuse. Parents complaining about their crying baby should be treated seriously and compassionately. Support from friends, neighbours, or relatives may be required for the parents to cope but if there is no one they can turn to then parents should be put in touch with local voluntary organizations like CRYSIS, La Leche, and the National Childbirth Trust who may be able to help.

Direct help to the parents can include encouraging parents to keep a diary of the baby's crying and their strategies of managing it. Problem-solving strategies can then be discussed with the parents and a systematic routine established.

References

1 Introduction: causes of behaviour problems

Barkley, R.A. (1981) *Hyperactive Children: A Handbook for Diagnosis and Treatment*, New York: Guilford.
Bates, J.E. (1980) 'The concept of difficult temperament', *M-P Quart. 26*: 299–319.
Bax, M. and Hart, H. (1976) 'Health needs of preschool children', *Arch. Dis. Child. 51*: 848.
Brown, G. and Harris, T. (1978) *Social Origins of Depression*, London: Tavistock.
Butler, N.R. and Golding, J. (eds) (1986) *From Birth to Five: A Study of the Health and Behaviour of Britain's Five Year Olds*, London: Pergamon.
Cantwell, D.P., Baker, L. and Mattison, R.E. (1980) 'Psychiatric disorders in children with speech and language retardation', *Arch. Gen. Psychiat. 37*: 423–5.
Carr, J. (1980) *Helping Your Handicapped Child*, Harmondsworth: Penguin.
Child Development Project (1987) School of Applied Social Studies, University of Bristol.
Dowdney, L., Skuse, D., Rutter, M. and Mrazek, D. (1985) 'Parenting qualities, concepts, measures and origins', in J.E. Stevenson (ed.) *Recent Research in Developmental Psychopathology*, Oxford: Pergamon.
Earls, F. (1980) 'Prevalence of behaviour problems in three year old children: a cross-national replication', *Arch. Gen. Psychiat. 37*: 1,153–7.
—— (1982) 'Cultural and national differences in the epidemiology of behaviour problems in preschool children', *Cult. Med. and Psychiat. 6*: 45–56.
Frommer, E. (1973) 'The importance of childhood experience in relation to problems of marriage and family building', *Brit. J. Psychiat. 123*: 573, 157–66.
Garmezy, N. (1985) 'Stress-resistant children: the search for protective

factors', in J.E. Stevenson (ed.) *Recent Research in Developmental Psychopathology*, Oxford: Pergamon.

Graham, P., Rutter, M. and George, S. (1973) 'Temperamental characteristics as predictors of behaviour disorders in children', *Amer. J. Orthopsychiat. 43*: 320–39.

Jenkins, S., Bax, M. and Hart, H. (1980) 'Behaviour problems in pre-school children', *J. Child Psychol. Psychiat. 21*: 5–17.

Lee, C.L. and Bates, J.E. (1985) 'Mother–child interaction at age two years and perceived difficult temperament', *Child Devel. 56*: 1,314–25.

McLean, P.D. (1976) 'Parental depression: incompatible with effective parenting', in E.J. Mash, L.C. Handy and L.A. Hamerlynck (eds) *Behaviour Modification Approaches to Parenting*, New York: Brunner/Mazel.

Patterson, G.R. (1982) *Coercive Family Process: A Social Learning Approach* (vol. 3), Eugene, Oreg: Castalia.

Pound, A., Cox, A., Puckering, C. and Mills, M. (1985) 'The impact of maternal depression on young children', in J.E. Stevenson (ed.) *Recent Research in Developmental Psychopathology*, Oxford: Pergamon.

Pringle, M.K. (1975) *The Needs of Children*, London: Hutchinson.

Rachman, S.J. (1979) 'The concept of required helpfulness', *Behav. Res. Ther. 17*: 1–6.

Radke-Yarrow, M. and Kuczynski, L. (1983) 'Perspectives and strategies in child-rearing: studies of rearing in normal and depressed mothers', in D. Magnusson and V. Allen (eds) *Human Development: Interactional Perspectives*, New York and London: Academic Press.

Richman, N. (1978) 'Depression in mothers of young children', *J. Roy. Soc. Med. 71*: 489–93.

Richman, N., Stevenson, J. and Graham, P.J. (1982) *Pre-School to School: A Behavioural Study*, London: Academic Press.

Rutter, M. (1979) 'Protective factors in children's responses to stress and disadvantage', in M.W. Kent and J. Rolf (eds) *Primary Prevention of Psychopathology, Vol. III: Social Competence in Children*, Hanover, NE: University Press of New England.

Rutter, M. and Madge, N. (1976) *Cycles of Disadvantage*, London: Open Books.

Rutter, M., Quinton, D. and Liddle, C. (1983) 'Parenting in two generations: looking backwards and looking forwards', in N. Madge (ed.) *Families at Risk*, London: Heinemann Educational.

Skuse, D. and Cox, A. (1985) 'Parenting of the pre-school child: clinical and social implications of research into past and current disadvantage', in J.E. Stevenson (ed.) *Recent Research in Developmental Psychopathology*, Oxford: Pergamon.

Starte, G.A. (1975) 'The poorly communicating two year old and his family', *J. Roy. Coll. Gen. Pract. 25*: 800.

Stevenson, J. and Richman, N. (1976) 'The prevalence of language delay in a population of three year old children and its association with general retardation', *Dev. Med. Child Neurol. 18*: 431–41.

—— (1978) 'Behaviour, language and development in three year old children', *J. Aut. Child Schizophren.* 8: 299–313.

Stevenson, J., Richman, N. and Graham, P. (1985) 'Behaviour problems and language abilities at three years and behavioural deviance at eight years', *J. Child Psychol. Psychiat.* 26: 215–30.

Thomas, A. and Chess, S. (1977) *Temperament and Development*, New York: Brunner/Mazel.

Thomas, A., Chess, S. and Birch, H.G. (1968) *Temperament and Behaviour Disorders in Children*, New York: New York University Press.

Thomas, A., Chess, S. and Korn, S.J. (1983) 'The reality of the difficult temperament', *M-P Quart.* 28: 1–20.

Vaughn, B., Deinard, A. and Egeland, B. (1980) 'Measuring temperament in paediatric practice', *J. Paediat.* 96: 510–14.

Wallerstein, J.S. and Kelly, J.B. (1980) *Surviving the Break-up: How Children and Parents Cope with Divorce*, New York: Basic Books.

Wolkind, S.N. and DeSalis, W. (1982) 'Infant temperament, maternal mental states and child behavioural problems', in R. Porter and G.M. Collins (eds) *Temperamental Differences in Infants and Young Children*, London: Pitman.

2 Assessment of the problem

Bamford, J.M. and Saunders, E. (1985) *Hearing Impairment, Auditory Perception and Language Disabilities*, London: Edward Arnold.

Barker, P. (1986) *Basic Family Therapy* (2nd edn), London: Collins.

Bax, M., Hart, H. and Jenkins, S. (1983) 'The behaviour, development and health of the young child: implications for care', *Brit. Med. J.* 286: 1,793–6.

Bayley, N. (1969) *Bayley Scales of Infant Development*, New York: The Psychological Corporation of New York.

Bishop, D. (1984) *Test for Reception of Grammar*, Manchester: University of Manchester.

Bowen, M. (ed.) (1978) *Family Therapy in Clinical Practice*, New York: Jason Aronson.

Burnham, J. (1986) *Family Therapy*, London: Tavistock.

Coppersmith, E.I. (1985) 'Teaching trainees to think in triads', *J. Marr. and Fam. Ther.* 11: 61–6.

Cunningham, C. and Davis, H. (1985) *Working with Parents: Frameworks for Collaboration*, Milton Keynes: Open University Press.

De'Ath, E. and Pugh, G. (1986) *Working With Parents: A Training Resource Pack*, London: National Children's Bureau.

Douglas, J. (1979) 'Behavioural work with families', *J. Fam. Ther. 1*: 371–81.

——(1981) 'Behavioural family therapy and the influence of a systems framework', *J. Fam. Ther.* 3: 327–39.

Eisenson, J. (1986) *Language and Speech Disorders in Children*, New York: Pergamon.

Garvey, C. (1977) *Play*, London: Fontana.

Gelfand, D.M. and Hartman, D.P. (1984) *Child Behaviour Analysis and Therapy*, New York: Pergamon.

Gorell-Barnes, G. (1984) *Working with Families*, Basingstoke: Macmillan.

Griffiths, R. (1954) *The Abilities of Babies*, London: University of London Press.

Herbert, M. (1981) *Behavioural Treatment of Problem Children: A Practice Manual*, London: Academic Press.

Jerger, S., Jerger, J., Alford, B.R. and Abrams, S. (1983) 'Development of speech intelligibility in children with recurrent otitis media', *Educ. and Hearing 4*: 138–45.

Ling, D. (1972) 'Rehabilitation of cases with deafness secondary to otitis media', in A. Glovig and K.S. Gerwin (eds) *Otitis Media. Proc. Nat. Conf.*, Springfield, Ill: Charles C. Thomas.

Lowe, M. (1975) 'Trends in the development of representative play in infants from 1–3 years: an observational study', *J. Child Psychol. 16*: 33–48.

McAuley, R. and McAuley, P. (1977) *Childhood Behaviour Problems*, London: Macmillan.

McCarthy, D. (1970) *McCarthy Scales of Children's Abilities*, New York: The Psychological Corporation of New York.

McConkey, R. (1985) *Working with Parents: A Practical Guide for Teachers and Therapists*, London: Croom Helm.

Mash, E. and Terdale, L. (eds) (1981) *Behavioural Assessment of Childhood Disorders*, New York: Guilford.

Mason, H.C. and O'Byrne, P. (1984) *Applying Family Therapy*, Oxford: Pergamon.

Matterson, E.M. (1975) *Play with a Purpose for the Under Sevens* (2nd edn), Harmondsworth: Penguin.

Minuchin, S. (1974) *Families and Family Therapy*, Cambridge, Mass: Harvard University Press.

Mittler, P. and Mittler, H. (1982) *Partnership With Parents*, Stratford: National Council for Special Education.

Newson, J. and Newson, E. (1979) *Toys and Playthings*, Harmondsworth: Penguin.

Paradise, J.L. (1981) 'Otitis media during early life. How hazardous to development? A critical view of the evidence', *Pediat. 68*: 868–73.

Reichman, J. and Healey, W. (1983) 'Hearing disabilities and conductive hearing loss involving otitis media', *J. Hearing Disabil. 16* (5): 272–8.

Reynell, J. (1977) *Reynell Developmental Language Scales* (revised), Windsor: NFER/Nelson.

Sak, R. and Ruben, R.J. (1981) 'Recurrent middle ear effusion in childhood: implications of temporary auditory deprivation for language learning', *Annals of Otology, Rhinology and Laryngology 89*: 303–11.

Shah, N. (1981) 'Treatment of conductive deafness in children', in H.A. Beagley (ed.) *Audiology and Audiological Medicine Vol. 2*, Oxford: Oxford University Press.

Sheridan, M. (1973) *Children's Development: Progress from Birth to Five Years. The Stycar Sequences*, Windsor: NFER/Nelson.

——(1977) *Spontaneous Play in Early Childhood from Birth to Six Years*, Windsor: NFER/Nelson.

Silva, P.A., Kirkland, A., Simpson, A., Stewart, I.A. and Williams, S.M. (1983) 'Some development and behavioural problems associated with bilateral otitis media with effusion', *J. Learn Disab. 15*: 417–21.

Singer, J. (ed.) (1973) *The Child's World of Make-Believe*, New York: Academic Press.

Smyth, G.D.L. (1984) 'Management of otitis media with effusion: a review', *Am. J. Otology 5* (5): 344–9.

Stevenson, J.E. (ed.) (1985) *Recent Research in Developmental Psychopathology*, Oxford: Pergamon.

Truax, C.B. and Carkhuff, R.R. (1967) *Towards Effective Counselling and Psychotherapy*, Chicago, Ill: Aldine.

Webster, A. (1986) 'Update – the implications of conductive hearing loss in childhood', *ACPP Newsletter 8*: 4–14.

Webster, A., Saunders, E. and Bamford, J. (1984)'Fluctuating conductive hearing impairment', *J. Assoc. of Ed. Psychol. 6* (5): 6–19.

Wechsler, D. (1967) *The Preschool and Primary Scale of Intelligence*, New York: The Psychological Corporation of New York.

Wheldall, K., Mittler, P. and Hobsbaum, A. (1979) *Sentence Comprehension Test*, Windsor: NFER/Nelson.

Zinkus, P.W., Gottleib, M.I. and Shapiro, M. (1978) 'Developmental and psychoeducational sequelae of chronic otitis media', *Amer. J. Dis. Childh. 132*: 1,100–4.

3 Positive parenting

Bijou, S. and Baer, D. (1976) *Behaviour Analysis and Child Development*, Englewood Cliffs, NJ: Prentice-Hall.

Birnbrauer, J.S. (1978) 'Some guides to designing behavioral programs', in D. Marholin II (ed.) *Child Behavior Therapy*, New York: Gardner.

Forehand, R.L. and McMahon, R.J. (1981) *Helping the Non-Compliant Child: A Clinician's Guide*, New York: Guilford.

Herbert, M. (1981) *Behavioural Treatment of Problem Children*, London: Academic Press.

Holden, G.W. (1983) 'Avoiding conflict: mothers as tacticians in the supermarket', *Child Dev. 54*: 233–40.

McAuley, R. and McAuley, P. (1977) *Childhood Behavioural Problems,* London: Macmillan.

Sajwaj, T. and Dillon, A. (1976) 'Complexities of an "elementary" behaviour modification procedure: differential adult attention used for children's behavioural disorders', in B. Etzel, J. LeBlanc and D. Baer (eds) *New Developments in Behavioural Research: Theory, Methods and Application*. Hillsdale, NJ: Lawrence Erlbaum.

Shaffer, H.R. and Crook, C.K. (1980) 'Child compliance and maternal control techniques', *Dev. Psychol. 16*: 54–61.

Stayton, D.J., Hogan, R. and Ainsworth, M.D. (1971) 'Infant obedience and maternal behaviour: the origins of socialization reconsidered', *Child Dev. 42*: 1057–69.

4 Setting limits

Christopherson, E.R. (1986) 'Anticipatory guidance on discipline', *Ped. Cl. of N. Amer. 33*: 789–98.

Cummings, E.M., Zahn-Waxler, C. and Yarrow-Radke, M. (1981) 'Young children's responses to expressions of anger and affection by others in the family', *Child Dev. 52*: 1,274–82.

Douglas, J. (1988) 'Antisocial behaviour', in J. Douglas (ed.) *Emotional and Behavioural Problems in Young Children: A Multidisciplinary Approach to Identification and Management*, Windsor: NFER/Nelson.

Douglas, J. and Richman, N. (1984) *Coping with Young Children*, Harmondsworth: Penguin.

Dumas, J.E. and Wahler, R.G. (1983) 'Predictors of treatment outcome in parent training: mother insularity and socio-economic disadvantage', *Behavioural Assess. 5*: 301–13.

—— (1985)'Indiscriminate mothering as a contextual factor in aggressive-oppositional child behaviour "damned if you do and damned if you don't"', *J. Ab. Child. Psychol. 13*: 1–17.

Dunn, J. (1983) 'Sibling relationships in early childhood', *Child Dev. 54*: 787–811.

—— (1984) *Sisters and Brothers*, London: Fontana.

Dunn, J. and Kendrick, C. (1981) 'Social behaviour of young siblings in the family context: differences between same-sex and different sex dyads', *Child Dev. 52*: 1,265–73.

—— (1982) *Siblings: Love, Envy and Understanding*, Oxford: Blackwell.

Dunn, J. and Munn, P. (1985) 'Becoming a family member: family conflict and the development of social understanding in the second year', *Child Dev. 56:* 480–92.

Forehand, R.L. and McMahon, R.J. (1981) *Helping the Non-Compliant Child: A Clinician's Guide*, New York: Guilford.

Herbert, M. (1981) *Behavioural Treatment of Problem Children: Practice Manual*, London: Academic Press.

Jenkins, S., Owen, C., Bax, M. and Hart, H. (1984) 'Continuities in common behavioural problems in preschool children', *J. Child Psychol. Psychiat. 25*: 75–89.

Kagan, J. (1982) *The Second Year*, Cambridge, Mass: Harvard University Press.

Kitzinger, S. (1979) *The Experience of Breastfeeding*, Harmondsworth: Penguin.

Newson, J. and Newson, E. (1976) *Seven Year Olds in the Home Environment*, Harmondsworth: Penguin.

Patterson, G.R. (1976) 'The aggressive child: victim and architect of a coercive system', in E.J. Mash, L.A. Hamerlynck and L.M. Handy (eds) *Behaviour Modification and Families I: Theory and Research*, New York: Brunner/Mazel.

—— (1980) 'Mothers: the unacknowledged victims', *Monogr. of the Soc. for Res. in Child Dev. 45* (5) serial no. 186.

—— (1982) *Coercive Family Process: A Social Learning Approach (Vol. 3)*, Eugene, Oreg: Castalia.

—— (1984) 'Siblings: fellow travelers in coercive family processes', in R. Blackmore (ed.) *Advances in the Study of Aggression*, New York: Academic Press.

—— (1986) 'The contribution of siblings to training for fighting: a microsocial analysis', in D. Olweus, J. Block and M. Radke-Yarrow (eds) *Development of Antisocial and Prosocial Behaviour*, London: Academic Press.

Patterson, G.R., Reid, J.B., Jones, R.R. and Conger, R.E. (1975) *A Social Learning Approach to Family Intervention: Families with Aggressive Children*, Eugene, Oreg: Castalia.

Reid, J.B., Taplin, P.S. and Lorber, R. (1981) 'A social interactional approach to the treatment of abusive families', in R.B. Stuart (ed.) *Violent Behaviour: Social Learning Approaches to Prediction, Management and Treatment*, New York: Brunner/Mazel.

Richman, N., Stevenson, J. and Graham, P.J. (1982) *Pre-School to School: A Behavioural Study*, London: Academic Press.

Rosenthal, P.A. and Doherty, M.B. (1984) 'Serious sibling abuse by preschool children', *J. Amer. Acad. Child Psychiat. 23*: 186–90.

Snyder, J.J. (1977) 'A reinforcement analysis of intervention in problem and non-problem children', *J. Abnorm. Psychol. 86*: 528–35.

Wahler,R.G. and Dumas, J.E. (1986) 'Maintenance factors in coercive mother–child interaction: the compliance and predictability hypothesis', *J. App. Behav. Anal. 19*: 13–22.

Wahler, R.G. and Graves, M.G. (1983) 'Setting events in social networks – ally or enemy in child behaviour therapy?', *Behav. Ther. 14*: 19–36.

Wahler, R.G., Hughes, J.B. and Gordon, J.S. (1981) 'Chronic patterns of mother–child coercion: some differences between insular and non-insular families', *Anal. and Interv. in Dev. Disabil. 1*: 145–56.

Wells, K.C. and Forehand, R. (1981) 'Childhood behavioural problems in the home', in S.M. Turner, S. Calhoun and H.E. Adams (eds) *Handbook of Clinical Behavior Therapy*, New York: Wiley.

5 Eating and feeding difficulties

Bernbaum, J.D., Pereira, G.R., Watkins, J.B. and Peckham, G.J. (1983) 'Non-nutritional sucking during gavage feeding enhances growth and maturation in premature infants', *Ped. 71*: 41–5.

Berwick, D.M., Levy, J.C. and Kleinerman, R. (1982) 'Failure to thrive: diagnostic yield of hospitalisation', *Arch. Dis. Childh. 57*: 347–51.

Blackman, J.A., Christy, L.A. and Nelson, O.T.R. (1985) 'Reinstituting oral feedings in children fed by gastrostomy tube', *Clin. Ped. 24*: 434–8.

Butler, N.R. and Golding, J. (eds) (1986) *From Birth to Five: A Study of Health and Behaviour of Britain's Five Year Olds*, London: Pergamon.

Casey, P.H., Bradley, R. and Wartham, B. (1984) 'Social and non-social home environments and infants with non-organic failure to thrive',*Ped. 73*: 348–53.

Chatoor, I. and Egan, J. (1983) 'Non-organic failure to thrive and dwarfism due to food refusal: a separation disorder', *J. Amer. Acad. Child Psychiat. 22*: 294–301.

Chatoor, I., Dickson, L., Schaefer, S. and Egan, J. (1985) 'A development classification of feeding disorders associated with failure to thrive: diagnosis and treatment', in D. Drotar (ed.) *New Directions in Failure to Thrive: Implications for Research and Practice*, New York: Plenum.

Cohen, E.A., Gelfand, D.M. and Dodd, D.K. (1980) 'Self-control practices associated with weight loss maintenance in children and adolescents', *Behav. Ther. 11*: 26–37.

Crawford, P.B., Keller, C.A. and Hampton, M.C. (1974) 'An obesity index for six month old children', *Amer. J. Clin. Nutr. 27*: 706–11.

Crockenburg, S. (1981) 'Infant irritability, mother responsiveness and social support influences in the security of infant–mother attachment', *Child Dev. 52*: 857–65.

Dietz, W.H. (1981) 'Obesity in infants, children and adolescents in the US – II: Causality', *Nutr. Res. 1*: 193.

—— (1984) 'Obesity in infancy', in R.B. Howard and H.S. Winter (eds) *Nutrition and Feeding of Infants and Toddlers*, Boston/Toronto: Little, Brown.

Douglas, J. and Richman, N. (1984) *Coping with Young Children*, Harmondsworth: Penguin.

Drotar, D. (ed.) (1985) *New Directions in Failure to Thrive: Implications for Research and Practice*, New York: Plenum.

Drotar, D., Woychik, J., Mantz-Clumprer, C., Bricknell, C., Negray, J., Wallace, M. and Malone, C.A. (1985) 'The family context of failure to thrive', in D. Drotar (ed.) *New Directions in Failure to Thrive: Implications for Research and Practice*, New York: Plenum.

Egan, J., Chatoor, I. and Rosen, G. (1980) 'Non-organic failure to thrive: pathogenesis and classification', *Clin. Proc. Ch. Hosp. Nat. Med. Cent. 34*: 173–82.

Epstein, L.H., Wing, R., Koeske, R., Androsik, F. and Ossip, D. (1981) 'Child and parent weight loss in family-based behaviour modification programmes', *J. Consult. and Clin. Psychol. 49*: 674–85.

Epstein, L.H., Wing, R.R., Woodall, K., Penner, B.C., Kress, M.J. and Koeske, R. (1985) 'Effects of family-based behavioural treatment on obese 5 to 8 year old children', *Behav. Ther. 16*: 205–12.

Euler, G. (1982) 'Non-medical management of the failure to thrive child in a paediatric in-patient setting', in P.J. Accardo (ed.) *Failure to Thrive in Infancy and Early Childhood*, Baltimore, Md: University Park Press.

Evans, S., Reinhart, J. and Succoop, R. (1972) 'Failure to thrive: a study of 45 children and their families', *J. Amer. Acad. Child Psychiat. 11*: 440–57.

Finney, J.W. (1986) 'Preventing common feeding problems in infants and young children', *Ped. Clins. N. Amer. 33*: 775–88.

Garn, S.M. and Clark, D.C. (1976) 'Trends in fatness and the origins of obesity. Ad hoc committee to review the 10 state nutrition survey', *Ped. 57*: 443–56.

Geertsma, M.A., Hyams, J.S., Pelletier, J.M. and Reiter, S. (1985) 'Feeding resistance after parental hyperalimentation', *Amer. J. Dis. Childh. 139*: 255–6.

Glaser, H.H., McHeagarty, M.C., Dullard, D.M. and Piychik, E.L. (1968) 'Physiological and psychological development of children with early failure to thrive', *J. Ped. 73*: 690–8.

Goldbloom, R.B. (1984) 'Failure to thrive', *Ped. Clin. N. Amer. 29*: 151–64.

Goldson, E., Bentovim, A. and Milla, P.J. (1985a) 'Failure to thrive: another approach', *Clin. Res. 33*: 110a.

Goldson, E., Milla, P.J. and Bentovim, A. (1985b) 'Failure to thrive: a transactional issue', *Family Systems 3*: 205–12.

Green, W.H., Campbell, M. and David, R. (1984) 'Psychosocial dwarfism: a critical review of the evidence', *J. Amer. Acad. Child Psychiat. 23*: 39–48.

Harden, B.L., Mandell, F. and Russo, D.C. (1986) 'Feeding induction in children who refuse to eat', *Amer. J. Dis. Childh. 140*: 52–4.

Harris, S.C. (1982) 'Non-organic failure to thrive syndromes', in P.J. Accardo (ed.) *Failure to Thrive in Infancy and Early Childhood*, Baltimore: University Park Press.

Hertzler, A.A. (1983a) 'Children's food patterns – a review: I. Food preferences and feeding problems', *J. Amer. Dietetic Assocn. 83*: 551–4.

—— (1983b) 'Children's food patterns – a review: II. Family and group behavior', *J. Amer. Dietetic Assocn. 83*: 555–60.

Homer, C. and Ludwig, S. (1981) 'Categorization of etiology of failure to thrive', *Amer. J. Dis. Childh. 135*: 848–51.

Howard, R.B. (1984) 'Nutrition and toddler feeding', in R. Howard and H.S. Winter, *Nutrition and Feeding in Infants and Toddlers*, Boston/ Toronto: Little, Brown.

Illingworth, R.S. and Lister, J. (1964) 'The critical or sensitive period with specific reference to certain feeding problems in infants and children', *Journal of Pediatrics 65*: 839–48.

Israel, A.C., Stolmaker, L. and Andrain, C.A. (1985) 'The effects of training parents in general child management skills on a behavioural weight loss program for children', *Behav. Ther. 16*: 169–80.

Iwaniec, D. and Herbert, M. (1982) 'The assessment and treatment of children who fail to thrive', *Social Work Today 13*: 8–12.

Iwata, B.A., Riordan, M.M., Wohl, M.K. and Finney, J.W. (1982) 'Paediatric feeding disorders: behavioural analysis and treatment', in P.J. Accardo (ed.) *Failure to Thrive in Infancy and Early Childhood*, Baltimore, Md: University Park Press.

Jenkins, J. and Milla, P. (1988) 'Feeding problems and failure to thrive', in N. Richman and R. Lansdown (eds) *Problems of Preschool Children*, Chichester: Wiley.

Kahn, E.J. (1973) 'Obesity in children', in N. Kiell (ed.) *The Psychology of Obesity: Dynamics and Treatment*, Springfield, Ill: Charles C. Thomas.

Kirtland, J. and Gurr, M.I. (1979) 'Adipose tissue hypercellularity – a review: 2. The relationship between cellulocity and obesity', *Int. J. Obesity 3*: 15–55.

Klesges, R.C., Coates, T.J., Brown, G., Sturgeon-Tillisch, J., Moldenhauer-Klesges, L.M., Holzer, B., Woolfrey, J. and Vollmer, J. (1983) 'Parental influences on children's eating behaviour and relative weight', *J. Appl. Behav. Anal. 16*: 371–8.

Knittle, J.C., Timmers, K. and Ginsburg-Fellner, F. (1979) 'The growth of adipose tissue in children and adolescents', *J. Clin. Invest. 63*: 239–46.

Kotelchuck, M. (1980) 'Non-organic failure to thrive: the status of interactional and environmental etiologic theories', *Advanc. Behav. Paed. 1*: 24–51.

Lewis, J.A. (1982) 'Oral motor assessment and treatment of feeding difficulties', in P.J. Accardo (ed.) *Failure to Thrive in Infancy and Early Childhood*, Baltimore, Md: University Park Press.

Lieberman, A.F. and Birch, M. (1985) 'The etiology of failure to thrive: an interactional developmental approach', in D. Drotar (ed.) *New Directions in Failure to Thrive: Implications for Research and Practice*, New York: Plenum.

Linscheid, T.R. and Rasnake, L.K. (1985) 'Behavioural approaches to the treatment of failure to thrive', in D. Drotar (ed.) *New Directions in Failure to Thrive: Implications for Research and Practice*, New York: Plenum.

McGuinn Koepke, J. and Thyer, B.A. (1985) 'Behavioral treatment of failure to thrive in a two year old', *Child Welfare League of America LXIV*: 511–16.

Maloney, M.J. and Klykylo, W.M. (1983) 'An overview of anorexia nervosa, bulimia and obesity in children and adolescents', *This Journal 22*: 99–107.

Mason, E. (1976) 'Obesity in pet dogs', *Vet. Rec. 86*: 612.

Palmer, S., Thompson, R.J. and Linscheid, T.R. (1975) 'Applied behavioural analysis in the treatment of childhood feeding problems', *Dev. Med. Child Neurol. 17*: 333–9.

Poskitt, E.M.E. (1980) 'Obese from infancy: a re-evaluation', *Top. Paed. 2*: 81–9.

Powell, G.F. and Low, J. (1983) 'Behaviour in non-organic failure to thrive', *Dev. and Behav. Peds.* 4: 26–33.

Richman, N. (1988) 'Feeding problems', in J. Douglas (ed.) *Emotional and Behavioural Problems in Young Children: A Multi-Disciplinary Approach to Identification and Management*, Windsor: NFER/Nelson.

Richman, N., Stevenson, J. and Graham, P.J. (1982) *Pre-School to School: A Behavioural Study*, London: Academic Press.

Schwartz, J.L., Niman, C.W. and Gisel, E.G. (1984) 'Tongue movements in normal preschool children during eating', *Amer. J. Occup. Ther.* 38: 87–93.

Senediak, C. and Spence, S.H. (1985) 'Rapid versus gradual scheduling of the therapeutic contact in a family based weight control programme for children', *Behav. Psychother.* 13: 265–87.

Shapiro, L.R., Crawford, P.B. and Clarke, M.J. (1984) 'Obesity prognosis in a longitudinal study of children from age six months to nine years', *Amer. J. Public Health* 74: 968–72.

Skuse, D. (1985) 'Non-organic failure to thrive: a reappraisal', *Arch. Dis. Childh.* 60: 173–8.

Spence, S.H. (1986) 'Behavioural treatments of childhood obesity', *J. Child Psychol. Psychiat.* 27: 447–53.

Taitz, L. (1971) 'Infantile over-nutrition among artificially fed infants in the Sheffield region', *Brit. Med. J.* 1: 315–16.

—— (1977) 'Obesity in pediatric practice: infantile obesity', *Ped. Clin. N. Amer.* 24: 107–22.

Tanner, J.M. and Whitehouse, R.H. (1975) *Growth and Development Charts*, Ware, Herts: Castlemead Publications.

Thompson, R.J., Palmer, S. and Linscheid, T.R. (1977) 'Single subject design and interactional analysis in the behaviour of a child with a feeding problem', *Child Psychiat. and Hum. Dev.* 8: 43–53.

Waxman, M. and Stunkard, A.J. (1980) 'Caloric intake and expenditure of obese boys', *J. Peds.* 96: 187–93.

Woolston, J.L. (1983) 'Eating disorders in infancy and early childhood', *Amer. Acad. Child Psychiat.* 22: 114–21.

—— (1987) 'Obesity in infancy and early childhood', *Amer. Acad. J. Child and Adol. Psychiat.* 26 (2): 123–6.

6 Toilet training

American Psychiatric Association (1980) *Diagnostic and Statistical Manual of Mental Disorders* (3rd edn), Washington, DC: American Psychiatric Association.

Ashkenazi, Z. (1975) 'The treatment of encopresis using a discriminative stimulus and positive reinforcement', *J. Behav. Ther. and Exper. Psychol.* 6: 1551–7.

Azrin, N.H., Sneed, J.J. and Foxx, R.M. (1974) 'Dry bed: a rapid elimination of childhood enuresis', *Behav. Res. and Ther.* 12: 147–56.

Bach, R. and Moylan, J.J. (1975) 'Parent administered behaviour therapy for inappropriate urination and encopresis: a case study', *J. Behav. Ther. and Exper. Psychiat.* *6*: 239–41.

Bakwin, H. (1973) 'The genetics of enuresis', in I. Kolvin, R.C. MacKeith and S.R. Meadow (eds) *Bladder Control and Enuresis: Clinics in Developmental Medicine Nos 48/49*, London: Spastics International Medical Publications.

Bakwin, H. and Bakwin, R.M. (1972) *Clinical Management of Behavioural Disorders in Children* (4th edn), Philadelphia, Pa: W.B. Saunders.

Balson, P.M. (1973) 'Case study – encopresis: a case with symptom substitution', *Behav. Ther.* *4*: 134–6.

Bellman, M. (1966) 'Studies on encopresis', *Acta Ped. Scand. Suppl. 170*.

Berg, I. (1979) 'Day wetting in children', *J. Child Psychol. Psychiat.* *20*: 167–73.

Berg, I. and Jones, K.V. (1964) 'Functional faecal incontinence in children', *Arch. Dis. Childh.* *39*: 465–72.

Berg, I., Fielding, D. and Meadow, R. (1977) 'Psychiatric disturbance, urgency and bacteriuria in children with day and night wetting', *Arch. Dis. Childh.* *52*: 651–7.

Berg, I., Forsythe, I., Holt, P. and Watts, J. (1983) 'A controlled trial of "Senokot" in faecal soiling treated by behavioural methods', *J. Child Psychol. Psychiat.* *24*: 543–9.

Blackwell, B. and Currah, J. (1973) 'The psychopharmacology of nocturnal enuresis', in I. Kolvin, R.C. MacKeith and S.R. Meadow (eds) *Bladder Control and Enuresis: Clinics in Developmental Medicine Nos 48/49*, London: Spastics International Medical Publications.

Blechman, E.A. (1979) 'Short and long term results of positive home based treatment of childhood chronic constipation and encopresis', *Child. Behav. Ther.* *1*: 237–47.

Butler, N.R. and Golding, J. (eds) (1986) *From Birth to Five: A Study of Health and Behaviour of Britain's Five Year Olds*, London: Pergamon.

Cooper, C. (1973) 'Giggle micturition', in I. Kolvin, R.C. MacKeith and S.R. Meadow (eds) *Bladder Control and Enuresis: Clinics in Developmental Medicine Nos 48/49*, London: Spastics International Medical Publications.

Davis, H.M., Mitchell, W.S. and Marks, F.M. (1977) 'A pilot study of encopretic children treated by behaviour modification', *Practitioner* *219*: 228–300.

de Jonge, G.A. (1973) 'The urge syndrome', in I. Kolvin, R.C. MacKeith and S.R. Meadow (eds) *Bladder Control and Enuresis: Clinics in Developmental Medicine Nos 48/49*, London: Spastics International Medical Publications.

de Vries, M. and de Vries, R.M. (1977) 'Cultural relativity in toilet training readiness: a perspective from East Africa', *Ped.* *60*: 170–7.

Dische, S. (1973) 'Treatment of enuresis with an enuresis alarm', in I. Kolvin, R.C. MacKeith and S.R. Meadow (eds) *Bladder Control and Enuresis: Clinics in Developmental Medicine Nos 48/49*, London: Spastics International Medical Publications.

Doleys, D.M. (1978) 'Assessment and treatment of enuresis and encopresis in children', in M. Hersen, R.M. Eisler and P.M. Miller (eds) *Progress in Behaviour Modification Vol. 6*, New York: Academic Press.

—— (1983) 'Enuresis and encopresis', in T.H. Ollendick and M. Hersen (eds) *Handbook of Child Psychopathology*, New York: Plenum.

Doleys, D.M. and Arnold, S. (1975) 'Treatment of childhood encopresis by full cleanliness training', *Ment. Retard. 13*: 14–16.

Douglas, J.W.B. (1973) 'Early disturbing events and later enuresis', in I. Kolvin, R.C. MacKeith and S.R. Meadow (eds) *Bladder Control and Enuresis: Clinics in Developmental Medicine Nos 48/49*, London: Spastics International Medical Publications.

Douglas, J. (1981) 'Behavioural family therapy and the influence of a systems framework', *J. Fam. Ther. 3*: 327–39.

Douglas, J. and Richman, N. (1984) *Coping with Young Children*, Harmondsworth: Penguin.

Drillien, C.M. (1964) *The Growth and Development of the Prematurely Born Infant*, Baltimore: Williams & Wilkins.

Fergusson, D.M., Horwood, L.J. and Shannon, F.T. (1986) 'Factors relating to the age of attainment of nocturnal bladder control: an eight year longitudinal study', *Ped. 78*: 884–90.

Foxx, R.M. and Azrin, N.H. (1973) 'Dry pants: a rapid method of toilet training children', *Behav. Res. and Ther. 11*: 435–42.

Graham, P. (1973) 'Depth of sleep and enuresis: a critical review', in I. Kolvin, R.C. MacKeith and S.R. Meadow (eds) *Bladder Control and Enuresis: Clinics in Developmental Medicine Nos 48/49*, London: Spastics International Medical Publications.

—— (1986) *Child Psychiatry: A Developmental Approach*, Oxford: Oxford Medical Publications.

Halliday, S., Meadow, S.R. and Berg, I. (1987) 'Successful management of daytime enuresis using alarm procedures: a randomly controlled trial', *Arch. Dis. Childh. 62*: 132–7.

Heinstein, M. (1966) *Child Rearing in California*, Bureau of Maternal and Child Health, State of California, Department of Public Health.

Hersov, L. (1985) 'Faecal soiling', in M. Rutter and L. Hersov (eds) *Child and Adolescent Psychiatry* (2nd edn), Oxford: Blackwell.

Houts, A.C., Liebert, R.M. and Padawer, W. (1983) 'A delivery system for the treatment of primary enuresis', *J. Abnorm. Child Psychol. 11*: 513–20.

Jolly, H. (1976) 'A paediatrician's view on the management of encopresis', *Proc. Roy. Soc. Med. 69*: 21–2.

Lask, B. (1985) *Children's Problems: A Parent's Guide to Understanding and Tackling Them*, London: Dunitz.

Leach, P. (1975) *Babyhood*, Harmondsworth: Penguin.

Levine, M.D. (1975) 'Children with encopresis: a descriptive analysis', *Ped. 56*: 412–16.

—— (1982) 'Encopresis: its potential evaluation and alleviation', *Ped. Clin. N. Amer. 29*: 315–30.

Levine, M.D. and Bakow, H. (1976) 'Children with encopresis: a study of treatment outcome', *Ped. 58*: 845–52.

Lovibond, S.H. and Coote, M.A. (1971) 'Enuresis', in G.C. Costello (ed.) *Symptoms and Pathology*, New York: Wiley.

MacKeith, R.C. (1968) 'A frequent factor in the origins of primary nocturnal enuresis: anxiety in the third year of life', *Dev. Med. Child Neurol. 10*: 465.

MacKeith, R.C., Meadow, R. and Turner, R.K. (1973) 'How children become dry', in I. Kolvin, R.C. MacKeith and S.R. Meadow (eds) *Bladder Control and Enuresis: Clinics in Developmental Medicine Nos 48/49*, London: Spastics International Medical Publications.

Meadow, S.R. and Berg, I. (1982) 'Controlled trial of imipramine in diurnal enuresis', *Arch. Dis. Childh. 57*: 714–16.

Miller, F.J.W., Court, S.D.M., Walton, W.S. and Knox, E.G. (1960) *Growing Up in Newcastle-upon-Tyne*, Oxford: Oxford University Press.

Mountjoy, P.T., Ruben, D.H. and Bradford, T.S. (1984) 'Recent technological advancements in the treatment of enuresis', *Behav. Mod. 8*: 291–315.

Newson, J. and Newson, E. (1965) *Patterns of Infant Care in an Urban Community*, Harmondsworth: Pelican.

O'Brien, S., Ross, C.V. and Christopherson, E.R. (1986) 'Primary encopresis: evaluation and treatment', *J. Appl. Behav. Anal. 19*: 137–45.

Rappaport, L.A. and Levine, M.D. (1986) 'The prevention of constipation and encopresis: a developmental model and approach', *Ped. Clin. N. Amer. 33*: 859–86.

Richman, N., Stevenson, J. and Graham, P.J. (1982) *Pre-School to School: A Behavioural Study*, London: Academic Press.

Savage, D.C.L., Wilson, M.I., Ross, E.M. and Fee, W.M. (1969) 'Asymptomatic bacteriuria in girl entrants to Dundee primary schools', *Brit. Med. J. 3*: 75–80.

Schmitt, B.D. (1982a) 'Daytime wetting (diurnal enuresis)', *Ped. Clin. N. Amer. 29*: 9–20.

—— (1982b) 'Nocturnal enuresis: an update on treatment', *Ped. Clin. N. Amer. 29*: 21–35.

Starfield, B. and Mellits, E.D. (1968) 'Increase in functional bladder capacity and improvement in enuresis', *J. Ped. 72*: 483.

Stein, Z. and Susser, M. (1967) 'Social factors in the development of sphincter control', *Dev. Med. Child Neurol. 9*: 692–706.

Sweets, P.M., Lancioni, G.E., Ball, S. and Oliva, D.S. (1985) 'Shaping self-initiated toileting in infants', *J. Appl. Behav. Anal. 18*: 303–8.

Taitz, L.S., Wales, J.K.H., Urwin, O.M. and Molnar, D.M. (1986) 'Factors associated with outcome in management of defecation disorders', *Arch. Dis. Childh. 61*: 472–7.

Taylor, P.D. and Turner, R.K. (1975) 'A clinical trial of continuous, intermittent and overlearning "bell and pad" treatment for nocturnal enuresis', *Behav. Res. and Ther. 13*: 281–93.

Turner, R.K. (1973) 'Conditioning treatment of nocturnal enuresis: present status', in I. Kolvin, R.C. MacKeith and S.R. Meadow (eds) *Bladder Control and Enuresis: Clinics in Developmental Medicine Nos 48/49*, London: Spastics International Medical Publications.

Verhulst, F.C., van der Lee, J.H., Akkerhuis, G.W., Sanders-Woudstra, J.A.R., Timer, F.C. and Donkhorst, I.D. (1985) 'The prevalence of nocturnal enuresis: do DSM III criteria need to be changed? A brief research report', *J. Child Psychol. Psychiat. 26*: 989–93.

Wakefield, M.A., Woodbridge, C., Steward, J. and Croke, W.M. (1984) 'A treatment programme for faecal incontinence', *Dev. Med. Child Neurol. 26*: 613–16.

Weir, K. (1982) 'Night and day wetting among a population of three year olds', *Dev. Med. Child Neurol. 24*: 479–84.

Yeates, W.K. (1973) 'Bladder function in normal micturition', in I. Kolvin, R.C. MacKeith and S.R. Meadow (eds) *Bladder Control and Enuresis: Clinics in Developmental Medicine Nos 48/49*, London: Spastics International Medical Publications.

Young, G. and Morgan, R.T.T. (1972) 'Overlearning in the conditioning treatment of enuresis', *Behav. Res. and Ther. 10*: 147.

—— (1973) 'Analysis of the factors associated with the extinction of a conditioned response', *Behav. Res. and Ther. 11*: 219.

Young, I. and Goldsmith, A. (1972) 'Treatment of encopresis in a day treatment programme', *Psychother. Theory Res. Prac. 9*: 231–5.

Zaleski, A., Gerrard, J.W. and Shokeir, M.H.K. (1973) 'Nocturnal enuresis: the importance of a small bladder capacity', in I. Kolvin, R.C. MacKeith and S.R. Meadow (eds) *Bladder Control and Enuresis: Clinics in Developmental Medicine Nos 48/49*, London: Spastics International Medical Publications.

7 Bedtime and sleep problems

Anders, T.F. and Weinstein, P. (1972) 'Sleep and its disorders in infants and children', *Ped. 50*: 312–24.

Bernal, J.F. (1973) 'Night waking in infants during the first fourteen months', *Dev. Med. Child Neurol. 15*: 760–9.

Blurton-Jones, N., Rossetti-Ferreira, M.C., Farquar-Brown, M. and MacDonald, L. (1978) 'The association between perinatal factors and later night waking', *Dev. Med. Child Neurol. 20*: 427–34.

Butler, N.R. and Golding, J. (eds) (1986) *From Birth to Five: A Study of Health and Behaviour of Britain's Five Year Olds*, London: Pergamon.

Clements, J., Wing, L. and Dunn, G. (1986) 'Sleep problems in handicapped children: a preliminary study', *J. Child Psychol. Psychiat. 27*: 399–407.

Douglas, J. (1988) 'Sleep disturbance', in J. Douglas (ed.) *Emotional and Behavioural Problems in Young Children: A Multidisciplinary Approach to Identification and Management*, Windsor: NFER/Nelson.

Douglas, J. and Richman, N. (1984) *My Child Won't Sleep*, Harmondsworth: Penguin.
—— (1985) *Sleep Management Manual*, London: Department of Psychological Medicine, Hospital for Sick Children.
Farnes, J. and Wallace, C. (1987) 'Pilot study for a sleep clinic', *Health Visitor 60*: 41–3.
Jenkins, S., Bax, M. and Hart, H. (1980) 'Behaviour problems in preschool children', *J. Child Psychol. Psychiat. 21*: 5–19.
Jolly, H. (1977) *Book of Child Care*, London: Sphere.
Ounsted, M.K. and Hendrick, A.M. (1977) 'The first born child: patterns of development', *Dev. Med. Child Neurol. 19*: 446–53.
Richman, N. (1981a) 'A community survey of characteristics of 1–2 year olds with sleep disruptions', *Amer. Acad. Child Psychiat. 20*: 281–91.
—— (1981b) 'Sleep problems in young children: annotation', *Arch. Dis. Childh. 56*: 491–3.
—— (1985a) 'A double-blind trial of drug treatment in young children with waking problems', *J. Child Psychol. Psychiat. 26*: 591–8.
—— (1985b) 'Prevalence and treatment of sleep problems in young children', in J.E. Stevenson (ed.) *Recent Research in Developmental Psychopathology*, Oxford: Pergamon.
Richman, N., Douglas, J., Hunt, H., Lansdown, R. and Levere, R. (1985) 'Behavioural methods in the treatment of sleep disorders: a pilot study', *J. Child Psychol. Psychiat. 26*: 581–90.
Richman, N., Stevenson, J. and Graham, P. (1975) 'Prevalence and patterns of psychological disturbance in children of primary age', *J. Child Psychol. 6*: 101–13.
Richman, N., Stevenson, J. and Graham, P.J. (1982) *Pre-School to School: A Behavioural Study,* London: Academic Press.
Sallustro, F. and Atwell, C.W. (1978) 'Body rocking, head banging and head rolling in normal children', *J. Ped. 93:* 704–8.
Sanger, S., Weir, K. and Churchill, E. (1981) 'Treatment of sleep problems: the use of behaviour modification techniques by health visitors', *Health Visitor 54*: 421–3.
Thornton, P., Walsh, J., Webster, J. and Harries, C. (1984) 'The sleep clinic', *Nursing Times* 14 March, 40–3.

8 Emotional problems

Azrin, N.H., Nunn, R.G. and Frantz-Renshaw, S. (1980) 'Habit reversal treatment of thumbsucking', *Behav. Res. and Ther. 18*: 395–9.
Black, D. (1979) 'Early help for the bereaved child avoids later problems', *Modern Medicine*, May.
—— (1987) 'The bereaved child', in J.D. Pollitt (ed.) *Psychiatric Emergencies in Family Practice*, Lancaster: MTP Press.
Black, D. and Urbanowicz, M. (1985) 'Bereaved children: family intervention', in J.E. Stevenson (ed.) *Recent Research in Developmental Psychopathology*, Oxford: Pergamon.

—— (1987) 'Family intervention with bereaved children', *J. Child Psychol. Psychiat. 28*: 467–76.

Boniface, D. and Graham, P. (1979) 'The three year old and his attachment to a special soft object', *J. Child Psychol. Psychiat. 20*: 217–24.

Caplan, M.G. and Douglas, V.I. (1969) 'Incidence of parental loss in children with depressed mood', *J. Child Psychol. Psychiat. 10*: 225–34.

Christensen, A.P. and Sanders, M.R. (1987) 'Habit reversal and differential reinforcement of other behaviour in the treatment of thumb sucking: an analysis of generalisation and side effects', *J. Child Psychol. Psychiat. 28*: 281–95.

Clowes-Hollins, V. and King, N. (1982) 'Parents and siblings as behaviour modifiers in control of a common developmental problem (thumb-sucking)', *J. Clin. Child Psychol. 11*: 231–3.

Davidson, P.O., Haryett, R.D., Sandilands, M. and Hansen, F.C. (1967) 'Thumbsucking – habit or symptom?', *J. Dent. Child 34*: 252–9.

Donovan, C.F. (1984) 'Life changes – divorce', *Brit. Med. J. 289*: 597–600.

Elizur, E. and Kauffman, M. (1983) 'Factors influencing the severity of childhood bereavement reactions', *Amer. J. Orthopsychiat. 53*: 668–76.

Emde, R.N. (1980) 'Levels of meaning for infant emotions', in W.A. Collins (ed.) *Development of Cognition, Affect and Social Relationships*, Minnesota Symposia on Child Psychology (Vol. 13: 1–37), Hillsdale, NJ: Lawrence Erlbaum.

Fine, S. (1987) 'Children in divorce, custody and access situations: an update', *J. Child Psychol. Psychiat. 28*: 361–4.

Gilby, R. and Pederson, D. (1982) 'The development of the child's concept of the family', *Can. J. Behav. Sci. 14*: 110–21.

Harris, S.L. and Ferrari, M. (1983) 'Developmental factors in child behaviour therapy', *Behav. Ther. 14*: 54–72.

Haryett, R.D., Hansen, F.C. and Davidson, P.O. (1970) 'Chronic thumbsucking: a second report on treatment and its psychological effects', *Amer. J. Orthodon. 57*: 164–78.

Hetherington, E.M., Cox, M. and Cox, R. (1979) 'Family intervention and social, emotional and cognitive development of children following divorce', in L. Vaughn and T.B. Brazelton (eds) *The Family Setting Priorities*, New York: Science and Medical.

Hildebrand, J. (1988) 'Surviving marital breakdown', in J. Douglas (ed.) *Emotional and Behavioural Problems in Young Children: A Multi-disciplinary Approach to Identification and Management*, Windsor: NFER/Nelson.

Johnson, W.F., Emde, R.N. and Pannabecker, B.J. (1982) 'Maternal perception of infant emotion from birth through 18 months', *Inf. Behav. Dev. 5*: 313–22.

Kalter, N. and Plunkett, J.W. (1984) 'Children's perceptions of the causes and consequences of divorce', *Amer. Acad. Child Psychiat. 23*: 326–34.

Kalter, N., Pickar, J. and Lesowitz, M. (1984) 'School based development facilitation groups for children of divorce: a preventative intervention', *Amer. J. Orthopsychiat. 54*: 613–23.

Kane, B. (1979) 'Children's concept of death', *J. Genet. Psychol. 134*: 141–53.

Kastenbaum, R. and Aisenberg, R. (1972) *The Psychology of Death*, New York: Springer.

Kauffman, M. and Elizur, E. (1979) 'Children's bereavement reactions following death of the father', *Int. J. Fam. Ther. 1*: 203–29.

Klinnert, M.D., Campos, J.J., Sorce, J.F., Emde, R.N. and Svedja, M. (1983) 'Emotions as behaviour regulators: social referencing in infancy', in R. Plutchik and H. Kellerman (eds) *Emotions in Early Development* (Vol. 2), New York: Academic Press.

Knight, M.F. and McKenzie, H.S. (1974) 'Elimination of bedtime thumbsucking in home settings through contingent reading', *J. Appl. Behav. Anal. 7*: 33–8.

Lansdown, R. and Benjamin, G. (1985) 'The development of the concept of death in children aged 5–9 years', *Child: Care, Health and Development 11*: 13–20.

Lassen, M.K. and Fluet, N.R. (1978) 'Elimination of nocturnal thumbsucking by glove wearing', *J. Behav. Ther. and Exper. Psychiat. 9*: 85.

Lewis, M., Shilton, P. and Fuqua, R.W. (1981) 'Parental control of nocturnal thumbsucking', *J. Behav. Ther. and Exper. Psychiat. 12*: 87–90.

McGurk, H. and Glachan, M. (1987) 'Children's conception of the continuity of parenthood following divorce', *J. Child Psychol. Psychiat. 28*: 427–35.

Marks, I. (1987a) 'The development of normal fear: a review', *J. Child Psychol. Psychiat. 28*: 667–97.

—— (1987b) *Fears, Phobias and Rituals*, New York: Oxford University Press.

Newson, J., Newson, E. and Mahalski, P. (1982) 'Persistent infant comfort habits and their sequelae at 11 and 16 years', *J. Child Psychol. Psychiat. 23*: 421–36.

Ozturk, M. and Ozturk, O.M. (1977) 'Thumbsucking and falling asleep', *Brit. J. Med. Psychol. 50*: 95–103.

Passman, R.H. and Halonen, J.S. (1979) 'A developmental survey of young children's attachments to inanimate objects', *J. Genet. Psychol. 134*: 165–78.

Piaget, J. (1961) *Judgement and Reasoning in the Child*, Pallerman, NJ: Littlefield, Adams.

Raphael, B. (1982) 'The young child and the death of a parent', in C.M. Parkes and J. Stevenson-Hinde (eds) *The Place of Attachment in Human Behaviour*, London: Tavistock.

Reilly, T.P., Hasazi, J.E. and Bond, L.A. (1983) 'Children's conceptions of death and personal mortality', *J. Ped. Psychol. 8*: 21–31.

Richards, M.P.M. (1982) 'Post-divorce arrangements for children: a psychological perspective', *J. Soc. Welf. Law 5*: 133–51.

Rosenheim, E. and Reicher, R. (1985) 'Informing children about a parent's terminal illness', *J. Child Psychol. Psychiat.* 26: 995–8.

Rustin, L. (1987) *Assessment and Therapy Programme for Dysfluent Children*, Windsor: NFER/Nelson.

Rustin, L., Purser, H. and Rowley, D. (eds) (1987) *Progress in the Treatment of Fluency Disorders*, London: Taylor & Francis.

Rutter, M. (1984) *Maternal Deprivation Reassessed* (2nd edn), Harmondsworth: Penguin.

Smilansky, S. (1981) *Death Conception by Children*, Ach (Hebrew), Haifa, Israel.

Stacey, M., Dearden, R., Pill, R. and Robinson, D. (1970) *Hospitals, Children and their Families: A Pilot Study*, London: Routledge & Kegan Paul.

Steinman, S.B., Zemmelman, S.E. and Knoblauck, T.M. (1985) 'A study of parents who sought joint custody following divorce: who reaches agreement and sustains joint custody and who returns to court', *J. Amer. Acad. Child Psychiat.* 24: 554–62.

Tryon, A.F. (1968) 'Thumb sucking and manifest anxiety: a note', *Child Dev.* 39: 1,159–63.

Van Eerdewegh, M.M., Bieri, M.D., Parrilla, K.H. and Clayton, P. (1982) 'The bereaved child', *Brit. J. Psychiat.* 140: 23–9.

Van Eerdewegh, M.M., Clayton, P. and Van Eerdewegh, P. (1985) 'The bereaved child: variables influences early psychopathology', *Brit. J. Psychiat.* 147: 188–94.

Wallerstein, J. (1985) 'Children of divorce – emerging trends', *Psychiat. Clin. N. Amer.* 8: 837–55.

Wallerstein, J. and Kelly, J. (1980) *Surviving the Break-up: How Children and Parents Cope with Divorce*, New York: Basic Books.

Waters, B. and Dimock, J. (1983) 'A review of research relevant to custody and access disputes', *Aus. and N. Zeal. J. of Psychiat.* 17: 181–9.

Zill, N. (1984) *Happy, Healthy and Insecure*, New York: Doubleday.

9 The overactive and hyperactive child

American Psychiatric Association (1980) *Diagnostic and Statistical Manual of Mental Disorders* (3rd edn), Washington, DC: American Psychiatric Association.

Barkley, R.A. (1981) *Hyperactive Children: A Handbook for Diagnosis and Treatment*, New York: Guilford.

Barkley, R.A. and Cunningham, C.E. (1979) 'The effects of Ritalin on the mother–child interaction of hyperactive children', *Arch. Gen. Psychiat.* 36: 201–08.

Befera, M.S. and Barkley, R.A. (1985) 'Hyperactive and normal girls and boys: mother–child interaction, parent psychiatric status and child psychopathology', *J. Child Psychol. Psychiat.* 26: 439–53.

Bornstein, P.H. and Quevillon, R. (1976) 'The effects of a self instructional package on overactive pre-school boys', *J. Appl. Behav. Anal. 9*: 179–88.

Conners, C.K. (1969) 'A teacher rating scale for use in drug studies with children', *Amer. J. Psychiat. 126*: 885–8.

—— (1970) 'Symptom patterns in hyperkinetic, neurotic and normal children', *Child Dev. 41*: 667–82.

—— (1973) 'Rating scales for use in drug studies with children', *Psychopharm. Bull. (Special issue: Pharmacotherapy of Children)*: 24–84.

—— (1975) 'Controlled trial of methylphenidate in preschool children with minimal brain dysfunction', *Int. J. Ment. Health 4*: 61–74.

Conrad, P. (1976) *Identifying Hyperactive Children: The Medicalization of Deviant Behavior*, Lexington, Mass: Lexington Books.

Douglas, V.I. (1983) 'Attentional and cognitive problems', in M. Rutter (ed.) *Developmental Neuropsychiatry*, Edinburgh: Churchill Livingstone; New York: Guilford.

Douglas, V.I., Barr, R.G., O'Neill, M.E. and Britton, B.G. (1986) 'Short term effects of methylphenidate on the cognition, learning and academic performance of children with attention deficit disorder in the laboratory and the classroom', *J. Child Psychol. Psychiat. 27*: 191–212.

Egger, J., Carter, C.M., Graham, P.J., Gumley, D. and Soothill, J.F. (1985) 'Controlled trial of oligoantigenic treatment in the hyperkinetic syndrome', *Lancet i*: 540–5.

Feingold, B.F. (1973) *Introduction to Clinical Allergy*, Springfield, Ill: Charles C. Thomas.

—— (1975) *Why Your Child is Hyperactive*, New York: Random House.

Goyette, C.H., Conners, C.K. and Ulrich, R.F. (1978) 'Normative data on revised Conners' Parent and Teacher rating scales', *J. Abnorm. Child Psychol. 6*: 221–36.

Harley, J.P., Roy, R.S., Tomasi, L., Eichman, P.L., Matthews, L.G., Chun, R., Cheeland, C.S. and Traisman, E. (1978a) 'Hyperkinesis and food additives: testing the Feingold hypothesis', *Ped. 61*: 818–28.

Harley, J.P., Matthews, C.G. and Eichman, P.L. (1978b) 'Synthetic food colors and hyperactive children: a double-blind challenge experiment', *Ped. 62*: 975–83.

Harvey, P. (1984) 'Annotation: lead and children's health, recent research and future questions', *J. Child Psychol. Psychiat. 25*: 517–22.

Lansdown, R. and Yule, W. (1986) (eds) *The Lead Debate: The Environment, Toxicology and Child Health*, London: Croom Helm.

Mattes, J.A. and Gittelman, R. (1981) 'Effects of artificial food colourings in children with hyperactive symptoms', *Arch. Gen. Psychiat. 38*: 714–18.

Nichols, P.L. and Chen, T.C. (1981) *Minimal Brain Dysfunction: A Prospective Study*, Hillsdale, NJ: Lawrence Erlbaum.

Ottenbacher, K.J. and Cooper, H.M. (1983) 'Drug treatment of hyperactivity in children', *Dev. Med. Child Neurol. 25*: 358–66.

Rapoport, J.L. and Ferguson, B. (1981) 'Biological validation of the hyperkinetic syndrome', *Dev. Med. Child Neurol. 23*: 667–82.

Rapp, D.J. (1979) *Allergies and the Hyperactive Child*, New York: Sovereign.

Rutter, M. (1983) 'Introduction: concepts of brain dysfunction syndromes', in M. Rutter (ed.) *Developmental Neuropsychiatry*, Edinburgh: Churchill Livingstone; New York: Guilford.

Safer, D.J. and Allen, R.R. (1976) *Hyperactive Children: Diagnosis and Management*, Baltimore, Md: University Park Press.

Schachar, R., Rutter, M. and Smith, A. (1981) 'The characteristics of situationally and pervasively hyperactive children: implications for a syndrome definition', *J. Child Psychol. Psychiat. 22*: 375–92.

Schacher, R., Taylor, E., Weiselberg, M., Thorley, G. and Rutter, M. (1988) 'Effect of methylphenidate on family function and relationships', *J. Amer. Child Psychiat.* (in press).

Schleifer, M., Weiss, G., Cohen, N.J., Elman, M., Cvejic, H. and Kruger, E. (1975) 'Hyperactivity in preschoolers and the effect of methylphenidate', *Amer. J. Orthopsychiat. 45*: 35–70.

Soothill, J.F. (1983) 'The atopic child', in J.F. Soothill, A.R. Hayward and C.B.S. Wood (eds) *Paediatric Immunology*, Oxford: Blackwells.

Taylor, E.A. (1979) 'The use of drugs in hyperkinetic states: clinical issues', *Neuropharmac. 18*: 951–8.

—— (1984) 'Diet and behaviour', *Arch. Dis. Childh. 59*: 97–8.

—— (1985a) 'Syndromes of overactivity and attention deficit', in M. Rutter and L. Hersov (eds) *Child and Adolescent Psychiatry* (2nd edn), Oxford: Blackwells.

—— (1985b) *The Hyperactive Child: A Parent's Guide*, London: Martin Dunitz.

—— (1986a) 'Overactivity, hyperactivity and hyperkinesis: problems and prevalence', in E.A. Taylor (ed.) *The Overactive Child: Clinics in Developmental Medicine No. 97*, Oxford: Spastics International Medical Publications.

—— (1986b) 'Impulsiveness, defiance and conduct problems', in E.A. Taylor (ed.) *The Overactive Child: Clinics in Developmental Medicine No. 97*, Oxford: Spastics International Medical Publications.

—— (1986c) 'The causes and development of hyperactive behaviour', in E.A. Taylor (ed.) *The Overactive Child: Clinics in Developmental Medicine No. 97*, Oxford: Spastics International Medical Publications.

—— (1986d) 'The basis of drug treatment', in E.A. Taylor (ed.) *The Overactive Child: Clinics in Developmental Medicine No. 97*, Oxford: Spastics International Medical Publications.

—— (ed.) (1986e) *The Overactive Child: Clinics in Developmental Medicine No. 97*, Oxford: Spastics International Medical Publications.

—— (1988) 'Psychopharmacology in childhood', *ACPP Newsletter 10*: 3–6.

Weiss, B. (1982) 'Food additives and environmental chemicals as sources of childhood behavior disorders', *J. Amer. Acad. Child Psychiat. 21*: 144–52.

Yule, W. (1986) 'Behavioural treatments', in E.A. Taylor (ed.) *The Overactive Child: Clinics in Developmental Medicine No. 97*, Oxford: Spastics International Medical Publications.

Yule, W., Lansdown, R., Millar, I.B. and Urbanowicz, M.A. (1981) 'The relationship between blood lead concentrations, intelligence and attainment in a school population: a pilot study', *Dev. Med. Child Neurol. 23*: 567–76.

Zukow, P.G., Zukow, A.H. and Bentler, P.M. (1978) 'Rating scales for the identification and treatment of hyperkinesis', *J. Consult. and Clin. Psychol. 46*: 213–22.

10 Crying babies

Anderson, G. (1983) 'Infantile colic: a possible solution', *Amer. J. Mat. Child Nursing 8*: 185.

Asnes, R.S. and Mones, R.L. (1982) 'Infantile colic: a review', *Dev. Behav. Ped. 4*: 57–62.

Barr, R.G., Kramer, M.S., Pless, I.B., Boisjoly, C. and Leduc, D.G. (1983) 'Feeding and temperament predispose to cry/fuss behavior at six weeks', *Amer. J. Dis. Childh. 137*: 541.

Bernal, J. (1972) 'Crying during the first ten days of life, and maternal responses', *Dev. Med. Child Neurol. 14*: 362–72.

Boukydis, C.F.Z. (1985) 'Perception of infant crying as an interpersonal event', in M. Lester and C.F.Z. Boukydis (eds) *Infant Crying: Theoretical and Research Perspectives*, New York: Plenum.

Brackbill, Y. (1973) 'Continuous stimulation reduces arousal level: stability of the effect over time', *Child Dev. 44*: 43–6.

Brackbill, Y., Douthill, T.C. and West, H. (1973) 'Psychophysiologic effects in the neonate of prone versus supine placement', *J. Ped. 83*: 83–4.

Brazelton, T.B. (1962) 'Crying in infancy', *Ped. 29*: 579–88.

—— (1985) 'Application of cry research to clinical perspectives', in M. Lester and C.F.Z. Boukydis (eds) *Infant Crying: Theoretical and Research Perspectives*, New York: Plenum.

Butler, N.R. and Golding, J. (eds) (1986) *From Birth to Five: A Study of Health and Behaviour of Britain's Five Year Olds*, Oxford: Pergamon.

Byrne, J.M. and Horowitz, F.D. (1981) 'Rocking as a soothing intervention: the influence of direction and type of movement', *Inf. Behav. and Dev. 4*: 207–18.

Carey, W.B. (1968) 'Maternal anxiety and infantile colic: is there a relationship?', *Clin. Ped. 7*: 590–5.

—— (1972) 'Clinical applications of infant temperament measurements', *J. Ped. 81*: 823–8.

—— (1983) '"Colic" or excessive crying in young infants', in M.D. Levine, W.B. Carey, A.C. Crocker and R.T. Gross (eds) *Developmental-Behavioural Paediatrics*, Philadelphia, Pa: W.B. Saunders.

Donovan, W.L. and Leavitt, A. (1985) 'Physiology and behaviour:

parents' response to the infant cry', in M. Lester and C.F.Z. Boukydis (eds) *Infant Crying: Theoretical and Research Perspectives*, New York: Plenum.

Dupuis, L. (1985) 'Dicyclomine: a recent orphan', *Drug Info. Bulletin: The Hospital for Sick Children (Toronto) 2(2)*: 1–3.

Evans, R.W., Fergusson, D.M., Allardyce, R.A. and Taylor, B. (1981) 'Maternal diet and infantile colic in breast fed infants', *Lancet i*: 1,340–2.

Frodi, A.M. (1985) 'When empathy fails: aversive infant crying and child abuse', in M. Lester and C.F.Z. Boukydis (eds) *Infant Crying: Theoretical and Research Perspectives*, New York: Plenum.

Frodi, A.M., Lamb, M.E., Leavitt, L., Donovan, W., Neff, C. and Sherry, D. (1978) 'Fathers' and mothers' responses to infant smiles and cries', *Inf. Behav. and Dev. 1*: 187–98.

Gray, P. (1987) *Crying Baby: How to Cope*, London: Wisebuy.

Hide, D.W. and Guyer, B.M. (1982) 'Prevalence of infant colic', *Arch. Dis. Childh. 57*: 561–2.

Hunziker, U.A. and Barr, R.G. (1986) 'Increased carrying reduces infant crying: a randomized controlled trial', *Ped. 77*: 641–8.

Jacobssen, I. and Lindberg, T. (1978) 'Cow's milk as a cause of infantile colic in breastfed infants', *Lancet ii*: 347–9.

—— (1983) 'Cow's milk proteins cause colic in breastfed babies: a double blind crossover study', *Paed. 71*: 268–9.

Kirkland, J. (1985) *Crying and Babies: Helping Families Cope*, Kent: Croom Helm.

Kirkland, J., Deane, F. and Brennan, M. (1983) 'About Crysos, a clinic for people with crying babies', *Fam. Rel. 32*: 537–43.

Korner, A.F. and Thoman, E.B. (1972) 'The relative efficacy of contact and vestibular proprioceptive stimulation in soothing neonates', *Child Dev. 43*: 443–53.

Lester, B.M. (1985) 'Introduction: there is more to crying than meets the ear', in M. Lester and C.F.Z. Boukydis (eds) *Infant Crying: Theoretical and Research Perspectives*, New York: Plenum.

Liebman, W.M. (1981) 'Infantile colic: association with lactose and milk intolerance', *J. Amer. Med. Assoc. 245*: 732–3.

Lipton, E.L., Steinschreider, A. and Richmond, J.B. (1965) 'Swaddling, a child care practice, historical, cultural and experimental observations', *Ped. 35*: 519–67.

Lounsbury, M.L. and Bates, J.E. (1982) 'The cries of infants of differing levels of perceived temperamental difficultness: acoustic properties and effects on the listener', *Child Dev. 53*: 677–86.

Meyer, J.E. and Thaler, M.M. (1971) 'Colic in low birthweight infants', *Amer. J. Dis. Childh. 122*: 25–7.

Michelsson, K. (1971) 'Cry analysis of symptomless, low birthweight neonates and of asphyxiated newborn infants', *Acta Paed. Scand. 216*: 1–45.

Michelsson, K., Sirvio, P. and Wasz-Höckert, O. (1977) 'Pain cry in full-term asphyxiated newborn infants correlated with late findings', *Acta Paed. Scand. 66*: 611–16.

Murray, A.D. (1979) 'Infant crying as an elicitor of parental behaviour: an examination of two models', *Psychol. Bull. 86*: 191–215.

—— (1985) 'Aversiveness is in the mind of the beholder: perception of infant crying by adults', in M. Lester and C.F.Z. Boukydis (eds) *Infant Crying: Theoretical and Research Perspectives*, New York: Plenum.

O'Donovan, J.C. and Bradstock, A.S. (1979) 'The failure of conventional drug therapy in the management of infant colic', *Am. J. Dis. Childh. 133*: 999–1,001.

Pritchard, P. (1986) 'An infant crying clinic', *Health Visitor 59*: 375–7.

Rebelsky, F. and Black, R. (1972) 'Crying in infancy', *J. Genet. Psychol. 121*: 49–57.

Rubin, S.P. and Prendergast, M. (1984) 'Infantile colic: incidence and treatment in a Norfolk community', *Child: Care, Health and Development 10*: 219–26.

St James-Roberts, I. and Wolke, D. (1984) 'Comparison of mothers with trained observers' reports of neonatal behavioural style', *Inf. Behav. and Dev. 7*: 299–310.

Taubman, B. (1984) 'Clinical trial of the treatment of colic by modification of parent–infant interaction', *Ped. 74*: 998–1,003.

Ter Vrugt, D. and Pederson, D.R. (1973) 'The effects of vertical rocking frequencies on the arousal level in two month old infants', *Child Dev. 44*: 205–9.

Thoman, E.B., Acebo, C. and Becker, P.T. (1983) 'Infant crying and stability in the mother–infant relationship: a system analysis', *Child Dev. 54*: 653–9.

Thomas, D.B. (1981) 'Aetiological associations in infantile colic: an hypothesis', *Austr. Paed. J. 17*: 292–5.

Wasz-Höckert, O., Michelsson, K. and Lind, O. (1985) 'Twenty-five years of Scandinavian research', in M. Lester and C.F.Z. Boukydis (eds) *Infant Crying: Theoretical and Research Perspectives*, New York: Plenum.

Weissbluth, M., Christoffel, K.K. and Davis, A.T. (1984) 'Treatment of infantile colic with dicyclomine hydrochloride', *Ped. 104*: 951–5.

Index